BLACK MEN

# SAGE FOCUS EDITIONS

# BLACK MEN

## Edited by
## LAWRENCE E. GARY

 SAGE PUBLICATIONS   Beverly Hills   London

This book is dedicated to my wife, Robenia Baker, and my children, Lisa Ché, Lawrence Charles Andre, and Jason Edward, for their understanding, patience, and support.

*For information address:*

SAGE Publications, Inc.
275 South Beverly Drive
Beverly Hills, California 90212

SAGE Publications Ltd
28 Banner Street
London EC1Y 8QE, England

Printed in the United States of Amerrica

**Library of Congress Cataloging in Publication Data**

Main entry under title:

Black men.
   (Sage focus editions ; 31)
   Includes bibliographies.
   1. Afro-American men--Addresses, essays, lectures.
I. Gary, Lawrence E.   I. Series.
E185.86.B526      305.3'08996073      81-9021
ISBN 0-8039-1654-X          AACR2
ISBN 0-8039-1655-8 (pbk.)

FIFTH PRINTING, 1985

# CONTENTS

# ACKNOWLEDGMENTS

In the production of any book, many detailed tasks have to be performed and there has to be the proper mix of ideas and energies. Eva M. Bell, Audrey B. Chapman, Denise S. Goins-Stockton, Sterlon A. Hawkins, Lorna E. Gougis, Frazier T. Jackson, Jean P. Durr, Emma Davis, Amybelle Wright, Doris Y. Wilkinson, Ingrid R. Gabriel, Brenda L. Davis, Linda Love, Lesa Garland, and others, so many that I cannot name, assisted me in the development of the manuscript. I am indebted to all of you and I thank you. I acknowledge a large debt of gratitude for the skill of Diane R. Williams, who provided editorial assistance. Her careful editing was an inspiration, convincing me that this book could be done.

Special thanks are due Greta L. Berry. She provided the administrative support for this project from the beginning to the end. In addition to keeping the manuscript moving and corresponding with the contributors, she helped with editing, typing, and checking references. She also provided warm support and encouragement.

I owe a debt of gratitude to Lucy C. Drayton for her invaluable technical aid as my research analyst. She spent numerous hours in libraries on my behalf. Going way beyond the call of duty, she always was willing to find difficult materials, to proof and reproof each chapter, to run all kinds of errands, and to give me constructive criticism on all aspects of this volume.

As a result of working on this book, I did not get a chance to visit my grandmother, Henrietta M. Gary, this year. I appreciate very much her understanding why this project was so important for me to complete.

I am gratefully indebted to the people whose contributions are included in this volume. Without their cooperation the book would not have been possible.

My appreciation goes to the Center for Minority Group Mental Health Programs, National Institute of Mental Health, which supports in part my research on the mental health of Black people (No. 5 RO1 MH-25551-07). The Chief of this Center, Dr. James Ralph, has been consistent in his support and guidance for the past seven years.

I would also like to thank three other persons. Dr. Lorraine A. Williams, Vice President for Academic Affairs, Howard University, who supported my sabbatical so that I could complete this piece of work; Louis A. Ramey of the Southern Regional Education Board, who encouraged me, every time he saw me, to pursue my interest in learning more about how Black men are coping with the pressures and stresses of our society; and Mr. Levi J. Delaine, my neighbor now deceased, for the inspiration he provided through the life he led.

# INTRODUCTION

In this volume, the editor and contributors examine some of the major issues affecting the behavior and status of Black men in the United States. About five years ago, the editor started asking questions about the future of Black families in general and his family in particular. At an annual family Thanksgiving dinner, a question was raised as to whether or not the Gary Family had made much progress over the past three generations. There followed a heated discussion centering on the difficulties faced by Black women in the editor's family, as they attempted to protect and nurture their children. Little attention was focused on the role of Black men in their families. When the Black man was discussed, his negative attributes were emphasized. Yet, the editor remembers many pleasant, as well as negative, interactions with the men in his family, including his brother, uncles, cousins, grandfather, and stepfather.

At a local barbershop two years later, the men there were trying to describe the role their fathers had played in their respective families. However, much of the discussion focused on the conflict between the mother and father.

As a result of these and similar experiences, the author began to seek more information on the role performance and contributions of Black men to their families and communities.

A review of health, social, and economic data on Black men revealed the necessity of a research conference in order to put some of these national statistics in perspective. In November 1979, under the directorship of the editor, the Mental Health Research and Development Center of the Institute for Urban Affairs and Research at Howard University sponsored a research conference, "The Black Male in America: Survival for the Future." The primary purpose of the conference was to provide a forum for scholars, leaders, and lay people critically to assess the current status of the Black male in the United States and to examine the implications and alternatives for the continued survival of the Black male in the future. Participants in the conference included noted researchers, scholars, practitioners, policy makers, students, and representatives from a variety of organizations, such as churches, fraternities, sororities, civic and social clubs, and recreational groups. Conference presentations focused on a range of topics in the following substantive areas: economics, health, education, family support systems, the military, the criminal justice system, the media, and the arts.

The conference discussion and findings underscored the need for a book on Black men. Despite the various roles Black men play in their families, they have received only marginal attention from social and behavioral scientists and practitioners. Although there has been an increase in the literature on various aspects of behavior in Black communities, much of this intellectual activity reflects a greater interest in studies on the Black family with a specific focus on Black women and their children.

As a result of the women's movement, considerable attention has been given to the role and status of Black women, as evidenced by the increasing number of books on Black females. These include *Tomorrow's Tomorrow: The Black Woman* (Ladner, 1971); *The Black Woman in America* (Staples, 1973); *Black Women in White America: A Documentary History* (Lerner, 1973); *All Our Kin* (Stack, 1974); *Beautiful, Also, Are the Souls of My Black Sisters: A History of Black Women in America* (Noble, 1978); *Black Macho and the Myth of the Super Woman* (Wallace, 1979); and *The Black Woman* Rodgers-Rose, 1980). Although these publications have added considerably to our knowledge of Black women and their families, to some extent they have created the impression in the minds of many people that the Black community functions primarily as a matriarchal family system. In fact, so little attention has been given to Black men as fathers and husbands that they have been referred to as the "phantom of American family studies" (Cazenave, 1979). Therefore, this volume is needed to communicate a more balanced presentation of family life in Black communities.

In order not to mislead the reader, it should be noted that there are some scholarly works on Black men. These include *Urban Blues* (Keil, 1966); *Nineteen Negro Men* (Rutledge and Gass, 1967); *Tally's Corner* (Liebow, 1967); *Soulside* (Hannerz, 1969); *Deep in the Jungle* (Abrahams, 1970); *The Black Male in America* (Wilkinson & Taylor, 1977); and *A Place on the Corner* (Anderson, 1978). While these works have helped us to gain a better understanding of the role of Black men in their families and communities, for the most part they have tended to be social-problem-oriented in that they have focused primarily on social positions and role enactment problems. Moreover, much of the social science literature on the Black male has focused on his absence from his family (Burton & Whiting, 1961; Earl & Lohmann, 1978; Herzog, 1972; Hetherington, 1966; Rubin, 1974; Shinn, 1978). One consequence of this emphasis is that we have not accumulated much knowledge on the effects on the family of those fathers who are present.

Another deficiency in the research on Black men is the tendency of social scientists to study primarily low-income Black men (Abrahams, 1970; Anderson, 1978; Liebow, 1967; Rutledge & Gass, 1967). A recent exception to this is Cazenave's (1979) study of 54 Black middle-class fathers. Other research on Black men has included social problems in areas such as crime, employment, social services, and the readjustment of veterans (Fendrich, 1972; Gelber, 1974; Hopkins, 1973; Strayer & Ellenhorn, 1975).

Although research on the Black male has improved over the past decade, many studies have continued to be narrowly focused, methodologically limited, and sometimes lacking in cultural sensitivity. Review of most of these studies indicates that two continuing problems in past research have been small sample sizes or nonprobability sampling techniques. As a result of these problems, social scientists and practitioners have perpetuated many myths, stereotypes, and distortions about Black men. As a subject of research, the Black male has been cast in a restricted role set that, to a large extent, has been pathological in nature. This role set has depicted Black males as "street-corner men," pimps, deserters, criminals, hustlers, or ineffective family figureheads. Moreover, the Black male has been projected as psychologically impotent and castrated, dependent, incredulous, nebulous, irresponsible, and suspicious.

To some degree, the mass media, by relying on the social science literature, have also projected a negative image of the Black man. Since television has become a powerful socialization agent in our society, it is interesting to see how this institution has portrayed Black men. A recent study by the U. S. Commission on Civil Rights (1977) showed that between 1969 and 1974 only 8.6 percent of television's major and minor characters in dramatic roles were nonwhite males, compared to 65.3 percent who were white males. Moreover, 75 percent of the nonwhite male characters were not depicted as husbands, and 53.8 percent of those who were portrayed as very poor were nonwhite males. In contrast to white males, more nonwhite males were represented as service workers or were associated with criminal activities.

Television has had tremendous effect on American families, especially on children from low-income, nonwhite communities. In general, television's portrayal of Black men revolves around their being nonfamily, poor, nonprofessional, and unlawful. This distortion is another indication of the victimization of Black males. Further, it may well be a manifestation of discriminatory employment practices, since few Black males occupy executive-level positions or head the programming departments of television stations. One can argue that these practices and policies have had a negative effect on the socialization of many Black males for family life.

Therefore, an important purpose of this anthology is to present data that will dispel some of the myths and misconceptions about the Black male. In addition, this volume will attempt to define and to discuss a range of issues and problems confronting Black men and their families from the perspective of the Black community.

Another function of this book is to clarify and differentiate between the issues raised by the men's liberation movement and the special needs and concerns of Black men. In the past decade, there has been a significant increase in the literature on the role of men in the American society (Farrell, 1974; Fasteau, 1975; Goldberg, 1977; Hapgood, 1979; Hoffman, 1980; Kriegel, 1979; Nichols, 1975; Pleck & Pleck, 1980: Tiger, 1969). However, most of the literature has documented the privileges, experiences, and disadvantages of being a white middle-class male in our society. Very little attention has been focused on the unique concerns or needs of the Black male. In their book, *Men and Masculinity,* Pleck and Sawyer (1974: 2) state:

> This book deals mainly with the experience of males who are white, middle-class, heterosexual and live in the United States. This is a distinctly advantaged group with disproportionate access to society's wealth and respect.

In this regard, the theme that guides this book is institutional racism rather than sexism and classism. It is suggested that "these basic 'isms' . . . should not be conceptually lumped together for analysis and for problem-solving because they are, in fact, different in terms of history, dynamics, and intensity; and as such, the solutions are also different" (Hopkins, 1979: 260).

Longres and Bailey (1979) used an institutional sexism perspective in their review essay on men's issues. In general, this frame of reference focuses on practices and policies by which males have certain privileges at the expense of females. In this respect, an institutional sexism framework views men as victims and as oppressors. This book will not view Black men as oppressors of Black women, for it is clear that the racial subordination of Black men has negated their advantages as males (although it should be understood that some Black men do oppress some Black women). In a discerning analysis of the impact of sex and race on Black men, Staples (1978: 169-170) writes:

> In the case of Black men, their subordination as a racial minority has more than cancelled out their advantages as males in the larger society.

Any understanding of their experiences will have to come from an analysis of the complex problems they face as Blacks and as men. Unlike white males, they have few privileges in this society.

The classism-theoretical perspective for explaining the economic and social suffering of Black people, as advocated by Gershman (1980) and Wilson (1978), has created much controversy in recent years. This scheme suggests that neither sexism nor racism can adequately describe the poverty and the despair in Black communities. Rather, it suggests that the problems of Black people, including Black men, can best be explained in terms of class and economic trends. While this approach has some merit, it does not adequately deal with the fact that Black and white men operate in two different psychological milieus. Furthermore, this approach has many theoretical, methodological, and structural problems that have to be resolved.

In this volume, the editor and contributors will examine problems confronting Black men from an institutional racism premise (Clark, 1980; Gary, 1978; Stewart & Scott, 1978). According to Staples (1978: 170),

> the experiences of males and females, Black and white, in their lives are critical and different from each other. Black men face certain problems related to institutional racism and environments which often do not prepare them very well for the fulfillment of masculine roles.

In other words, rather than view Black men as oppressors, we see them as victims of racism. Pettigrew (1973: 274-275) defines institutional racism as

> that complex of institutional arrangements that restrict the life choices of Black Americans in comparison to those of white Americans. . . . Institutional racism avidly supports individual racism. . . . Racist institutions need not be headed by racists nor designed with racist intentions to limit Black choices. . . . The restrictive consequence is the important fact rather than formal intentions.

How racism operates to eliminate Black men from the Black community or to render them ineffective in their role performances in a variety of settings has been addressed in Stewart and Scott's (1978) penetrating article, "The Institutional Decimation of Black American Males." There are cooperative and connectional relations among institutions in their strategies for destroying Black males. The major institutions of our society use racist techniques for reducing the survival rate of Black males. Black males are born into their families with a certain potential for development. To a large extent, their potential is developed or underdeveloped primarily as a function of the behavior of social institutions. Due to the racial oppression of external institutions, many Black families have had a difficult time preparing Black men for useful roles in our society. Often, difficult family relationships result from the pressures and frustrations Black men experience dealing with these institutions, especially in the areas of education and economics. According to Stewart and Scott (1978), these institutions induce certain types of behavioral responses, basically aggressive responses to social and economic frustrations. Thus, these men use a variety of psychological and social coping mechanisms, including suicide, homicide, crime and vice, drugs, and alcohol, for dealing with the racial oppression of these institutions. Of course, many Black men have been able to cope successfully with the problems of living in a racist society. Unfortunately, too many Black men, in comparison to white men, do not succeed.

In this book, for the most part, our comparative reference is white men, rather than Black women, because white men have the power to maintain a racist social system. Given this orientation and the data available, it becomes clear that Black men are not like white men on many significant institutional measures, and that race, rather than sexism or classism, is a more powerful variable for understanding the behavior of Black men in the American society.

The volume is divided into four major sections, each preceded by an introduction. In Part I there is a comparison between white and Black men on a range of indicators such as sex ratio, age distribution, marital and family status, educational attainment, income, criminal victimization, mortality, morbidity, and mental health. In this comparative analysis, Black men find themselves on the negative side of most social and health indicators.

Part II examines the relationships of Black men with their families. There is a discussion of the impact of race and sex on the socialization of Black male children. How Black fathers interact with their children is described by one author. In addition, one chapter contains a study of problems and concerns of unwed adolescent fathers. The concept of Afrocentricity is used to develop a perspective on family relationships. There is also a chapter on the interpersonal relations between Black men and women.

Part III is devoted to the psychosocial dynamics of the Black male. This section addresses some of the adaptation strategies used by Black men as they attempt to operate within their environment. Among the issues discussed are stress, social support systems, alcohol abuse, and suicide. Another chapter provides insight into how Black men use support systems as coping strategies.

Part IV reviews the way Black men relate to the major social institutions in our society. Both public schools and higher educational institutions are discussed in terms of their impact on the educational experiences of Black men. One chapter examines the incarceration of Black men. How social services under the auspices of the government function to undermine the role of Black men in their families is also reviewed. The religious experience of Black men concludes the analysis of the impact of selected institutions on Black men.

The concluding section is a brief summary of directions and priorities for improving the quality of Black men's lives. There is a discussion of the need for more research in this important area so that appropriate internal and external strategies can be developed for the purpose of reducing the high-risk status of Black men in the American society.

The editor and contributors do not claim to cover all past, present, and future problems and issues affecting Black men. We emphasize contemporary concerns, realizing that historical background plays a role in understanding current issues. A variety of topics are covered in this volume. Most of the chapters are revised presentations from the 1979 research conference on Black men. Including both theoretical and research articles, the work is interdisciplinary in scope. Among the disciplines and professions represented in this publication are education, epidemiology, history, political science, psychology, social work, and sociology.

It is the editor's hope that this book will serve as a resource for those who are training to become teachers, social workers, psychologists, psychiatrists, counselors, nurses, and social scientists; those who are involved in training professional workers; those who are involved in planning, designing, and funding programs directed at solving problems in the Black community; and lay persons, political leaders, community organizers, ministers, and others who are committed to improving the quality of life for all Black people.

–Lawrence E. Gary

## REFERENCES

Abrahams, R. *Deep in the jungle.* Chicago: Aldine, 1970.

Anderson, E. *A place on the corner.* Chicago: University of Chicago Press, 1978.

Burton, R., & Whiting, J. The absent father and cross sex identity. *Merrill-Palmer Quarterly,* 1961, *7,* 85-95.

Cazenave, N. Middle-income Black fathers: An analysis of the provider roles. *The Family Coordinator,* 1979, *28,* 583-592.

Clark, K. The role of race. *New York Times Magazine,* October 1980, pp. 25-35.

Earl, L., & Lohmann, M. Absent fathers and Black male children. *Social Work,* 1978, *23,* 413-415.

Farrell, W. *The liberated man.* New York: Bantam Books, 1974.

Fasteau, M. *The male machine.* New York: McGraw-Hill, 1975.

Fendrich, J. Returning Black Vietnam era veterans. *Social Service Review,* 1972, *46,* 60-75.

Gary, L. (Ed.) *Mental health: A challenge to the Black community.* Philadelphia: Dorrance, 1978.

Gelber, S. *Black men and businessmen: The growing awareness of a social responsibility.* Port Washington, NY: Kennikat, 1974.

Gershman, C. A matter of class. *New York Times Magazine,* October 1980, 24, 92-109.

Goldberg, H. *The hazards of being male: Surviving the myth of masculine privilege.* New York: Signet, 1977.

Hannerz, U. *Soulside.* New York: Columbia University Press, 1969.

Hapgood, F. *Why males exist.* New York: William Morrow, 1979.

Hetherington, E. Effects of paternal absence on sex-typed behavior in Negro and white males. *Journal of Personality and Social Psychology,* 1966, *4,* 87-91.

Herzog, E. *Boys in fatherless families.* Washington, DC: U. S. Department of Health, Education and Welfare, 1972.

Hoffman, S. *The classified man: Twenty-two types of men.* New York: Coward, McCann & Geoghegan, 1980.

Hopkins, T. The role of the agency in supporting Black manhood. *Social Work,* 1973, *18,* 53-58.

Hopkins, T. Another conflict. *Social Work,* 1979, *24,* 259-260.

Keil, C. *Urban blues.* Chicago: University of Chicago Press, 1966.

Kriegel, L. *On men and manhood.* New York: Hawthorn, 1979.

Ladner, J. *Tomorrow's tomorrow: The Black woman.* Garden City, NY: Doubleday, 1971.

Lerner, G. *Black women in white America: A documentary history.* New York: Vintage, 1973.

Liebow, E. *Tally's corner.* Boston: Little, Brown, 1967.

Longres, J., & Bailey, R. Men's issues and sexism: A journal review. *Social Work,* 1979, *24,* 26-32.

Nichols, J. *Men's liberation: A new definition of masculinity.* New York: Penguin, 1975.

Noble, J. *Beautiful, also, are the souls of my Black sisters: A history of Black women in America.* Englewood Cliffs, NJ: Prentice-Hall, 1978.

Pleck, E., & Pleck, J. (Eds.). *The American man.* Englewood Cliffs, NJ: Prentice-Hall, 1980.

Pleck, J., & Sawyer, J. (Eds.). *Men and masculinity.* Englewood Cliffs, NJ: Prentice-Hall, 1974.

Pettigrew, T. Racism and mental health of white Americans. In C. Willie, B. Kramer, & B. Brown (Eds.), *Racism and mental health.* Pittsburgh: University of Pittsburgh Press, 1973, 274-275.

Rodgers-Rose, L. *The Black woman.* Beverly Hills, CA: Sage Publications, 1980.

Rubin, R. Adult male and the self attitudes of Black children. *Child Study Journal,* 1974, *4,* 33-46.

Rutledge, A., & Gass, G. *Nineteen Negro men.* San Francisco: Jossey-Bass, 1967.

Shinn, M. Father absence and children's cognitive development. *Psychological Bulletin,* 1978, *85,* 295-324.

Stack, C. *All our kin.* New York: Harper & Row, 1974.

Staples, R. *The Black woman in America.* Chicago: Nelson-Hall, 1973.

Staples, R. Masculinity and race: The dual dilemma of Black men. *Journal of Social Issues,* 1978, *34,* 169-183.

Strayer, R., & Ellenhorn, L. Vietnam veterans: A study exploring adjustment patterns and attitudes. *Journal of Social Issues,* 1975, *31,* 81-93.

Stewart, J., & Scott, J. The institutional decimation of Black American males. *Western Journal of Black Studies,* 1978, *2,* 82-93.

Tiger, L. *Men in groups.* New York: Random House, 1969.

U. S. Commission on Civil Rights. *Window dressing on the set: Women and minorities in television.* Washington, DC: Government Printing Office, 1977.

Wallace, M. *Black macho and the myth of the super woman.* New York: Dial Press, 1979.

Wilkinson, D., & Taylor, R. *The Black male in America.* Chicago: Nelson-Hall, 1977.

Wilson, W. *The declining significance of race.* Chicago: University of Chicago Press, 1978.

# PART I
## SOCIAL AND HEALTH INDICATORS

In this section, Gary examines selected statistical data collected by the federal government and presents them in a manner that describes the current social and health conditions and trends of Black men in the United States. He uses a framework that compares Black men with white men on a range of indicators. Acknowledging that there are some limitations in using government statistics, the author provides the necessary background information to assist the reader in understanding and appreciating the content presented in subsequent chapters.

In developing a social profile of Black men, Gary reveals that in 1978 there were 12 million Black males, of which 7.3 million were adults. Although there has been an increase in the Black male population since 1960, he finds that the sex ratio—that is, the number of males per 100 females—has been declining over the past hundred years. This finding takes into consideration the fact that Black men have consistently been undercounted by the U.S. Bureau of the Census. Further, Gary indicates that in comparison to white males the Black male population is younger and a larger percentage of them are single, either never having married or not presently married (i.e., widowed, divorced, or separated). In examining the family status, the author notes that there have been some significant changes in the role of men in the traditional family unit in Black communities. Changes in the educational and economic levels of Black men are also discussed. Unable to earn an adequate income in our economy, many Black men are forced to engage in criminal activities or to join the armed forces, Gary suggests. Although Black men are less likely to be involved in the political process or professional organizations than are white men, the author observes that Black men have developed their own voluntary organizations and associations.

In discussing the health status of Black men, Gary examines the differences between Black and white men in the following areas: (1) mortality, (2) morbidity, (3) accidents and injuries, and (4) mental disorders. After a brief review of the concept of health status, the author finds that Black males have a lower life-expectancy rate and a higher age-adjusted death rate than white males have. Moreover, of the leading causes of death for men, he says that Black males have a higher death rate than white males for all of them except two: suicide and arteriosclerosis. The sudden rise in cancer deaths and the low survival rates among Black men after the discovery of the disease are discussed. Although some differences in morbidity rates between white and Black men were noted, Gary indicates that the lifestyles of Black men are related to many of their health problems. In addition, the author discloses that the mental health of Black men is poor on a number of measures in comparison to that of white men. Gary concludes his chapter by discussing the relationship between the major causes of death among Black males and associated behavioral risk factors.

# 1

## A SOCIAL PROFILE

Lawrence E. Gary

In this chapter, consideration will be given to the social and demographic characteristics of Black men in the United States. As mentioned earlier, there seems to be an impression in the minds of many people that the Black community is composed primarily of Black women and their children. In a provocative essay Jackson (1971) asked, "Where are the Black men?" Although the ratio of Black males to Black females has been declining for many years, there were 12,108,000 Black males in the United States in 1978. This figure represented 47.5 percent of the total Black population (U.S. Bureau of the Census, 1979a).

There is no doubt that Black men are an integral part of Black communities. It is important for us to describe the current social conditions under which these men function in our society. More specifically, in this chapter, we plan to develop a profile on Black men in terms of population growth and distribution, marital and family status, educational attainment, employment and income, and social participation. Health status is discussed in Chapter 2. Moreover, an in-depth analysis of education and training and economics is contained in Chapters 12, 13, and 14.

In developing this profile, it was necessary to exercise considerable judgment in selecting from the enormous body of available data. The primary data sources for this study include the U.S. Bureau of the Census, the U.S. Bureau of Labor Statistics, the U.S. Department of Justice (Federal Bureau of Investigation), and the National Center for Education Statistics. In addition, two government publications, *The Social and Economic Status of the Black Population in the United States 1790-1978* (U.S. Bureau of the Census, 1979b) and *Social Indicators 1976* (U.S. Department of Commerce, 1977), have been most useful in developing this chapter. Since the data in this chapter were obtained from a variety of sources, one has to be aware of sampling errors (values from samples compared to those from complete enumeration of particular population groups) and nonsampling errors (refusals of respondents, undercounts of certain groups, poorly designed instruments, falsification of records, incorrect recording of information, and so forth). Where appropriate, we shall mention data limitations as different information is presented.

In keeping with the basic theme of this volume, major comparisons will be made between Black and white men, rather than between Black men and women. In some cases, comparisons can be made only between Blacks and whites. Moreover, much of the social data collected by various departments of the federal government have been categorized in terms of white and nonwhite. When this is the case, appropriate acknowledgement of this fact will be made. This social profile will provide a framework for helping us to understand the high psychosocial and economic risk status of Black men in our society. Further, it will document the social frustration of Black men that often leads to unhealthy adaptations. Finally, these social indicators will help us to see the interlocking relationship between Black families and social institutions such as the economy, social services, education, the military, and the penal system.

## POPULATION GROWTH AND DISTRIBUTION

As indicated earlier, in 1978, there were over 12 million Black men, compared to 92 million white men. In other words, Black males accounted for about 11.3 percent of the male population in the United States (U.S. Bureau of the Census, 1979a). In 1960, the Black male population was 9 million, compared to 78 million for white men. These data suggest that since 1960, the Black male population has increased by 33.3 percent, whereas the white male population has increased by only 18 percent.

As indicated in Table 1.1, the age distribution of the Black male population has shown some changes since 1960, in comparison to little change for the white male population. In 1978, the median age for Black males was 23.2 years, but it was 29.4 years for white males. In other words, the Black male population is younger than is the white male population. The proportion of the Black male population below the age of 21 years was 48 percent, compared to 37 percent for the white male population in 1978. On the other hand, 10 percent of the white male population was 65 years and older, but the corresponding percentage for the Black male population was only 7 percent in 1978. These data suggest that the age dependency ratio (the ratio of persons under 14 years of age and those persons 65 years of age and older—defined as dependents—to those persons between 14 and 65 years of age—defined as economically productive) is much higher for Black males than it is for white males. In 1978, 36 percent of Black males can be defined as being dependent, compared to 31 percent of white males.

Over the past hundred years, the U.S. Bureau of the Census has enumerated more Black females than it has Black males. The sex ratio (the number of males per 100 females) was 96.2 for the Black community in 1870 and 90.6 in 1978 (U.S. Bureau of the Census, 1979a, 1979b). In comparison, the sex ratio was 95.3 for the white community in 1978. As implied in Table 1.1, the sex ratio is particularly problematic for the Black community during the marriage and childbearing ages. However, this is not the case for the white community. Jackson (1971) has further analyzed sex ratio for the Black community in terms of regions and states. She has shown that the sex ratio varies according to city, state, and region, and that it has an impact on family stability and behavior. In Chapter 4, Braithwaite discusses the impact of the imbalance in the sex ratio on female and male relationships in Black communities. Some caution must be exercised in accepting the census data with respect to the sex ratio. It has been shown that the U.S. Bureau of the Census undercounted the number of Black people, especially Black males, in the 1970 decennial census (Rodgers-Rose, 1980; Siegal, 1973; U.S. Department of Commerce, 1977). It has been suggested that the corrected sex ratio should be 95, instead of 91 (U.S. Bureau of the Census, 1979b).

## MARITAL AND FAMILY STATUS

In 1975, 38 percent of the Black male population 14 years of age and older was single, but only 28 percent of the white male population in this same age group was classified as single. What is interesting to note, as shown in Table 1.2, is that, in 1940, Black and white men had similar marital statuses. For white men 14 years of age and older, the percentage married increased from 61 in 1940 to 66 in 1975. However, for Black men the trend was the reverse; that is, there was a decrease in the percentage of married Black men. Black men are more likely to be divorced than are white men. In 1978, 6.9 percent of Black males 18 years of age and over were divorced, compared to 2.4 percent in 1960 and 3.6 percent in 1970 (U.S. Bureau of the Census, 1979a). As shown in Table 1.2, divorce has become more common and widowhood less common for both groups between 1940 and 1975. It

## TABLE 1.1
### Selected Population Characteristics of the
### U.S. Male Population by Race

|  | Black Male | White Male |
|---|---|---|
| 1. Total population in millions, 1978 | 12.0 | 92.0 |
| 2. Total population in millions, 1970 | 10.0 | 87.0 |
| 3. Total population in millions, 1960 | 9.0 | 78.0 |
| 4. Median age in years, 1978 | 23.2 | 29.4 |
| 5. Median age in years, 1970 | 21.0 | 27.6 |
| 6. Median age in years, 1960 | 22.4 | 29.4 |
| 7. Percentage of population under 22 years of age, 1978 | 48.0 | 37.0 |
| 8. Percentage of population 65 years of age 1978 and older, | 7.0 | 10.0 |
| 9. Percentage of population considered dependents, 1978 | 36.0 | 31.0 |
| 10. Males per 100 females, 1978 | 90.6 | 95.3 |
| 11. Males under 14 years of age per 100 females, 1978 | 101.6 | 104.8 |
| 12. Males 14-24 years of age per 100 females, 1978 | 96.1 | 102.4 |
| 13. Males 25-44 years of age per 100 females, 1978 | 84.0 | 98.8 |
| 14. Males 45-64 years of age per 100 females, 1978 | 86.1 | 92.8 |
| 15. Males 65 years of age and older per 100 females, 1978 | 71.2 | 67.9 |

SOURCE: U. S. Bureau of the Census. *Statistical Abstract of the United States: 1979* (100th ed.). Washington DC: Government Printing Office, 1979, pp. 28-29.

should be noted that income, education, region and age will have an impact on the divorce rate for a given population group, but a discussion of these issues is beyond the scope of this chapter (Glick, 1970; Glick and Norton, 1979).

The data tend to suggest that there has been a significant increase in the number and percentage of Black men who are single. When one combines single, divorced, or widowed into a category of unattached or not married, the data in Table 1.2 show that, in 1975, 46 percent of Black males over 14 years of age are so classified, compared to 33 percent for white males. This large percentage of unmarried Black males will have an impact on male and female relationships and on the need for social and mental health services for this high-risk group. Further, as is pointed out in Chapters 2 and 8, marital status is correlated with health behavior and other adaptation strategies.

## TABLE 1.2
## Marital Status of U.S. Males by Race

|  | Black Male | White Male |
|---|---|---|
| 1. Percentage of male population 14 years old and older single, 1975 | 38.0 | 28.0 |
| 2. Percentage of male population 14 years old and older married, 1975 | 53.0 | 66.0 |
| 3. Percentage of male population 14 years old and older divorced, 1975 | 4.0 | 3.0 |
| 4. Percentage of male population 14 years old and older unattached (single, divorce, widowed, etc.), 1975 | 46.0 | 33.0 |
| 5. Percentage of male population 14 years old and older single, 1940 | 33.0 | 33.0 |
| 6. Percentage of male population 14 years old and older married, 1940 | 61.0 | 61.0 |
| 7. Percentage of male population 14 years old and older divorced, 1940 | 1.0 | 1.0 |
| 8. Percentage of male population 14 years old and older widowed, 1940 | 6.0 | 4.0 |
| 9. Divorced males: all ages per 1000 married persons with spouse present, 1975 | 83.0* | 51.0 |
| 10. Divorced males 45-64 years of age per 1000 married persons with spouse present, 1975 | 116.0* | 55.0 |
| 11. Percentage of male population 14 years old and older widowed, 1975 | 4.0 | 2.0 |

SOURCE:   U.S. Bureau of the Census. *The Social and Economic Status of the Black Population in the United States 1790-1978.* Washington, DC: Government Printing Office, 1979, pp. 109-111; and U.S. Department of Commerce. *Social Indicators 1976.* Washington, DC: Government Printing Office, 1977, p. 68.

* Data refer to Black and other racial minorities.

Studies (Carter & Glick, 1976; Glick & Norton, 1979; Rosen et al., 1979; Gove, 1972) have consistently shown that unmarried (single, divorced, or widowed) persons are at a greater risk than are married persons for all types of social and health disabilities (mental illness, drug and alcohol abuse, arrest, imprisonment, unemployment, homicide, and so forth).

Although the social science literature has tended to focus on the Black male's absence from his family, it should be noted that in 1978 there were 5.8 million Black families in the United States, of which the majority (56.1 percent) were two-parent families; that is, both husband and wife are present

TABLE 1.3
Family Status of the U.S. Population by Race

|  | Black Male | White Male |
|---|---|---|
| 1. Percentage of own children living with both parents, 1960 | 75.0 | 93.0 |
| 2. Percentage of own children living with both parents, 1970 | 65.0 | 91.0 |
| 3. Percentage of own children living with both parents, 1978 | 49.4 | 85.7 |
| 4. Percentage of all families, husband-wife type, 1960 | 74.1 | 89.2 |
| 5. Percentage of all families, husband-wife type, 1970 | 68.1 | 88.7 |
| 6. Percentage of all families, husband-wife type, 1978 | 56.1 | 85.9 |
| 7. Percentage of all families, male-headed, no wife present, 1960 | 4.1 | 2.7 |
| 8. Percentage of all families, male-headed, no wife present, 1970 | 3.7 | 2.3 |
| 9. Percentage of all families, male-headed, no wife present, 1978 | 4.6 | 2.5 |
| 10. Percentage of husband-wife families where husband is 14-34 years old, 1960 | 28.0 | 27.0 |
| 11. Percentage of husband-wife families where husband is 65 years old and older, 1960 | 11.0 | 12.0 |
| 12. Percentage of husband-wife families where husband is 14-34 years old, 1975 | 32.0 | 30.0 |
| 13. Percentage of husband-wife families where husband is 65 years old and older, 1975 | 13.0 | 14.0 |

SOURCE: U.S. Bureau of the Census. *The Social and Economic Status of the Black Population in the United States 1790-1978.* Washington, DC: Government Printing Office, 1979, pp. 103, 105, 107, 175, and 178.

(U.S. Bureau of the Census, 1979b). Moreover, in the same year, approximately 4.6 percent of all families were headed by men, with no wife present. As indicated in Table 1.3, Black families are more likely to have no husband present than are white families. Between 1960 and 1978, Black husband-wife families declined from 74.1 percent to 56.1 percent of all Black families. By contrast, for whites the decline in husband-wife families has not been as significant. For example, in 1960, 89.2 percent of all white families were of the husband-wife type; in 1978 this family type had declined to 85.9 percent. In 1978, 85.7 percent of white children lived with both parents, compared to 49.4 percent for Black children. In both white and Black communities, there has been a decline in the percentage of children who live with both parents. However, the decline is much more significant for Black families. The data suggest that for both Blacks and whites the proportion of children living with both parents seems to be related to income (U.S. Bureau of the Census, 1979b). For example, in 1975, for Black families with incomes under $4,000, only 17 percent of the children lived with both parents, but for those families with incomes of $15,000 and more, 86 percent lived with their parents. A similar income effect is noted for white families, although at all income levels white children are more likely to live with both of their parents than are Black children.

In general, these data suggest that there has been a significant change in the structure of the traditional family unit in the Black community. First, a large number of Black men are not getting married. In addition, there is an increase in the divorce rate among Black men. While income, age, and regional factors influence marital and family status, it is becoming increasingly clear that family fragmentation is more pronounced in Black communities than it is in white communities. Part II of this volume discusses in some detail the consequences of these changes on family relationships.

## EDUCATION AND TRAINING

Education is considered to be a very important value in Black communities (Doddy, 1963; Gary & Favors, 1975; Staples, 1976). To a large extent, many Blacks see education as fundamental to their gaining the necessary economic resources for maintaining a reasonable quality of life. School enrollment rates for Black males are about the same as those for whites, especially since 1960 (see Table 1.4). Commenting on the school attendance behavior of Black people, the U.S. Bureau of the Census (1979b: 86) concludes:

> In the past 25 years (1950-1975), substantial increases have been noted in the proportion of Black youth enrolled in school above the compulsory attendance age. . . . The growth in enrollment experienced by the age group 5 to 13 years old is due both to the increased availability of kindergarten classes to Blacks . . . and to increased participation rates at the compulsory school ages 7 to 13.

The extension of formal schooling to Black men has resulted in a decline in the illiteracy rate from 10 percent in 1959 to 4 percent in 1969, as indicated in Table 1.4. In 1978, the median years of school completed was 11.6 for Black males, compared to 12.6 for white males. Although Black males' school enrollment rates are very similar to those for white males, Black males continue to lag behind their white counterparts on a variety of educational attainment measures including median years of school completed, percentage of high school graduates, percentage of college graduates, and literacy rates. In an article, "Boys: Endangered Species," Raspberry (1979) reviews some of the behavioral and institutional problems that boys must face as they advance through the public school system. In Chapter 13, Patton provides additional insight into this problem. Given the negative attitude of the public school system toward Black males, as indicated in Table 1.4, it should be no surprise that their dropout rate was 20.0 percent, compared to 12.4 for white males in 1977.

As shown in Table 1.4, the data indicate that Black men have been making gains in higher education, but they still lag behind their white counterparts. For example, in 1979, 8.3 percent of Black men 25 years of age and older had four years or more of college, compared to 21.4 percent for white men in that age group. Although there has been an increase in the number of Black men enrolled in college, they are quite a distance from reaching parity with white men. In 1978, 1.0 million Black adults were enrolled in college; of this number, 452,000 were Black men (U.S. Bureau of the Census, 1979a). In other words, Black males represented 44.3 percent of the Black adults enrolled in college. For the white community, males accounted for 52.9 percent of the adult college enrollment. While Black men and women are near parity in regard to college enrollment, Black men still lag behind white men. Once enrolled in college, Black men experience a variety of problems. In Chapter 14, Fleming examines the impact of higher education on Black males.

## EMPLOYMENT AND INCOME

How educational attainment benefits Black men is a continuing question that is asked by many in the Black community. Yankelovich (1979: 31) in an essay entitled "Who Gets Ahead in America," answered the question in the following manner:

> If you are "finishing" and have been persuaded to stay in school because "finishing high school will help you find a better job later on," forget what you have been told. Even for whites the economic advantages of finishing high school without going on to college are marginal at best; for Blacks, they count for almost nothing.

These conclusions are based on findings from a study conducted by Jencks and his colleagues. Apparently, the Black men who drop out of high school are making rational decisions based on these research observations. Nevertheless, the predictions for success in employment and income seem to be better for Black males who go to college. Commenting on this issue, Yankelovich (1979: 31) concludes:

> If you are Black and in college and suspect that finishing college is not going to help you economically, you are wrong. Buckle down, hang in there and finish at all costs. If it's money and a good job you are after, stay in college, no matter how you do it. . . . Economically it does not matter what you study, how you learn or where you go to college—as long as you finish.

Although data seem to support these assertions, some caution should be exercised in accepting them at face value. Nonetheless, data do show that education, especially at the college level, influences the direction of a number of economic status variables, such as unemployment rates, labor force participation rates, earnings, and so forth. Although college education has a positive impact on economic success for Black males, it should be noted that only 8.3 percent of them were college graduates in 1979 (see Table 1.4).

Given this reality, one should expect a high level of economic frustration for the vast majority of Black men. The data in Table 1.5 show that the labor force participation rate for civilian Black males has decreased from 83.4 percent in 1959 to 71.9 percent in 1979. For white males, the labor force participation rate was 78.6 percent in 1979. Commenting on the Black male participation rate in the labor market, Stewart and Scott (1978: 84) wrote:

> One source of frustration of employed Black males is the crowding of these workers into low-status occupations of which the associated wage rates are inadequate to provide for a standard of living significantly above the poverty level.

An examination of the occupational distribution of employed Black males indicates that the majority are blue-collar and service workers. In Table 1.5, one can observe that in 1977 over one-half (58 percent) of the employed Black males were blue-collar workers—for example, craft, operatives and non-farm laborers—while 17 percent were service workers. It should be noted that 3 percent of Black males were employed as farm workers and 23 percent were employed as white-collar workers (U.S. Bureau of the Census, 1979b). In contrast, during the same year, there were nearly twice as many (42 percent) white males employed in white-collar jobs, while less than half (45 percent) were blue-collar workers and 8 and 4 percent, respectively, were service or farm workers.

Not only have the majority of Black males occupied lower-status jobs than have white males, but they have also experienced high rates of unemployment over the last several decades. During the period of 1954-1974, the unemployment rate for Black males 20 years of age and older was either more than double or slightly less than double that of white males (U.S. Bureau of the Census, 1979b). As depicted in Table 1.5, the unemployment rate for Black males 20 years of age and older was 9.1 percent in 1979, but it was only 3.6 percent for white males in this age category. The data in this table also indicate that young Black males have had a much higher unemployment rate than has the Black male population as a whole. In 1979, the unemployment rate for Black males between the ages of 16 and 17 years old was 34.4 percent, but it was only 16.1 percent for white males in the same age

TABLE 1.4
Educational Profile of Males
by Race in the United States

|  | Black Male | White Male |
|---|---|---|
| 1. Median years of school completed, 1960 | 7.7 | 10.7 |
| 2. Median years of school completed, 1970 | 9.6 | 12.2 |
| 3. Median years of school completed, 1978 | 11.6 | 12.6 |
| 4. Percentage of illiterate in population 14 years old and older, 1959 | 10.0* | 2.0 |
| 5. Percentage of illiterate in population 14 years old and older, 1969 | 4.0* | 1.0 |
| 6. Percentage of persons 5 to 29 years old enrolled in school, 1960 | 66.0* | 69.0 |
| 7. Percentage of persons 5 to 29 years old enrolled in school, 1970 | 69.0* | 70.0 |
| 8. Percentage of persons 5 to 29 years old enrolled in school, 1975 | 69.0* | 64.0 |
| 9. Percentage of high school dropouts among persons 14 to 34 years old, 1970 | 30.4 | 14.4 |
| 10. Percentage of high school dropouts among persons 14 to 34 years old, 1977 | 20.0 | 12.4 |
| 11. Percentage of persons 25 years old and older, less than 4 years of high school, 1970 | 67.5 | 42.8 |
| 12. Percentage of persons 25 years old and older, less than 4 years of high school, 1979 | 50.8 | 29.7 |
| 13. Percentage of persons 25 years old and older with 4 years of high school, 1970 | 22.2 | 30.9 |
| 14. Percentage of persons 25 years old and older with 4 years of high school, 1979 | 29.5 | 33.1 |

## TABLE 1.4
### Educational Profile of Males
### by Race in the United States (Continued)

| | Black Male | White Male |
|---|---|---|
| 15. Percentage of persons 25 years old and older with 4 years of college or more, 1979 | 8.3 | 21.4 |
| 16. Percentage of persons 25 years old and older with 4 years of college or more, 1970 | 4.6 | 15.0 |
| 17. Percentage of total persons 14-34 years old enrolled in college by race, 1978 | 44.3 | 52.9 |
| 18. Percentage of total persons 14-34 years old enrolled in college by race, 1970 | 48.5 | 60.2 |

SOURCE:   U. S. Bureau of the Census. *Statistical Abstract of the United States 1979* (100th ed.). Washington, DC: Government Printing Office, 1979, pp. 145, 159; U.S. Bureau of the Census. *The Social and Economic Status of the Black Population in the United States 1790-1978*. Washington, DC: Government Printing Office, 1979, pp. 89, 92-93; National Center for Education Statistics. *Digest of Education Statistics 1979*. Washington, DC: Government Printing Office, 1979, p. 66; and U.S. Department of Commerce. Population Profile of the United States: 1979. *Current Population Reports, 1980, Series P-20, No. 350, p. 17.*

* Data include Black and other racial minorities.

category. Furthermore, young Black male veterans also experienced a high level of unemployment. In all cases, the unemployment rate for Black men is substantially higher than that for white men.

When Black men are able to find work, their earnings lag behind those of white men. In 1979, Black males had a median income that was $4,962 less than that of white males; the median incomes of Black and white males, respectively, were $13,068 and $18,030 (U.S. Department of Commerce, 1980a). The gap in median incomes between Black and white men was only $3,830 in 1978. The median income of Black male-headed families was $13,443, compared to $17,848 for their white counterparts in 1977. Further, in the same year, when wives were also in the paid labor force, the median Black family income was $17,008, compared to $20,518 for white families. Studies (Datcher, 1980; Duncan, 1969; Miller, 1966; Siegel, 1965) have shown consistently that Black men earn lower wages than do white men working in the same occupation. Commenting on wage differences between Black and white men, Stolzenberg (1975: 300) concluded:

It has been found repeatedly that Black men are less successful than their white counterparts in "converting" years of schooling into dollars or earnings, even when racial differences in schooling, family background, occupation and other factors are taken into consideration. Numerous analyses have also carried the argument that these racial differences in wage returns to schooling are not merely artifacts of hiring discrimination which keep educationally qualified Black men out

### TABLE 1.5
### Economic Profile of Male Population
### in the United States by Race

|  | Black Male | White Male |
|---|---|---|
| 1. Civilian Labor Force Participation rates for persons 16 years and older, 1979* | 71.9 | 78.6 |
| 2. Civilian Labor Force Participation rates for persons 16 years and older, 1969* | 76.9 | 80.2 |
| 3. Civilian Labor Force Participation rates for persons 16 years and older, 1959* | 83.4 | 83.8 |
| 4. Unemployment rates for civilians 20 years and older, 1979 | 9.1 | 3.6 |
| 5. Unemployment rates of male Vietnam-era veterans 20-24 years of age, 1979* | 20.5 | 9.8 |
| 6. Unemployment rates of male Vietnam-era nonveterans 20-24 years of age, 1979* | 15.6 | 6.9 |
| 7. Unemployment rates of persons 18 and 19 years old, 1979* | 29.6 | 12.3 |
| 8. Unemployment rates of persons 16 and 17 years old, 1979* | 34.4 | 16.1 |
| 9. Median family income, male-headed, 1977 | 13,443 | 17,848 |
| 10. Percentage of employed men who are white-collar workers, 1977 | 23.0 | 42.0 |
| 11. Percentage of employed men who are blue-collar workers, 1977 | 58.0 | 45.0 |
| 12. Percentage of employed men who are service workers, 1977 | 17.0 | 8.0 |
| 13. Percentage of employed men who are farm workers, 1977 | 3.0 | 4.0 |
| 14. Victimization rates for persons 12 and older, crimes of violence, 1977 | 57.4 | 45.3 |
| 15. Victimization rates for persons 12 and older, robbery, 1977 | 19.8 | 7.5 |

SOURCE: U.S. Department of Labor. *Employment and Training Report of the President.* Washington, DC: Government Printing Office, 1980, pp. 225-226, 230-231, 233-234, 254-255; U.S. Bureau of the Census *The Social and Economic Status of the Black Population in the United States 1790-1978.* Washington, DC: Government Printing Office, 1979, p. 190, 218; and U.S. Department of Justice. *Criminal Victimization in the United States.* Washington, DC: Government Printing Office, 1979, p. 13.

* These data include Black and other racial minorities. Blacks represent about 90 percent of those classified as Black and others.

of the more remunerative occupations; a number of studies have found racial differences in wage returns to schooling within occupational categories.

The economic system generates widespread frustration for many Black males. Due to their high level of unemployment, concentration in low-level occupations and low earnings in comparison to white men, other family members—including wives and children—are forced to enter the labor market or to seek public assistance in order to augment the earnings of the Black male. Even when the wife works, the median income of Black families still lags behind that of white families. For example, in 1978 the family income of Black male-headed households where the wife worked was about the same as that of white male-headed households where the wife did not work (U.S. Bureau of the Census, 1979b). In fact, regardless of the number of wage earners in the family, Blacks earned less than did their white counterparts. Moreover, some data suggest that affirmative action programs in employment have had a negative impact on the economic status of Black males. In their analysis of statistics collected by the Equal Employment Opportunity Commission (EEOC), Brimmer and Company (1980: 96) observed:

> White women are winning out over Blacks in competing for occupational upgrading. . . . In 1973, white women held 30 percent of the EEOC-reported jobs. By 1978, their participation was up to 31.7 percent. . . . The overall position of Black men actually deteriorated in the same period. They filled 6.4 percent of the jobs in 1973 and 2.6 percent of those in 1978.

It is believed that the Black male's frustration with the economic system leads to his disproportionate involvement with America's criminal justice system. It is assumed that there is a relationship between economic conditions and crime against property. Arrest data suggest that Blacks are arrested disproportionately for offenses that have a functional relationship to economic frustrations. In 1979, for example, 505,754 Blacks were arrested for property crimes. This figure represents 29.4 percent of those arrested for these offenses. In addition, Blacks accounted for 56.9 percent of those arrested for robbery, 52.6 percent of those arrested for prostitution and commercialized vice and 67.9 percent of those arrested for gambling in 1979. Similar statistics hold for offenses such as forgery and counterfeiting, fraud, stolen property (burglary, receiving and processing), and weapons and drug abuse violations (U.S. Department of Justice, 1980).

The data in Table 1.5 summarize the extent to which Black males are victimized by the economic system as reflected in the high incidence of crime in Black communities. For example, in 1977, the victimization rate for persons aged 12 years and older for crimes of violence was 57.4 percent for

TABLE 1.6
Persons in the U.S. Armed Forces, 1971-1980

| Year | Total | White Males | Black Males | White Females | Black Females |
|------|-------|-------------|-------------|---------------|---------------|
| 1980 | 2,036,672 | 1,507,569 | 358,865 | 129,374 | 40,864 |
| 1979 | 2,013,233 | 1,514,641 | 348,655 | 116,994 | 32,943 |
| 1978 | 2,047,880 | 1,586,622 | 327,966 | 107,775 | 25,517 |
| 1977 | 2,063,074 | 1,643,726 | 301,626 | 97,555 | 20,167 |
| 1976 | 2,070,424 | 1,672,763 | 288,623 | 91,165 | 17,873 |
| 1975 | 2,116,281 | 1,732,229 | 287,302 | 81,681 | 15,069 |
| 1974 | 2,150,618 | 1,789,166 | 286,995 | 63,562 | 10,895 |
| 1973 | 2,241,230 | 1,915,545 | 270,615 | 47,995 | 7,075 |
| 1972 | 2,311,300 | 2,014,774 | 252,028 | 39,279 | 5,219 |
| 1971 | 2,701,208 | 2,388,586 | 270,299 | 37,656 | 4,667 |

SOURCE:   U.S. Department of Defense, Equal Opportunity, unpublished data, 1981.

Black males, but it was 45.3 percent for white males. The victimization rate for robbery was 7.5 percent for white males aged 12 years old and over, and 19.8 percent for Black males in that age group in 1977. Moreover, Blacks in general have a much higher rate of incarceration than whites have. Further discussion of the impact of the criminal justice system on Black males is contained in Chapter 17. Nonetheless, these data suggest that economic pressures and frustration push a large number of Black males into the criminal justice system, which temporarily separates them from the Black community and their families.

Many Black men who have difficulties dealing with the economic system often join the armed forces. In discussing the involvement of Black men in the military, Stewart and Scott (1978: 87) commented, "The pressures which push Blacks into the penal correction system also push them into the enlisted ranks of the military. . . . Blacks that are nonfunctional in the civilian labor market may still be functional in the military establishment." Table 1.6 indicates that in 1980 there were 358,865 Black males in the military. This figure represents 17.6 percent of the total persons in the military. It is interesting to note that, while the number of white males in the armed forces is on the decline, it has increased for Black males. According to Carl Rowan (1980), Black volunteers for the armed forces have more formal schooling than do white volunteers.

The military experiences of Blacks have both positive and negative components (Moskos, 1973; Moskos & Janowitz, 1974; Stewart & Scott, 1978). On the positive side, the military provides steady income, good benefits, and opportunity for travel and advancement. On the other hand, Black men are overrepresented in the combat and services units. They have a higher expulsion rate than do their white counterparts. As pointed out in Chapter 18, many Black men are incarcerated in the military. According to Stewart and Scott (1978: 88), "channeling Black males into the military, then, complements operations of the public-assistance system in mitigating violent protests against the economic frustrations associated with civilian Blacks. Once Blacks leave the military, however, they are recaptured by civilian institutional decimation." The implication is that a large number of Black men have negative interactions in the armed forces. Once they return to civilian life, they continue to experience economic frustrations as reflected in the high unemployment rate for veterans, especially those who served during the Vietnam period (see Table 1.5). Of course, economic frustration will have consequences for the family life of Black men as well as for their adaptation strategies.

## SOCIAL PARTICIPATION

In developing a social profile of Black men, it is important to examine the extent to which they are actively involved in different forms of personal and community associations and activities. Unfortunately, there are not many data on the social participation of Black men. The government and other institutions and individuals have collected a great deal of information on family status, income and employment, health status, crime, education, and so forth. More consideration needs to be given to developing a data base on social participation on the part of Black men and women, for these data will provide us with the necessary information for developing more functional coping strategies for dealing with the negative institutional outcomes from the majority community.

One type of participation where some data have been collected is in the area of politics. In 1980, 68.3 percent of white men reported that they were registered to vote, compared to only 57.2 percent for Black men (see Table 1.7). In the same year, the majority (60.9 percent) of white men reported that they voted in the 1980 election, but less than half (47.5 percent) of Black men reported that they voted. In other words, in 1980, there were 7.3 million Black men of voting age, but only 3.5 million indicated that they voted. Furthermore, 3.1 million Black men were not registered to vote in 1980. While one can argue that Black men have some involvement in political activities, the data suggest that the majority of Black men of voting age are not very active in the political process in this country. As shown in Table 1.7, age has an impact on political behavior of both Black and white men. Younger men are less active in politics than are older men for both racial groups. It is also assumed that income, education, and family background

## TABLE 1.7
### Reported Voting and Registration of the
### Male Polulation of Voting Age by Race, 1980

| Age | Percentage Reported Registered | | Percentage Reported Voted | |
|---|---|---|---|---|
| | White Male | Black Male | White Male | Black Male |
| 18-20 | 45.4 | 35.6 | 36.2 | 25.9 |
| 21-24 | 53.1 | 42.8 | 43.5 | 30.9 |
| 25-34 | 62.4 | 53.4 | 55.0 | 43.8 |
| 35-44 | 70.5 | 63.4 | 64.3 | 54.1 |
| 45-54 | 75.5 | 62.8 | 69.3 | 54.2 |
| 55-64 | 80.4 | 68.7 | 74.1 | 60.1 |
| 65-74 | 81.1 | 72.2 | 73.9 | 63.2 |
| 75 and older | 77.5 | 69.6 | 67.2 | 54.6 |
| All ages above 18 | 68.3 | 57.2 | 60.9 | 47.5 |

SOURCE:  U.S. Department of Commerce. Voting and Registration in the Election of November 1980. *Current Population Reports* (Population Characteristics, Series P-20, No. 359, advance copy). Washington, DC: U.S. Bureau of the Census, January 1981, pp. 4-5.

influence political activities for both white and Black men. It is clear, however, that Black men are less likely to be involved in political participation than are white men.

One important outcome of the political process is the election of officials. Table 1.8 shows the number of persons elected at the federal government level. In 1979, white men represented 93.1 percent of the persons in the House of Representatives and 99 percent of the persons in the Senate. There were no Black men in the Senate, and they represented only 3.2 percent of the persons in the House of Representatives. The picture is about the same for the 97th Congress (1981); that is, both houses of Congress are basically composed of white males. Given their population size, Black people are distressingly underrepresented in the Congress. A similar pattern exists for high-level appointments in all branches of the federal government.

At the state and local levels of government, Black people are also underrepresented. In 1979, there were 4,607 Black Americans who held popularly elected offices in the United States; of this number, 80 percent were newly elected (Joint Center for Political Studies, 1979). There has been a significant increase in the number of Black elected officials at all levels. For example, in 1969 there were 1,124 Black elected officials, but by 1975 there were 3,503. In 1980 there were over 4,912 Black elected officials in 44 states, the District of Columbia, and the Virgin Islands ("Number of Black Elected Officials up

### TABLE 1.8
### Members of Congress by Race and Sex, 1979

|  | Male | | | Female | | | Total |
|---|---|---|---|---|---|---|---|
|  | Black | White | Total | Black | White | Total |  |
| Congress Representatives | 14 | 404* | 418 | 2 | 14 | 16 | 434 |
| Senators | 0 | 99* | 99 | 0 | 1 | 1 | 100 |
| Representatives | 14 | 503 | 517 | 2 | 15 | 17 | 534 |

SOURCE:   Joint Center for Political Studies. *National Roster of Black Elected Officials,* Vol. 9.
Washington, DC: Joint Center for Political Studies, 1979; and U.S. Bureau of the
Census. *Statistical Abstract of the United States 1979* (100th ed.). Washington, DC:
Government Printing Office, 1979, p. 509.

NOTE:   Figures exclude vacancies and representatives from the Virgin Islands.

* These figures include other racial groups (2 senators and 3 representatives).

by 6.6 Percent," 1980). It should be noted that for federal, state, and local government levels, Black elected women held a larger share of Black elected offices than white women held. Related to this fact is that the proportion of Black men holding elected offices has declined from 88 percent in 1969 to 80 percent in 1980. It is estimated that there are over 490,265 elected state and local government officials (U.S. Bureau of the Census, 1979a). Given this fact, one can observe that Black people are grossly underrepresented at these levels of government. In evaluating the functions of Black elected officials, the Joint Center for Political Studies (1979) concluded:

> Black elected officials tend to have fewer resources to deal with the problems and needs of their constituents than do white elected officials. At the top levels of government, where elected officials wield considerable power and are routinely provided a variety of professional support services with which to administer their power, there are relatively few Black elected officials.

Historically, in the Black community, great emphasis has been placed on the importance of participating in voluntary associations (Layng, 1978; Orum, 1966; Ross and Wheeler, 1971; Yearwood, 1980). According to Tomeh (1973: 99),

> studies . . . show higher participation rates for Blacks at all social levels, especially lower class. For whatever reasons, Blacks have indeed become joiners. The rise of a wide range of Black associations in recent years indicates that voluntary associations are not the preserve of the white middle-class. . . . Whatever the case may be, the response of Blacks to segregation appears to be quite the opposite of indifference and apathy.

Often, Black people, including Black men, have used voluntary organizations to solve personal and community problems. In addition, these organizations serve as service centers, information exchanges, forums for job and business-related issues, and support mechanisms in personal development. Hard comparative data on the participation rates of Black and white men in voluntary associations are not available. Nonetheless, we are aware of a variety of organizations that have a high level of involvement on the part of Black men (see the list of some of these organizations in Table 1.9).

Black men have not held as many executive positions and offices in traditional professional associations and organizations, such as the American Medical Association, American Bar Association, American Economic Association, American Legion, American Dental Association, Chamber of Commerce of the United States, and the National Rifle Association of America, as have white men. It was estimated that in 1978, there were more than 13,589 national associations covering a range of areas such as health, social welfare, commerce and business, public affairs, recreation, labor unions, veterans, and education (U.S. Bureau of the Census, 1979a). For the most part, Black people do not play important roles in these organizations.

In many cases, Blacks have developed their own organizations and associations. The church and fraternal organizations have provided many opportunities for Black men to exercise their leadership skills and for self-expression and personal achievement. Several writers (Franklin, 1974; Hill, 1972; Staples, 1976) have pointed out the significant role played by Black churches in helping Black people, including men, to cope with societal pressures and stresses. In Chapter 16, Tinney provides us with specific insight into the role of the church in the life of Black men.

Fraternal organizations have been one formal mechanism Black men have used to operationalize the value of mutual aid. According to McPherson et al. (1971: 158), "next to the church, the fraternal and mutual benefit societies were the most [important] social institutions in the Black community." In his book, *The Negro in America,* Frazier (1957: 378) reached a similar conclusion:

> The fraternal organizations offered economic relief in time of sickness and provided decent burials. . . . The organization and growth of mutual aid associations and secret fraternal societies among Negroes have been in response to social and economic forces within Negro life as well as the result of the relations of the races.

In any social profile of Black men, consideration must be given to sports. As with other areas of social participation, there are very little hard data on the participation of the Black male in sports except in professional, collegiate, and secondary school areas. But if one drives through any Black

TABLE 1.9
List of Selected Organizations with
High Levels of Black Male Involvement

*Business and Commerce*

American Association of Blacks in Energy
Interracial Council for Business Opportunity
National Alliance of Postal and Federal Employees
National Association of Black Accountants
National Association of Black Manufacturers
National Association of Broadcasters
National Association of Market Developers
National Association of Minority Contractors
National Association of Real Estate Brokers
National Bankers Association
National Business League
National Funeral Directors and Morticians Association
National Insurance Association
National Newspaper Publishers Association
Opportunities Industrialization Centers of America
United Mortgage Bankers of America

*Civic and Civil Rights*

Affirmative Action Association of America
Congress of Racial Equality
Congressional Black Caucus
Frontiers Internationsl
National Association for the Advancement of Colored People
National Black Veterans Organization
National Conference of Black Lawyers
National Conference of Black Mayors
National Urban League
One Hundred Black Men, Inc.
People United to Save Humanity
Southern Christian Leadership Conference
United Black Fund
Veterans Association, Inc.

*Fraternal Organizations*

Alpha Phi Alpha Fraternity, Inc.
Ancient and Accepted Scottish Rite Masons

*(continued)*

community and observes, there will be some Black males involved in a variety of sports. In the 1975 Health Interview Survey (HIS), there were several questions concerning the participation in sports by adults 20 years old and over (National Center for Health Statistics, 1978). It was discovered that 43.2 percent of white males were involved in at least one type of sport, compared to 29.2 percent for nonwhites. As one would expect, age and income

## TABLE 1.9
### List of Selected Organizations with
### High Levels of Black Male Involvement (Continued)

Ancient Egyptian Order of the Mystic Shrine
Federalism of Masons of the World, Inc.
Grand United Order of Odd Fellows
Improved Benevolent Protective Order of Elks of the World
Kappa Alpha Psi Fraternity, Inc.
Omega Psi Phi Fraternity, Inc.
Phi Beta Sigma Fraternity, Inc.
Prince Hall Masons (Prince Hall Grand Lodge)
Tuskegee Airmen

*Professionals*

Afro-American Patrolmen's League
Association of Black Psychologists
Association for the Study of Afro-American Life and History
Black Music Association
Black Psychiatrists of America
National Alliance of Black School Educators
National Association of Black Social Workers, Inc.
National Association for Equal Opportunity in Higher Education
National Association for Health Services Executives
National Association of Negro Musicians
National Bar Association
National Medical Association
National Pharmaceutical Association, Inc.
National Society of Black Engineers

*Religious*

African Methodist Episcopal Church
African Methodist Episcopal Zion Church
Christian Methodist Episcopal Church
Church of God in Christ
Ethiopian Hebrew Congregation
National Baptist Convention of America
National Baptist Convention, U.S.A., Inc.
National Conference of Black Churchmen, Inc.
National Primitive Baptist Convention, Inc.
National United Church Ushers Association of America, Inc.
Progressive National Baptist Convention, Inc.
World Community of Islam in the West

SOURCE: L. S. Yearwood (Ed.). *Black Organizations: Issues on Survival Techniques.* Lanham, Md: University Press of America, 1980; H. A. Ploski and E. Kaiser. *The Negro Almanac.* New York: The Bellwether Co., 1971; and D. J. Jones and W. H. Matthews (Ed). *The Black Church: A Community Resource.* Washington, DC: Institute for Urban Affairs and Research, 1977.

influence the degree to which a person was active in organized sports. Higher-income persons were more likely to be involved in sports than were lower-income persons. As age increases, the level of involvement in sports decreases. Further analysis of data is not possible since the data were not broken down by racial and sex groups. But the data did suggest that Black men are more likely to be involved in basketball than they were to be involved in swimming, tennis, or golf. Bowling, softball, and baseball are also favorite sports of Black men.

Several studies (Anderson, 1976; Liebow, 1967) suggest that Black men spend a great deal of their leisure time in unorganized activities, such as playing checkers and chess, shooting pool, and gambling. These recreational activities take place in pool rooms, bars, and barbershops. Moreover, many Black men spend time in informal settings with their friends, talking and playing around on "the corner" or on "the block." One has to appreciate the fact that these informal networks provide cognitive and affective services to those men who are in need of help. According to Gary (1978: 39),

> Many Black people with personal problems customarily turn to informal organizations. . . . These informal groups . . . such as barbershops, peer groups, gangs, and storefront churches make up the social network of the Black community. . . . These informal organizations . . . have enabled many Blacks to develop the necessary talent for functioning in a hostile racist environment.

While these informal networks include recreational activities, many Black males are very much involved in professional and semiprofessional sports.

In their book, *Jock: Sports and Male Identity,* Sabo and Runfola (1980) discuss some of the negative consequences of placing so much emphasis on sports in the American society. They examine the interrelationships among sexism, racism, violence, and sports. In most Black communities, one can find young Black males preparing themselves for the professional world of sports. Many Black parents and their male children believe that sports are the most democratic area of our society (Sabo & Runfola, 1980). These parents believe that athletics constitute the main mechanism by which their sons will achieve manhood. The media, especially television, have promoted cultural stereotypes of Black males as athletic and sexual supermen. Although professional sports have helped many Black males to achieve recognition and to earn good salaries, there is ample evidence that Black athletes are victims of racial oppression (Edwards, 1969; Johnson & Marple, 1973; Pascal & Radding, 1972). Commenting on racism in sports, Eitzen and Yetman (1977: 13) conclude:

> Despite some indication of change, discrimination against Black athletes continues in American team sports; sports are not a meritocratic realm where race is ignored. . . . If discrimination occurs in a public area, one

so generally acknowledged to be discrimination free and one where a premium is placed on individual achievement rather than race, how much more subtly pervasive must discrimination be in other areas of American life, where personal interaction is crucial and where the actions of power wielders are not subject to public scrutiny.

## CONCLUDING COMMENTS

The data in this chapter show that there have been notable changes in the demographic and social characteristics of Black men over the past twenty years in comparison to white men. Contrary to myths projected by the media and the social science literature, Black men are an integral part of Black communities. As of 1978, there were 12 million Black males, of which 7.3 million were adults, that is, 18 years old or older. Although there is a growth in the male population, the sex ratio, that is, the number of males per 100 females, has been declining during this century. The imbalance in the sex ratio is particularly problematic for the Black community during the marriage and childbearing ages. Moreover, there has been a significant increase in the number of Black men who are single compared to white men who are single. Given the employment and income conditions of Black men, one can understand why the Black family seems to be breaking down.

Many Black men do not earn adequate incomes to provide for their families. Black men have made some gains in higher education and in employment, but data suggest that affirmative action programs directed at white women have eroded some of their advancements. There is much evidence to suggest that the economic frustration of Black men has led some of them to engage in criminal activities in order to support themselves and their families. In addition, many Black men who have difficulties dealing with the economic system join the armed forces, but once enlisted they continue to experience racial oppression. They learn some skills in the armed forces, but often those skills are not transferable to the civilian world of work. The data show that the unemployment rate is higher for Black than for white veterans. The data also suggest that the basic institutions of our society have developed techniques for systematically making a large percentage of Black males useless for fulfilling their family obligations.

Although the government has not collected many data on the social participation of Black males, we were able to identify some areas where they have had a more positive experience. Black men have developed their own voluntary associations and organizations, especially in the areas of fraternities and benefit societies, civic and professional organizations, and the church. In the political arena, Black men are grossly underrepresented at all levels of the government. Also, Black men experience considerable social discrimination in the area of professional sports. One can conclude that the data indicate that Black men, in comparison to white men, have had a difficult time protecting themselves from the pressures of the major institutions in our society, and these institutional outcomes have had negative consequences for family relationships in Black communities.

# REFERENCES

Anderson, E. *A place on the corner.* Chicago: University of Chicago Press, 1976.

Brimer and Company. Facts and figures: A statistical profile of Black economic development. *Black Enterprise,* 1980, *11,* 96.

Carter, H., & Glick, P. *Marriage and divorce: A social and economic study* (Revised edition). Cambridge, MA: Harvard University Press, 1976.

Datcher, L. Effects of community, family and education on earnings of Black and white men. *Review of Black Political Economy,* 1980, *10,* 291-394.

Doddy, H. The progress of the Negro in higher education. *Journal of Negro Education,* 1963, *32*(4), 485.

Duncan, O. Inheritance of poverty or inheritance of race? In D. P. Moynihan (Ed.), *Understanding poverty.* New York: Basic Books, 1969, 85-110.

Edwards, H. *The revolt of the Black athlete.* New York: Macmillan, 1969.

Eitzen, D., & Yetman, N. Immune from racism? Blacks still suffer from discrimination in sports. *Civil Rights Digest,* 1977, *9,* 2-13.

Franklin, J. *From slavery to freedom: A history of Negro Americans* (4th edition). New York: Knopf, 1974.

Frazier, E. *The Negro in America* (Rev. ed.). New York: Macmillan, 1957.

Gary, L. (Ed.). *Mental health: A challenge to the Black community.* Philadelphia: Dorrance, 1978.

Gary, L., & Favors, A. (Eds.). *Restructuring the educational process: A Black perspective.* Washington, DC: Institute for Urban Affairs and Research, 1975.

Glick, P. Marriage and marital stability among Blacks. *Milbank Memorial Fund Quarterly,* 1970, *63,* 100-103.

Glick, P., & Norton, A. Marrying, divorcing and living together in the U.S. today. *Population Bulletin,* 1979, *32,* 4-38. (Updated reprint)

Gove, W. The relationship between sex roles, marital roles, and mental illness. *Social Forces,* 1972, *51,* 34-44.

Hill, R. *The strengths of Black families.* New York: Emerson Hall, 1972.

Jackson, J. Where are the men? *The Black Scholar,* 1971, *3,* 30-41.

Johnson, N., & Marple, D. Racial discrimination in professional basketball: An empirical test. *Sociological Focus,* 1973, *6,* 6-18.

Joint Center for Political Studies. *National roster of Black elected officials* (Vol. 9). Washington, DC: Author, 1979.

Jones, D., & Matthews, W. (Eds.). *The Black church: A community resource.* Washington, DC: Institute for Urban Affairs and Research, 1977.

Layng, A. Voluntary associations and Black ethnic identity. *Phylon,* 1978, *39,* 171-179.

Liebow, E. *Tally's corner.* Boston: Little, Brown, 1967.

McPherson, J., Holland, L., Banner, J., Weiss, N., & Bell, M. *Blacks in America: Bibliographic essays.* Garden City, NY: Doubleday, 1971.

Miller, H. *Income distribution in the United States.* Washington, DC: Government Printing Office, 1966.

Moskos, C. The American dilemma in uniform: Race in the armed forces. *Annals of the American Academy of Political and Social Science,* 1973, *406,* 94-106.

Moskos, C., & Janowitz, M. Racial composition in the all volunteer force. *Armed Forces and Society,* 1974, *1,* 109-123.

National Center for Education Statistics. *Digest of education statistics 1979.* Washington, DC: Government Printing Office, 1979.

National Center for Health Statistics. Exercise and participation in sports among persons 20 years of age and over: United States. *Advance Data,* 1978, *19.*

Number of Black elected officials up by 6.6 percent. *Focus,* 1980, *8* (12), 6.

Orum, A. A reappraisal of the social and political participation of Negroes. *American Journal of Sociology,* 1966, *76,* 32-46.

Pascal, A., & Radding, Z. The economics of racial discrimination in organized baseball. In A. Pascal (Ed.), *Racial discrimination in economic life.* Lexington, MA: D. C. Heath, 1972.

Ploski, H., & Kaiser, E. *The Negro almanac.* New York: Bellwether, 1971.

Raspberry, W. Boys: Endangered species? *The Washington Post,* March 1979, p. A23.

Rodgers-Rose, L. *The Black woman.* Beverly Hills, CA: Sage Publications, 1980.

Rosen, B., Goldsmith, H., & Redick, R. Demographic and social indicators: Uses in mental health planning in small areas. *World Health Statistics,* 1979, *32*(1), 11-102.

Ross, J., & Wheeler, R. *Black belonging: A study of social correlates of work relations among Negroes.* Westport, CT: Greenwood, 1971.

Rowan, C. Moshe Dayan insults Black GIs. *New York Amsterdam News,* December 1980, p. 17.

Sabo, D., & Runfola, R. *Jock: Sports and male identity.* Englewood Cliffs, NJ: Prentice-Hall, 1980.

Siegal, J. *Estimates of coverage of the population by sex, race and age in the 1970 census.* Paper presented at the annual meeting of the Population Association of America, New Orleans, Louisiana, April 26, 1973.

Siegal, P. On the cost of being a Negro. *Sociological Inquiry,* 1965, *35,* 41-57.

Staples, R. *Introduction to Black sociology.* New York: McGraw-Hill, 1976.

Stewart, J., & Scott, J. The institutional decimation of Black American males. *Western Journal of Black Studies,* 1978, *2,* 82-92.

Stolzenberg, R. Education, occupation and wage differences between white and Black men. *American Journal of Sociology,* 1975, *81,* 299-323.

Tomeh, A. Formal voluntary organizations: Participation, correlates and interrelationships. *Sociological Inquiry,* 1973, *43*(3), 89-110.

U.S. Bureau of the Census. *Statistical abstract of the United States: 1979* (100th ed.). Washington, DC: Government Printing Office, 1979. (a)

U.S. Bureau of the Census. *The social and economic status of the Black population in the United States 1790-1978* (Special Studies Series P-23, No. 80). Washington, DC: Government Printing Office, 1979. (b)

U.S. Department of Commerce. *Social indicators 1976.* Washington, DC: Government Printing Office, 1977.

U.S. Department of Commerce. Money, income and poverty status of families and persons in the United States: 1979. *Current Population Reports* 1980, Series P-60, No. 125, advance report. (a)

U.S. Department of Commerce. Population profile of the United States: 1979. *Current Population Reports,* 1980, Series P-20, No. 350, p. 17. (b)

U.S. Department of Commerce. Voting and registration in the election of November 1980. *Current Population Reports, Population Characteristics,* 1981, Series P-20, No. 359, advance copy.

U.S. Department of Defense. Washington, DC: Department of Defense, Equal Opportunity, 1981. (Unpublished data)

U.S. Department of Justice. *Criminal victimization in the United States.* Washington, DC: Government Printing Office, 1979.

U.S. Department of Justice. *Crime in the United States.* Washington, DC: Government Printing Office, 1980.

U.S. Department of Labor. *Employment and training report of the president.* Washington, DC: Government Printing Office, 1980.

Yankelovich, D. Who gets ahead in America. *Psychology Today,* July 1979, pp. 28-34; 40-44.

Yearwood, L. (Ed.). *Black organizations: Issues and survival techniques.* Lanham, MD: University Press of America, 1980.

# 2

## HEALTH STATUS

Lawrence E. Gary

An important challenge facing Black men in the United States is their health. Black men, women and children, from an historical perspective, have waged a tremendous struggle against their social and physical environments in the attempt to survive and to maintain a healthy state in a society that has been hostile to their existence. The problem addressed in this chapter is whether a difference exists in the health status and behavior of Black as opposed to white men in the American society. The specific topics discussed are (1) mortality, (2) morbidity, (3) accidents and injuries, and (4) mental disorders. Moreover, where data are available appropriate attention will be given to how marital status, age, and income impact on each topic discussed.

Admittedly, the topics and concerns of this chapter are broad. We shall narrow our scope by focusing on adult males rather than on male children and on nationwide rather than on regional, state, or local data. Although some attention will be given to trends, our primary emphasis will be on the most recent data available.

The development of this chapter entails secondary analysis of various data bases of the National Center for Health Statistics with some references to current studies. The specific information sources used at the Center were: (1) vital statistics data, (2) the National Health Interview Survey (NHIS), (3) the Health and Nutrition Examination Survey (HANES), (4) the Health Examination Survey (HES), (5) the Master Facility Inventory, (6) the Hospital Discharge Survey (HDS, 1980), and (7) other surveys (e.g., by the U.S. Department of Health, Education and Welfare). Most of the information on mental health was taken from surveys of mental health facilities sponsored by the Divisions of Biometry and Epidemiology of the National Institute of Mental Health.

In relying on various data sources, it is necessary to mention relevant limitations. For example, terms such as "disadvantaged," "racial minorities," "nonwhites," and "other than white" have been used in some of these data bases in describing health status and behavior. With such reporting, it becomes difficult to make comparisons among the various nonwhite groups. Although Blacks account for about 90 percent of the nonwhite groups, using this category for estimates of health characteristics of the Black population can be misleading. In addressing the problem of using data published for the nonwhite category as a proxy for data on the Black population, Wilson and Danchik (1980: 13) concluded:

> The results suggest that for many of the health variables presented in NHIS publications such an approximation can be used. For mortality data, the "other than white" rates can serve as an alternate for Black rates for expectancy up to about 65, for age-specific and age-adjusted mortality rates for all "causes.". . . Condition specific age-adjusted mortality rates for the total "other than white" population can, however, reflect a different relationship to the white population than rates for Blacks, as was found in cases of heart disease mortality.

In this chapter, the terms "nonwhite" and "Black" will be used interchangeably, even though there are limitations to this practice. However, when data on Black and white men are presented in the tables, the appropriate term will be used; that is, we shall utilize the same terminology as was presented in the original data sets.

In addition to the problem of categorization of the data, one has to be aware of sampling errors. Consequently, particular care must be exercised in the interpretation of data based on a relatively small number of cases or on small differences between estimates. Moreover, one has to be aware of the problem of the census undercount of Black people, especially of Black males (Rodgers-Rose, 1980; Siegal, 1973; U.S. Bureau of the Census, 1979). The census undercount problem is important because certain health status rates are based on population data. There is also the problem of interpretation of the data, especially when there is interaction among various independent variables. While these limitations are important, it is possible to use these data for the purpose of projecting the overall health condition of Black males.

## THE CONCEPT OF HEALTH STATUS

It is becoming increasingly clear that there are many shortcomings of the modern definition of health as illustrated by "the clear bill of health," or the absence of symptoms, orientation imprinted in the minds of the public through the annual physical examination (Bloomfield & Kory, 1978). Moreover, diseases such as cancer, emphysema, or arthritis begin years before they are detected, and when their symptoms appear, it is often too late. The "here today and gone tomorrow" belief is a reality when discussing one's health. In his book, *Causal Thinking in the Health Sciences,* Susser (1973) argues that "disease, illness and sickness are not synonymous." He views disease as a process that produces psychological and physiological symptoms, the consequence of which is impairment. Thus, illness results in disability and is viewed as a state of distress manifested by symptoms. Finally, sickness is defined as a state of social dysfunction, the consequence of which is a handicap. What this means is that "a person may have a disease, yet not be ill, or a person may be ill although no disease process can be identified" (Susser, 1973).

There has been much discussion of the appropriate definition of health (Maykovick, 1980; Mechanic, 1978; Wolinsky, 1980) and a lengthy discussion of this concept is beyond the scope of this chapter. It is clear, however, that one's definition of health affects what one does to make oneself healthy or ill and what we do socially to advance health (Bloomfield & Kory, 1978). Some examples of the various definitions of health are listed below:

(1) "The age-old view of health as the absence of disease" (Schwab & Schwab, 1978).

(2) "Health is a state of complete physical, mental and social well-being and not merely the absence of disease and infirmity" (World Health Organization, 1958).

(3) "A physical and mental state fairly free of discomfort and pain which permits the person concerned to function as effectively and as long as possible in the environment where chance or choice has placed him" (Dubos, 1965).

(4) "Health is a positive state of well-being. . . . It refers to a level of physical fitness and physical-emotional harmony that affords maximum resistance to disease and supports a sustained joy of living" (Bloomfield & Kory, 1978).

In a casual review of the above and other definitions of health, it is obvious that there is no satisfactory and scientifically useful definition of health. However, the public does not seem to be aware of this problem. Health has been used both as a noun and an adjective ("health care," "health behavior," and so forth). The implication is that it is necessary to define or measure health from a multidimensional perspective. In this chapter, health status is measured primarily in terms of mortality and morbidity. Although these measures subsume a variety of health conditions, they are not perfect. For example, dental health, genetic and reproductive health, health expenditures, and other elements of health status are not discussed. Despite the data

TABLE 2.1
Trends in Selected Mortality Indicators
of Males by Race, 1945-1977

| | Age-Adjusted Death Rate (per 1000 persons) | | | Life Expectancy at Birth | | |
| Year | White | Nonwhite* | Ratio of Nonwhite to White | White | Nonwhite* | Ratio of Nonwhite to White |
|------|-------|-----------|---------------------------|-------|-----------|---------------------------|
| 1945 | 10.7 | 14.5 | 1.36 | 64.4 | 56.1 | .87 |
| 1950 | 9.6 | 13.6 | 1.42 | 66.5 | 59.1 | .89 |
| 1955 | 9.1 | 11.9 | 1.13 | 67.4 | 61.4 | .91 |
| 1960 | 9.2 | 12.1 | 1.32 | 67.4 | 61.1 | .91 |
| 1965 | 9.1 | 12.2 | 1.34 | 67.6 | 61.1 | .90 |
| 1970 | 8.9 | 12.3 | 1.38 | 68.0 | 61.3 | .90 |
| 1975 | 8.1 | 11.0 | 1.36 | 69.4 | 63.6 | .92 |
| 1976 | 8.0 | 10.7 | 1.35 | 69.7 | 64.1 | .92 |
| 1977 | 7.8 | 10.5 | 1.35 | 70.0 | 64.6 | .92 |

SOURCE:  Office of Health Resources Opportunity. *Health of the Disadvantaged Chartbook II* (DHHS Publication No. HRA-80-633). Washington, D.C.: Government Printing Office, 1980, pp. 29-32.

* Since Blacks constitute about 90 percent of the nonwhite category, the term "Black" is used in the text for discussion of this and other relevant tables.

sources, limitations, and the absence of a comprehensive definition of health, the topic identified for discussion should provide an overall assessment of the health status of Black men.

## MORTALITY RATES

Life expectancy at birth, predictive of the individual life patterns, is a particularly useful measure of the health conditions of a given group in our society. In 1977 life expectancy at birth was 73.2 years for Americans, which is a record high. However, there are some notable differences when this measure is divided into subgroups by sex and race. As shown in Table 2.1, the life expectancy rates in 1977 were 64.6 years for Black men and 70.0 years for white men. These data show that white men lived 5.4 years longer than did their Black counterparts as of 1977. From an historical perspective, the gap between Black and white men has narrowed over the years. For example, in 1945 white men lived 8.3 years longer than did Black men; however, by 1977 the gap was 5.4 years. Since 1975 the life expectancy ratio of Black men to white men has remained basically the same, as indicated in Table 2.1.

TABLE 2.2
Death Rates of Males by Race and Age,
1977 (per 1000 persons)

| Age | White | Nonwhite | Differential |
| --- | --- | --- | --- |
| Under 1 | 14.3 | 27.8 | 1.94 |
| 1- 4 | 0.7 | 1.1 | 1.57 |
| 5-14 | 0.4 | 0.5 | 1.25 |
| 15-24 | 1.7 | 2.1 | 1.24 |
| 25-34 | 1.7 | 4.0 | 2.35 |
| 35-44 | 2.8 | 6.7 | 2.39 |
| 45-54 | 7.5 | 13.5 | 1.80 |
| 55-64 | 18.5 | 27.7 | 1.50 |
| 65-74 | 41.8 | 46.8 | 1.12 |
| 75-84 | 94.4 | 87.8 | .93 |
| 85 years and older | 180.4 | 112.9 | .63 |
| Age adjusted death rate | 7.8 | 10.5 | 1.35 |

SOURCE: Office of Health, Research, Statistics and Technology. *Final Mortality Statistics* (DHEW Publication No. [PHS] 79-1120 Vol. 28[1] Supplement). Hyattsville, MD: National Center for Health Statistics, May 11, 1979, pp. 15-16.

It is interesting to note that in 1977 the life expectancy rate for Black men was about the same as it was for white men in 1945! If one can assume that the life expectancy rate for white men will remain the same while that for Black men continues to increase at its present rate, it will take about 70 years before the two groups are at parity with respect to this measure.

The death rate alone is not a perfect measure of health status, however, a decrease in the death rate provides a good tool for assessing the overall health improvement in a population. The data in Table 2.1 show that the death rate for Black men is higher than that for white men. For example, in 1977 the age-adjusted death rate for Black men was 10.5, but it was 7.8 for white men—a differential of 1.35. Although the death rates for both groups have declined since 1945, the gap between the two groups has remained basically the same. The death rate for Black men in 1977 is almost identical to that for white men in 1945.

In Table 2.2 one can observe that Black males have higher death rates than their white counterparts, except at the age of 75 years and over. Age has an impact on the death rates and the resulting differential between the two groups. For example, in 1977 the death rate for Black males under 1 year of age was 27.8; however, it was 14.3 for white male children in that age group—a differential of 1.94. For the adult years 25 to 44, the death rate for Black men is twice as high as is that for white men. Furthermore, several studies (Carter & Glick, 1976; Geerken & Gove, 1974) have shown the effects of marital status on mortality rates. In an analysis of the impact of race, sex, and marital status on mortality rates, Geerken and Gove (1974: 578) concluded:

> The data support the view that marriage is slightly more advantageous for white men than for Black men, while being unmarried is slightly more disadvantageous for white men than for Black men.

Perhaps these data will shed some light on the shifting marital patterns in the Black community. In Chapter 1 we discussed the fact that Black men are more likely than are white men not to get married, or, conversely, the percentage of single males in the Black community is much higher than that in the white community.

## CAUSE OF DEATH

We shall now examine death rates for selected causes. Table 2.3 contains data on the leading causes of death in 1977 for Black and white men. Although the major causes of death for these two groups are similar, their ranking is different. For example, diseases of the heart and cancer were the number one and number two causes of death, respectively, for both Black and white men. On the other hand, homicide was the fifth leading cause of death for Black men, whereas for white men it was not even among the top ten causes. Also, Black males were much more likely than were white males to die from infant-related diseases. It is interesting to note that arteriosclerosis, bronchitis, emphysema, and asthma were among the leading causes of death for white men, but they were absent from the top causes of death for Black men. When age is introduced, a different cause-of-death pattern emerges. Accidents, suicide, and homicide are the top three causes of death for Black and white men between the ages of 15 and 24 years. Moreover, for men between the ages of 25 and 44 years, homicide was the number one cause of death for Black men, but it was ranked fifth for white men. Accidents were ranked as the number one cause of death for white men, compared to number two for Black men between the ages of 25 to 44 years. Diseases of the heart and cancer continued to be the main determinants of death for both Black and white men for the 25-to-44 age group. It should be noted that suicide has been increasing among Black men. In 1977, for Black men under 24 years of age, suicide was the number three cause of death, whereas it was number two for white men in the same age category. A detailed discussion of suicide is covered in Chapter 11 of this volume.

Table 2.4 provides information on age-adjusted death rates for males by causes in 1977. As Table 2.4 shows, except for suicide and arteriosclerosis,

## TABLE 2.3
### Ten Leading Causes of Death for Males by Rank Order, 1977

| | Rank Order | | | | | | |
|---|---|---|---|---|---|---|---|
| | Both Sexes and Races | White Male | Nonwhite Male | White Male 15-24 | Nonwhite Male 15-24 | White Male 25-44 | Nonwhite Male 25-44 |
| Diseases of the heart | 1 | 1 | 1 | 5 | 4 | 2 | 3 |
| Cancer | 2 | 2 | 2 | 4 | 5 | 3 | 4 |
| Cerebrovascular diseases | 3 | 3 | 4 | 8 | 8 | 7 | 7 |
| Accidents | 4 | 4 | 3 | 1 | 1 | 1 | 2 |
| Influenza and pneumonia | 5 | 5 | 7 | 7 | 6 | 9 | 8 |
| Diabetes | 6 | 9 | 9 | 9 | - | 8 | 9 |
| Cirrhosis of the liver | 7 | 7 | 8 | - | 9 | 6 | 5 |
| Arteriosclerosis | 8 | 10 | - | - | - | - | - |
| Suicide | 9 | 6 | 10 | 2 | 3 | 4 | 6 |
| Certain causes of infant mortality | 10 | - | 6 | - | - | - | - |
| Bronchitis, emphysema, asthma | - | 8 | - | - | 9 | - | - |
| Homicide | - | - | 5 | 3 | 2 | 5 | 1 |
| Nephritis and nephrosis | - | - | - | 10 | 10 | - | 10 |
| Congenital anomalies | - | - | - | 6 | 7 | 10 | - |

SOURCE: Office of Health Research, Statistics and Technology. *Final Mortality Statistics 1977* (DHEW Publication No. [PHS] 79-1120 Vol. 28 [1] Supplement). Hyattsville, MD: National Center for Health Statistics, May 11, 1979, p. 20; and U. S. Department of Health and Human Services. *Vital Statistics of the United States 1977*. Vol. II, Mortality Part B. Washington, DC: Government Printing Office, 2979, pp. 134-151.

TABLE 2.4
Selected Age-Adjusted Death Rates for Males
by Causes of Death and by Race, 1977
(per 100,000 persons)

| | Nonwhite Male | White Male | Differential |
|---|---|---|---|
| Diseases of the heart | 297.8 | 294.0 | 1.01 |
| Cancer | 205.4 | 160.0 | 1.28 |
| Cerebrovascular diseases | 79.8 | 50.5 | 1.58 |
| Accidents | 84.5 | 63.2 | 1.34 |
| Influenza and pneumonia | 29.6 | 18.1 | 1.64 |
| Suicide | 12.6 | 20.6 | .61 |
| Cirrhosis of the liver | 31.4 | 16.7 | 1.88 |
| Bronchitis, emphysema, asthma | 12.3 | 8.1 | 1.52 |
| Diabetes | 16.3 | 9.8 | 1.66 |
| Arteriosclerosis | 6.4 | 7.2 | .89 |
| Homicide | 60.1 | 8.8 | 6.83 |
| Tuberculosis | 5.7 | 1.2 | 4.75 |
| Hypertension | 4.6 | 1.6 | 2.88 |

SOURCE: Office of Health, Research, Statistics and Technology. *Final Mortality Statistics 1977* (DHEW Publication No. [PHS] 79-1102, Vol. 28,1, Supplement). Hyattsville, MD: National Center for Health Statistics, May 11, 1979, p. 31.

the age-adjusted death rates were higher for Black men than they were for white men. The differentials for causes of death between the two groups are especially noticeable for hypertension, tuberculosis, homicide, cirrhosis of the liver, diabetes, influenza, pneumonia, and stroke. Overall, Black male deaths accounted for 12.8 percent of the total male deaths in 1977. Moreover, as noted in Table 2.5, Black male deaths as a percentage of total male deaths for selected diseases are considerably above the average for syphilis (48.8), tuberculosis (33.7), homicide (48.2), certain causes of mortality in early infancy (30.1), and cirrhosis of the liver (17.1).

With respect to trends in the male age-adjusted death rates for selected causes, some interesting patterns emerge, as revealed in Table 2.6. For example, in 1950 the age-adjusted death rate for diseases of the heart was 407.5 for Black males and 381.1 for white males—a differential of 1.07. By 1977, the differential rates were about the same, as shown in Table 2.4. However, after further analysis one can observe substantial differences between the death rates for diseases of the heart for the two groups,

*(text continued on p. 58)*

## TABLE 2.5
## Number of Male Deaths by Cause and Race, 1977

| | Number of Deaths White Male | Percentage of Total White Male Deaths | Number of Deaths Nonwhite Male | Percentage of Total Nonwhite Male Deaths | Total Male Deaths | Black Male Deaths as Percentage of Total Male Deaths |
|---|---|---|---|---|---|---|
| Diseases of the heart | 358,734 | 39.3 | 37,748 | 28.3 | 396,482 | 9.5 |
| Cancer | 185,152 | 20.3 | 25,307 | 18.9 | 210,459 | 12.0 |
| Cerebrovascular diseases | 66,962 | 7.3 | 10,389 | 7.8 | 77,351 | 13.4 |
| Accidents | 61,004 | 6.7 | 10,931 | 8.2 | 71,935 | 15.2 |
| Influenza and pneumonia | 23,665 | 2.6 | 3,953 | 3.0 | 27,618 | 14.3 |
| Suicide | 19,531 | 2.1 | 1,578 | 1.2 | 21,109 | 7.5 |
| Cirrhosis of the liver | 16,727 | 1.8 | 3,440 | 2.6 | 20,167 | 17.1 |
| Bronchitis, emphysema, asthma | 15,084 | 1.7 | 1,023 | 0.8 | 16,107 | 6.4 |
| Diabetes | 11,621 | 1.3 | 2,011 | 1.5 | 13,632 | 14.8 |
| Arteriosclerosis | 10,694 | 1.2 | 954 | 0.7 | 11,648 | 8.2 |

## TABLE 2.5
## Number of Male Deaths by Cause and Race, 1977

| | Number of Deaths White Male | Percentage of Total White Male Deaths | Number of Deaths Nonwhite Male | Percentage of Total Nonwhite Male Deaths | Total Male Deaths | Black Male Deaths as Percentage of Total Male Deaths |
|---|---|---|---|---|---|---|
| Homicide | 7,951 | 0.9 | 7,404 | 5.5 | 15,355 | 48.2 |
| Certain causes of infant mortality | 9,405 | 1.0 | 4,043 | 3.0 | 13,448 | 30.1 |
| Hypertension | 2,171 | 0.2 | 578 | 0.4 | 2,749 | 21.0 |
| Syphilis | 62 | 0.0 | 59 | 0.0 | 121 | 48.8 |
| Tuberculosis | 1,343 | 0.1 | 684 | 0.5 | 2,027 | 33.7 |
| Other causes | 122,564 | 13.5 | 23,471 | 17.6 | 146,035 | 16.1 |
| Total of all causes | 912,670 | 100.0 | 133,573 | 100.0 | 1046,243 | 12.8 |

SOURCE: Office of Health Research, Statistics and Technology. *Final Mortality Statistics 1977* (DHEW Publication No. [PHS] 79-1102 Vol. 28 [1] Supplement). Hyattsville, MD: National Center for Health Statistics, May 11, 1979, pp. 20, 28-29.

TABLE 2.6
Trends in the Male Age-Adjusted Death Rates
for Selected Causes by Race, 1950-1975
(per 100,000 persons)

| | Nonwhite Male | White Male | Differential |
|---|---|---|---|
| Diseases of the heart | | | |
| 1975 | 307.0 | 308.0 | .99 |
| 1970 | 350.8 | 347.6 | 1.01 |
| 1965 | 376.1 | 368.6 | 1.02 |
| 1960 | 368.3 | 375.4 | .98 |
| 1955 | 369.2 | 367.4 | 1.00 |
| 1950* | 407.5 | 381.1 | 1.07 |
| Cancer | | | |
| 1975 | 199.7 | 157.2 | 1.27 |
| 1970 | 185.3 | 154.3 | 1.20 |
| 1965 | 173.3 | 148.0 | 1.17 |
| 1960 | 154.8 | 141.6 | 1.09 |
| 1955 | 138.7 | 137.4 | 1.00 |
| 1950* | 125.8 | 130.9 | .96 |
| Cerebrovascular diseases | | | |
| 1975 | 89.3 | 57.4 | 1.56 |
| 1970 | 113.5 | 68.8 | 1.65 |
| 1965 | 134.2 | 73.8 | 1.82 |
| 1960 | 135.2 | 80.3 | 1.68 |
| 1955 | 136.2 | 82.7 | 1.65 |
| 1950* | 144.0 | 87.0 | 1.66 |
| Accidents | | | |
| 1975 | 90.7 | 64.8 | 1.40 |
| 1970 | 115.7 | 76.2 | 1.52 |
| 1965 | 109.3 | 75.4 | 1.45 |
| 1960 | 101.1 | 70.6 | 1.43 |
| 1955 | 106.5 | 77.7 | 1.37 |
| 1950* | 107.1 | 81.0 | 1.32 |
| Influenza and pneumonia | | | |
| 1975 | 33.5 | 21.0 | 1.60 |
| 1970 | 50.1 | 26.0 | 1.93 |
| 1965 | 52.3 | 26.9 | 1.94 |
| 1960 | 68.0 | 31.0 | 2.19 |
| 1955 | 50.8 | 22.3 | 2.28 |
| 1950* | 63.4 | 27.1 | 2.34 |
| Cirrhosis of the liver | | | |
| 1975 | 32.1 | 17.9 | 1.80 |
| 1970 | 31.3 | 18.8 | 1.66 |
| 1965 | 23.3 | 15.6 | 1.49 |
| 1960 | 14.9 | 14.4 | 1.03 |
| 1955 | 10.3 | 12.9 | .80 |
| 1950* | 9.0 | 11.6 | .78 |

### TABLE 2.6
### Trends in the Male Age-Adjusted Death Rates
### for Selected Causes by Race, 1950-1975 (Continued)
### (per 100,000 persons)

|          | Nonwhite Male | White Male | Differential |
|----------|---------------|------------|--------------|
| Diabetes |               |            |              |
| 1975     | 17.9          | 10.7       | 1.67         |
| 1970     | 20.4          | 12.7       | 1.61         |
| 1965     | 18.1          | 11.9       | 1.52         |
| 1960     | 16.1          | 11.6       | 1.39         |
| 1955     | 11.2          | 10.9       | 1.03         |
| 1950*    | 11.8          | 11.3       | 1.04         |

SOURCE:   Office of Health Resources Opportunity. *Health Status of Minorities and Low-Income Groups* (DHEW Publication No. HRA 79-627). Washington, DC: Government Printing Office, 1979, pp. 91-92, 112, 115, 121, 126, 156.

\* Based on enumerated population adjusted for age bias in the population of races other than white.

especially for the 25-to-29 age group. The data in Tables 2.4 and 2.6 refer to nonwhite males, and we have been using this term interchangeably with Black males, as discussed earlier. Recently, the National Center for Health Statistics was able to separate the heart disease death rates for Black males from those of other nonwhite males. As indicated in Table 2.7, age has an impact on heart disease death rate patterns for males. For example, Black males between the ages of 1 and 39 years were twice as likely as were white males to die as a result of heart disease. Between the ages of 40 and 64 years, the relative differences in heart disease death rates decreased. White men 65 years and older had a higher mortality rate than did Black men of this same age category. These statistics clearly pinpoint the problem of using data pertaining to nonwhite males as a proxy for data on Black men.

In Table 2.6, other trend data show that, between 1950 and 1975, the death rates for strokes, influenza, and pneumonia declined for both groups, although Black males continue to have a higher death rate as a result of these diseases. Although the death rate for diabetes decreased for white men between 1950 and 1975, it increased for Black men. For example, in 1950, the death rate for this condition was 11.8 for Black men, but by 1975 it had grown to 17.9, an increase of 51.7 percent.

The data in Table 2.6 indicate that Black men are more likely than are white men to die from cancer, especially cancer of the lungs, stomach, larynx, prostate, tongue, pancreas, esophagus, small intestine, and penis (Enterline, 1979; Miller & Miller, 1980; Silverberg & Poindexter, 1979; Slater, 1974). However, Black men have not always had a higher cancer death rate than white

TABLE 2.7
Male Death Rates for Diseases of the Heart
According to Age, 1977 (per 100,000 persons)

| Age | White Male | Other* Male | Black Male | Ratio of Black Male to White Male |
|---|---|---|---|---|
| Under 25 years | 2.5 | 5.1 | 5.4 | 2.16 |
| 25-29 | 6.2 | 18.9 | 20.8 | 3.35 |
| 30-34 | 14.7 | 35.2 | 40.3 | 2.74 |
| 35-39 | 41.1 | 83.8 | 93.2 | 2.27 |
| 40-44 | 102.6 | 171.4 | 188.0 | 1.83 |
| 45-49 | 210.3 | 290.9 | 322.3 | 1.53 |
| 50-54 | 382.2 | 494.6 | 536.8 | 1.40 |
| 55-59 | 614.1 | 752.9 | 805.3 | 1.31 |
| 60-65 | 1004.0 | 1177.6 | 1247.6 | 1.24 |
| 65 and older | 2894.8 | 2331.4 | 2491.1 | .86 |
| Age-adjusted | 294.0 | 297.8 | 322.4 | 1.10 |

SOURCE:  U.S. Department of Health and Human Services. *Health United States 1980* (DHHS Publication No. [PHS] 81-1232, prepublication copy). Hyattsville, MD: National Center for Health Statistics, 1980, pp. 208-210.

* Black males are included in this category.

men have had. For example, in 1950 the cancer death rate for Black men was 125.8, whereas for white men it was 130.9. Since 1950, there has been a 58.7 percent increase in the cancer death rate for Black men, in contrast to a 20.1 percent increase for white men. Moreover, recent studies have shown that Black men with cancer have lower survival rates than white men (Office of Health Resources Opportunity, 1979). In other words, Black men are less likely than are their white counterparts to survive cancer five years after the disease is detected. It has been shown that 46 percent of the white men with colon cancer survived at least five years, while Black men had a 34 percent overall survival chance with the same kind of cancer ("Blacks' Cancer Survival Rate is Lower," 1980).

Various theories have been advanced to explain the sudden increase in cancer deaths and low cancer survival rates for Black men. On the survival question, in addition to the possibility of a genetic interpretation, there have been suggestions that Black men are less likely to obtain the most modern cancer treatment and follow-up care. Moreover, some have theorized that this increase in cancer deaths might be due to changes in the lifestyle of Black men over the last decade (American Cancer Society, 1979; Slater, 1974). These changes include increased smoking, entry into industrial jobs, and migration to industrial cities. Cigarette-smoking is perhaps the single most important preventable cause of death. Studies have shown that Black men are much more likely than white men to smoke cigarettes at all age levels above 20 years (U.S. Department of Health, Education and Welfare, 1980). For example, in 1978 45.9 percent of Black men above the age of 20 years were smokers, compared to 37.7 percent of white men in the same age category. It should be noted that cigarette smokers have a 70 percent higher death rate from all causes of death than nonsmokers have. Finally, in an article, "Black Workers and Cancer," Rowland (1980) documented the linkages between cancer incidences among Black men and their occupational exposures of 20 or 30 years ago to carcinogens.

Misuse of alcohol plays a part in a substantial number of premature deaths, illnesses, and disabilities. It is estimated that alcohol abuse is a factor in more than 10 percent of all deaths in the United States and is associated with half of all traffic deaths, as well as cirrhosis of the liver and liver cancer. These conditions are prevalent among Black men. Recently, Gary (1980) discussed the relationship between alcohol and drug abuse, and homicide among Black men. The data suggest that more than 50 percent of the murder cases in the Black community involve alcohol or drugs. Furthermore, research indicates that the typical lower-income killer is a Black male under 30 years of age, whereas the typical middle or upper-income killer is a white male over 30 years of age. An interesting observation is that alcohol consumption is a factor in more than half of the lower-income homicides, but rarely is a factor in middle- and upper-income homicides. As shown in Table 2.4, Black men were six times more likely than were white men to die as a result of homicide—about 48 percent of all murder victims are Black men. The data also tend to show that Black men are primarily responsible for most of the homicides in Black communities. In other words, Black men are both victims and offenders (U.S. Department of Justice, 1980).

Black men are more likely than any other sex group to experience death as a result of personal injuries on the job. Due to the racist structure of the labor market, Black men work in some of the dirtiest and most dangerous jobs in this society. For example, a disproportionately high number of Black men work near open hearth furnaces and in industries, surrounded by toxins and contaminated waste. Davis (1977) has studied occupational hazards among Blacks and has shown that they face a 37-percent greater chance of suffering an occupational injury and a 20-percent greater chance of dying from a job-related injury than do whites. Moreover, one assumes that there is a relationship between job environment and the incidence of and death rates from certain diseases in the Black community. It is generally known that the death rates for tuberculosis, pneumonia, liver and stomach ailments, cancer, influenza, and hypertension are higher in the Black community than they are in the white community. It is clear that the impact of the environment on the health status of Blacks, especially Black men, cannot be ignored.

# MORBIDITY

As implied earlier, death in contrast to sickness is a relatively easy way to measure health status. In general, one must understand and appreciate the subjective nature of illness. In discussing morbidity as a component of health status, the subjective element is recognized. According to Mechanic (1978: 181), "measures of illness tend to cover a wide range of territory from a sense of well-being to a sense of distress, from acute to chronic illness and from disability to impairment." Therefore, in our discussion on health status from the perspective of morbidity, we shall include disability days, restricted activity, bed disability days, and the number of acute and chronic conditions. Also, there will be a brief discussion of mental disorders.

As used here, "disability" involves the inability to carry out customary roles (as employee, provider, parent, spouse, friend, and so forth) and customary duties required of these roles, and includes the degree of impairment and the number of disability days. A "restricted activity day" is a day in which a person reduces his or her usual activities for the whole day due to illness or injury. A "bed disability day" is a day in which a person loses the entire work day due to injury or illness. As shown in Table 2.8, in 1978 Blacks had 9.9 bed disability days per person, regardless of income, in comparison to 8.6 such days for whites. When one controls for income—that is, when income is greater than $10,000—the racial differential for bed days is narrowed considerably (U.S. Department of Health, Education and Welfare, 1980). In 1978, Blacks spent 17.9 days per person in restricted activity, compared to 22.9 days per person for whites. Again, the rate of restricted activity days for higher-income Blacks was very similar to that for whites.

In the National Health Survey, acute conditions are defined as "those illnesses and injuries of less than three (3) months duration for which medical attention was sought or which resulted in restricted activity" (Office of Health Resources Opportunity, 1979: 82). Table 2.9 contains information on the number of acute conditions per 100 males. As can be seen, Black men are less likely to suffer from acute conditions than are white men, and these findings hold true for all income age groups in the male population for both races. The data also show that high-income Black men have a higher number of acute conditions than their low-income counterparts, except for those aged 17 to 44 years. On the other hand, when one controls for age, the data suggest that low-income white men have a higher incidence of acute conditions than do their higher-income counterparts.

We have already discussed mortality rates for acute conditions such as pneumonia, influenza, and cirrhosis of the liver. There is some disagreement as to whether cirrhosis of the liver is a chronic or an acute condition. There is also an interaction problem when one discusses the "causes" of this disease. In other words, all alcoholics do not suffer from cirrhosis of the liver and all

## TABLE 2.8
### Selected Health Characteristics

|    |                                                                                      | Blacks | Whites |
|----|--------------------------------------------------------------------------------------|--------|--------|
| 1. | Percentage of population self-assessed health as fair or poor, 1978                  | 20.5   | 10.9   |
| 2. | Percentage of population unable to carry out major activity, 1978                    | 5.5    | 3.1    |
| 3. | Number of restricted activity days per person per year, 1978                         | 22.9   | 17.9   |
| 4. | Number of bed disability days per person per year, 1978                              | 9.9    | 6.8    |
| 5. | Percentage of persons with elevated blood pressure per 100 persons, 1971-1974        | 30.4*  | 18.5*  |
| 6. | Percentage of persons with chronic activity limitation, 1977                         | 4.7    | 3.5    |
| 7. | Percentage of persons with chronic activity limitation with income under $5000, 1977 | 8.6    | 9.9    |
| 8. | Percentage of persons with chronic activity limitation with income of $5000-$9999, 1977 | 4.5 | 6.1    |
| 9. | Percentage of persons with chronic activity limitation with income of $10000 and over, 1977 | 1.7 | 1.6 |

SOURCE:   U.S. Department of Health and Human Services. *Health United States 1980* (DHHS Publication No. [PHS] 81-1232, prepublication copy). Hyattsville, MD: National Center for Health Statistics, 1980, pp. 229-230; U.S. Department of Health, Education and Welfare. *Health United States 1979* (DHEW Publication No. [PHS] 80-1232). Washington, DC: Government Printing Office, 1979, p. 125. *Health of the Disadvantaged Chartbook II* (DHHS Publication No. [HRA] 80-633). Washington, DC: Government Printing Office, 1980, pp. 50-51.

* These figures refer to men only.

people with this disease are not alcoholics. There are interaction and interpretation problems when one analyzes an acute condition such as cirrhosis of the liver. Nevertheless, we do know that the incidence of alcoholism and cirrhosis of the liver is increasing in the Black community, particularly among Black men.

Earlier, it was shown that with respect to the leading chronic diseases except for arteriosclerosis, the health status of Black men is inferior to that of white men (U.S. Department of Health, Education and Welfare, 1980). Among the chronic diseases discussed were those of the heart, cancer, strokes, and diabetes. All of these conditions had higher prevalence rates for Black men than they did for white men. One particular chronic condition that has

## TABLE 2.9
### Number of Acute Conditions per 100 Male Persons by Race, Age, and Family Income, 1973

|  | White Male | Nonwhite Male | Total |
|---|---|---|---|
| All ages |  |  |  |
| All family incomes* | 177.6 | 126.8 | 171.3 |
| Under $5,000 | 171.8 | 128.8 | 160.9 |
| $5,000-$9,999 | 190.7 | 109.8 | 178.7 |
| $10,000 and over | 178.4 | 136.4 | 175.5 |
| Under 17 years of age |  |  |  |
| All family incomes* | 274.6 | 162.1 | 257.4 |
| Under $5,000 | 314.4 | 137.1 | 242.1 |
| $5,000-$9,999 | 280.8 | 139.4 | 254.7 |
| $10,000 and over | 270.3 | 182.6 | 264.1 |
| 17 to 44 years of age |  |  |  |
| All family incomes* | 163.3 | 119.3 | 158.1 |
| Under $5,000 | 188.4 | 180.7 | 186.7 |
| $5,000-$9,999 | 183.5 | 96.8 | 170.9 |
| $10,000 and over | 156.0 | 118.1 | 153.1 |
| 45 to 64 years of age |  |  |  |
| All family incomes* | 95.4 | 69.4 | 92.9 |

SOURCE: Office of Health Resources Opportunity. *Health Status of Minorities and Low-Income Groups* (DHEW Publication No. [HRA] 79-627). Washington, DC: Government Printing Office, 1979, p.87.

NOTE: Figures for 45 to 64 years of age by income do not meet standards of reliability or precision.

* Includes unknown income.

plagued the Black community is hypertension. For example, as indicated in Table 2.7, the latest Health Interview Survey (HIS) showed that 30.4 percent of all Black people had elevated blood pressure, compared to 18.5 percent for whites. Chronic conditions have a tremendous impact on one's ability to carry on certain activities such as working, going to school, or participating in community work. Black people were more likely than were whites to suffer chronic activity limitation which made them unable to carry on major activities; however, when income is controlled a slightly different pattern becomes evident. Among persons with incomes under $9999, whites had a higher chronic activity limitation rate than did Blacks. It would appear, therefore, that income differentials have a greater impact on activity limitation than do racial differentials. For both groups, as income increases, the number of persons unable to carry on major activities as a result of chronic diseases declines.

## MENTAL DISORDERS

There is substantial disagreement on the definition of mental health, or what constitutes mental illness (Gary, 1978). Commenting on this problem, the President's Commission on Mental Health (1978) concluded:

Documenting the total number of people who have mental health problems, the kind they have, how they are treated, and the associated financial costs is difficult not only because opinions vary on how mental health and mental illness should be defined, but also because the available data are often inadequate or misleading. This difficulty is compounded by the subjective nature of many mental health problems.

Despite the absence of a suitable definition of mental health, a major industry has developed in the mental health field (e.g., public and private mental hospitals and clinics, community mental health centers, and manpower—psychiatrists, psychologists, nurses, social workers, paraprofessionals, and others).

It is assumed that the incidence and prevalence of mental disorders are related to the level of stress and anxiety in our society (Gary, 1978; Mechanic, 1978; Wolinsky, 1980). We live in a stress-ridden society, one in which survival itself means experiencing varying degrees of stress. The notion of stress implies excessive exposure to forces that can harm a person's well-being. In relation to Blacks, the conditions under which they live make them particularly vulnerable to the impact of stress and anxiety-producing factors. Holmes and Rahe (1967) developed a rating scale for measuring the extent of readjustment necessary for responding to a stressful life event. Furthermore, it is assumed that too many stressful life events (pleasant and unpleasant) will increase the probability of one's susceptibility to illness. When we look at some of the events identified by Holmes and Rahe (1967)—the death of a spouse, divorce, imprisonment, job loss, and so forth—it is clear that the Black male has a high incidence of stressful life events. Therefore, one would expect to find a high prevalence of stress-related diseases and death rates among Black men.

In this chapter, we have clearly documented the fact that the health status of Black males is poor in comparison to that of white males. Their poor health status means that a large number of Black men will be removed from their families through death or will be unable to work due to serious physical and psychological disabilities. The high morbidity and mortality rates of Black men have had devastating effects on their emotional health as well as on the emotional health of their family members and friends. In the HIS, 70 percent of the white men had a positive score on psychological well-being, but only 54 percent of the Black men had a similar score (U.S. Department of

## TABLE 2.10
### Admissions Data for Selected
### Mental Health Facilities for Males, 1975

| Mental Health Facilities | Age-adjusted Admission Rates per 100,000 Population for Selected Mental Health Facilities | | Median Age of Admission to Selected Mental Health Facilities | |
|---|---|---|---|---|
| | White | Black | White | Black |
| Outpatient Psychiatric Services | 587.7 | 729.7 | 24.7 | 17.5 |
| Inpatient Psychiatric Services | | | | |
| State, county mental hospitals | 213.2 | 509.8 | 34.6 | 30.0 |
| Private mental hospitals | 56.9 | 41.3 | 36.2 | 28.6 |
| Nonfederal general hospitals | 206.4 | 237.3 | 34.2 | 27.7 |
| Public general hospitals | 64.0 | 122.1 | 32.4 | 25.7 |
| Nonpublic general hospitals | 142.4 | 156.2 | 35.4 | 29.2 |

SOURCE:   Office of Health Resources Opportunity. *Health of the Disadvantaged Chartbook II* (DHHS Publication No. [HRA] 80-633). Washington, DC: Government Printing Office, 1980, pp. 86, 89.

Health, Education and Welfare, 1980). Given this perspective, it should not be surprising that in 1975 Black males had the highest admission rates of all sex and racial groups to state and community mental hospital inpatient units (Office of Health Resources Opportunity, 1980). This admission rate was the case for all age groups in the Black male population. As indicated in Table 2.10, with the exception of private mental hospitals, Black men had a higher age-adjusted admission rate to outpatient psychiatric services, nonfederal general hospitals, public general hospitals, and nonpublic general hospitals than white men had in 1975. Moreover, the data in Table 2.10 show that Black men were admitted to mental health facilities at a younger age than were white men. For example, in 1975 the median age of admissions to outpatient psychiatric services for white men was 24.7 years, whereas for Black men it was 17.5 years.

Once admitted to mental health facilities, Black and white men experience significant differences in terms of primary diagnosis at the time of admission.

With respect to diagnoses in state and community inpatient units, Black men are three times more likely to be diagnosed as schizophrenic than are white men, as noted in Table 2.11. In addition, Black men are eight times more likely to be diagnosed as having childhood disorders and almost three times more likely to be classified as having organic brain syndromes than are white men. Of the ten major mental health diagnostic categories, white men had a higher rate than Black men had for only four depressive disorders, neuroses, transient situational disorders, and social maladjustment. The same diagnostic pattern held for those persons in outpatient services, except for those suffering personality disorders. In other words, in state and community outpatient units, white men were less likely than were Black men to have personality disorders, but for outpatient services the reverse was true. As shown in Table 2.11, the diagnostic distribution patterns for Black and white men are similar to those for men in outpatient and inpatient units of civilian mental health institutions. Black men are more likely than are white men to be diagnosed as having alcoholic disorders, drug disorders, and schizophrenia for all three mental health facilities under discussion. What is interesting to note is that the large percentage of Black men who are classified as having no mental disorder are in the outpatient facilities. In fact, this is the largest diagnostic category for Black men (27.5 percent), compared to that for white men (9.7 percent), for this type of facility. This, perhaps, further demonstrates the tremendous impact of stress on Black men and the corresponding level of disability. In other words, due to the social, political and economic frustrations faced by many Black men, they go to mental health outpatient facilities for help, but they are not really suffering from mental disorders. They are really victims of racism and oppression.


## CONCLUSION

In this chapter we have shown, through an analysis of secondary data collected by various governmental agencies, that the health status of Black men is very poor in comparison to that of white men. In many respects, the Black male's high-risk status in the health care system is similar to his status in the economy, the military, and the penal system, as we discussed in Chapter 1. Commenting on the responses of the health care system to the needs of Black men, Stewart and Scott (1978: 89) write:

> Blacks more often than others are forced to obtain medical aid through a secondary health care delivery system; that to a large extent consists of clinics which lack access to the most modern diagnostic and treatment techniques and are serviced by relatively less skilled physicians.

## TABLE 2.11
### Diagnostic Data for Selected Mental Health Facilities for Males, 1975

| Type of Disorder | Distribution of Admissions to State and County Mental Hospital Inpatient Units | | | | Distribution of Admissions to Outpatient Services by Diagnosis | | | | Distribution of Discharges from Veterans Administration Hospital Psychiatric Inpatient Units by Primary Diagnosis | | | |
| | Percentage distribution | | Rates per 100,000 population | | Percentage distribution | | Rates per 100,000 population | | Percentage distribution | | Rates per 100,000 population | |
| | White | Nonwhite | White | Nonwhite | White | Nonwhite | White | Nonwhite | White | Nonwhite | White | Nonwhite |
|---|---|---|---|---|---|---|---|---|---|---|---|---|
| Alcohol disorders | 37.1 | 29.5 | 79.5 | 131.1 | 6.0 | 8.1 | 35.8 | 65.1 | 42.5 | 33.4 | 84.2 | 99.6 |
| Drug disorders | 4.7 | 3.8 | 10.0 | 17.0 | 1.3 | 6.6 | 7.7 | 53.0 | 5.2 | 14.5 | 10.3 | 43.3 |
| Organic brain syndromes | 4.0 | 5.4 | 8.6 | 23.8 | 2.4 | 2.5 | 14.2 | 20.5 | 5.9 | 4.2 | 11.8 | 12.4 |
| Depressive disorders | 10.1 | 4.2 | 21.7 | 18.5 | 9.2 | 2.6 | 54.6 | 21.0 | 8.9 | 4.1 | 17.6 | 12.2 |
| Schizophrenia | 26.3 | 40.1 | 56.3 | 178.5 | 10.9 | 11.2 | 64.6 | 90.2 | 23.3 | 33.7 | 46.2 | 101.1 |
| Neuroses | 1.1 | * | 2.3 | * | 6.1 | 3.2 | 36.2 | 25.8 | 6.5 | 3.7 | 12.9 | 11.0 |
| Personality disorders | 7.9 | 7.6 | 16.9 | 33.6 | 12.3 | 5.6 | 73.0 | 44.8 | 4.5 | 3.5 | 8.9 | 10.4 |
| Childhood disorders | 1.1 | 4.5 | 2.4 | 19.9 | 15.9 | 13.1 | 94.6 | 106.0 | * | * | * | * |
| Transient situational disorders | 3.1 | * | 6.6 | * | 13.7 | 9.6 | 81.4 | 77.6 | 1.0 | 0.8 | 2.1 | 2.4 |

## TABLE 2.11
### Diagnostic Data for Selected Mental Health Facilities for Males, 1975

| Type of Disorder | Distribution of Admissions to State and County Mental Hospital Inpatient Units | | | | Distribution of Admissions to Outpatient Services by Diagnosis | | | | Distribution of Discharges from Veterans Administration Hospital Psychiatric Inpatient Units by Primary Diagnosis | | | |
| | Percentage distribution | | Rates per 100,000 population | | Percentage distribution | | Rates per 100,000 population | | Percentage distribution | | Rates per 100,000 population | |
| | White | Nonwhite | White | Nonwhite | White | Nonwhite | White | Nonwhite | White | Nonwhite | White | Nonwhite |
|---|---|---|---|---|---|---|---|---|---|---|---|---|
| Social maladjustment | 0.3 | * | 0.6 | * | 7.2 | 4.4 | 42.9 | 35.6 | 0.1 | 0.1 | 0.2 | 0.2 |
| No mental disorders | 1.7 | 0.8 | 3.7 | 3.4 | 9.7 | 27.5 | 57.4 | 222.1 | 0.2 | 0.3 | 0.4 | 0.8 |
| All others | 2.6 | 2.4 | 5.5 | 10.9 | 5.3 | 5.6 | 31.3 | 45.2 | 1.9 | 1.7 | 3.7 | 5.1 |
| All mental disorders | 100.0 | 100.0 | 214.2 | 444.5 | 100.0 | 100.0 | 593.8 | 806.9 | 100.0 | 100.0 | 198.3 | 298.4 |

SOURCE: Office of Health Resources Opportunity. *Health of the Disadvantaged Chartbook II* (DHHS Publication No. [HRA] 80-633). Washington, DC: ' Government Printing Office, 1980, pp. 82,84; and Veterans Administration 1975 Patient Treatment Files.

* Five or fewer sample cases. Does not meet standards of reliability.

## TABLE 2.12
### Major Causes of Black Male Deaths
### in 1977 and Associated Risk Factors

| | Percentage of all Black Male Deaths | Risk Factors |
|---|---|---|
| Heart Disease | 28.4 | Smoking, hypertension, lack of exercise, stress, family history, diabetes, and diet. |
| Cancer | 18.9 | Alcohol, worksite carcinogens, smoking, environmental carcinogens, and diet. |
| Accidents | 8.2 | Alcohol, drug abuse, speeding, no seat belts, traffic congestion, smoking, handgun availability, lack of code enforcement, and unsafe worksite. |
| Stroke | 7.8 | Smoking, hypertension, stress, and diet. |
| Homicide | 5.5 | Stress, alcohol, drug abuse, availability of handguns, and arguments. |
| Influenza and pneumonia | 3.0 | Smoking, vaccination status, and lack of code enforcement. |
| Certain causes of early infant mortality | 3.0 | Drug abuse, smoking, alcohol, diet, postnatal care, teenage pregnancy, lack of prenatal care, lack of code enforcement, low birth weight, and child abuse. |
| Cirrhosis of the liver | 2.6 | Alcohol abuse and stress. |
| Diabetes | 1.5 | Diet, obesity, and stress. |
| Suicide | 1.2 | Stress, alcohol, drug abuse, availability of handguns, and lack of support systems. |
| Other causes | 19.9 | Diet, smoking, overweight, stress, and hazards on jobs. |
| | 100.0 | |

SOURCE: U.S. Department of Health and Human Services. *Health United States—1980* (DHHS Publication No. [PHS] 81-1232, prepublication copy). Hyattsville, MD: National Center for Health Statistics, 1980, pp. 208-222. Office of Health Research, Statistics and Technology, *Final Mortality Statistics 1977* (DHEW Publication No. [PHS] 79-1102 Vol. 28 [1] Supplement). Hyattsville, MD: National Center for Health Statistics, May 11, 1979, pp. 20, 28-29.

While it is true that the health care system has played a role in preventing Black men from being more functional in their communities, the lifestyles of Black men have also contributed to their demise. It is becoming increasingly obvious that Black men as a population group smoke too many cigarettes, consume too much alcohol, have poor eating habits, have access to too many handguns, use too many drugs, work in too many unsafe environments, do not get enough exercise, and are exposed to too many stressful life events. These behavioral risk factors adversely affect their health and are responsible for much of the premature morbidity and mortality in Black communities, especially among Black men. Table 2.12 provides a simple overview of the linkages between the causes of death for Black men and risk factors. As a group, Black men must give more attention to disease prevention and health promotion. Moreover, in order to improve the health status of Black men, major reform in the health care delivery system will be necessary. Finally, in any effort to correct these problems, it will be necessary to involve all income and social groups in the Black male population as well as other groups within and outside the Black community.

# REFERENCES

American Cancer Society. *Proceedings of the national conference on meeting the challenge of cancer among Black Americans.* New York: Author, 1979.

Blacks' cancer survival rate is lower. *The Washington Post,* October 27, 1980, p. A5.

Bloomfield, H., & Kory, R. *The holistic way to health and happiness.* New York: Simon & Schuster, 1978.

Carter, H., & Glick, P. *Marriage and divorce: A social and economic study.* Cambridge, MA: Harvard University Press, 1976.

Davis, M. Occupational hazards and Black workers. *Urban Health,* 1977 (August), 16-18.

Dubos, R. *Man adapting.* New Haven, CT: Yale University Press, 1965.

Enterline, J. *A comparison of nonwhite cancer mortality among major U.S. metropolitan areas: 1969-1971.* Washington, DC: Cancer Coordinating Council, 1979.

Gary, L. (Ed.). *Mental health: A challenge to the Black community.* Philadelphia: Dorrance, 1978.

Gary, L. Role of alcohol and drug abuse in homicide. *Public Health Reports,* 1980, *95,* 553-554.

Geerken, M., & Gove, W. Race, sex and marital status: The effect on mortality. *Social Problems,* 1974, 567-580.

Holmes, T., Rahe, R. The social readjustment scale. *Journal of Psychosomatic Research,* 1967, *11,* 213-218.

Maykovick, M. *Medical sociology.* Sherman Oaks, CA: Alfred, 1980.

Mechanic, D. *Medical sociology* (2nd ed.). New York: Free Press, 1978.

Miller, M., & Miller, J. Cancer will kill 121 Blacks today. *Sepia,* 1980, *29,* 28-30.

Office of Health Research, Statistics and Technology. *Final mortality statistics, 1977* (DHEW Publication No. PHS 79-1120). Hyattsville, MD: National Center for Health Statistics, 1979.

Office of Health Resources Opportunity. *Health status of minorities and low-income groups* (DHEW Publication No. HRA 79-627). Washington, DC: Government Printing Office, 1979.

Office of Health Resources Opportunity. *Health of the disadvantaged chartbook II* (DHHS Publication No. HRA 80-633). Washington, DC: Government Printing Office, 1980.

President's Commission on Mental Health, *Health summary report to the President.* Washington, DC: Government Printing Office, 1978.

Rodgers-Rose, L. *The Black woman.* Beverly Hills, CA: Sage Publications, 1980.

Rowland, A. Black workers and cancer. *Labor Occupational Health Program Monitor,* 1980, *8,* 14-60.

Schwab, J., & Schwab, M. *Socio-cultural roots of mental illness: An epidemiologic survey.* New York: Plenum Medical, 1978.

Siegal, S. *Estimates of coverage of the population by sex, race and age in the 1970 census.* Presented at the annual meeting of the Population Association of America, New Orleans, April 26, 1973.

Silverberg, E., & Poindexter, C. *Cancer facts and figures for Black Americans.* New York: American Cancer Society, 1979.

Slater, J. The rise of cancer in Black men. *Ebony,* July 1974, pp. 92-94.

Stewart, J., & Scott, J. The institutional decimation of Black American males. *Western Journal of Black Studies,* 1978, *2,* 82-92.

Susser, M. *Causal thinking in the health sciences: Concepts and strategies of epidemiology.* New York: Oxford Universtiy Press, 1973.

U.S. Bureau of the Census. *Statistical abstract of the United States: 1979.* Washington, DC: Government Printing Office, 1979.

U.S. Department of Health and Human Services. *Health United States 1980.* (DHHS Publication No. PHS 81-1232, prepublication copy). Hyattsville, MD: National Center for Health Statistics, 1980.

U.S. Department of Health, Education and Welfare. *Health United States—1979* (DHEW Publication No. PHS 80-1232). Washington, DC: Government Printing Office, 1980.

U.S. Department of Justice. *Crime in the United States, 1979.* Washington, DC: Government Printing Office, 1980.

Wilson, R., & Danchick, K. *Comparison of Black and other than white data from the national health interview survey and mortality statistics.* Unpublished manuscript, 1980.

Wolinsky, F. *The sociology of health.* Boston: Little, Brown, 1980.

World Health Organization. *The first ten years of the World Health Organization,* Geneva: Author, 1958.

# PART II
# BLACK MEN AND THEIR FAMILIES

After reviewing the social data on the marital and family status of Black men, one can understand why there is so much concern about the quality of family life in Black communities. Asante describes the concept of Afrocentricity and its effects on how Black men relate to Black women. After differentiating between affairs and relationships, the author maintains that there are four important aspects of an Afrocentric relationship (sacrifice, inspiration, vision, and victory). The church as a negative factor in the relationships Black men have with Black women is discussed. Throughout his presentation, Asante integrates African history and philosophy with the experiences of Black Americans. He concludes his essay by suggesting that when a man and a woman become related in a physical, emotional, and spiritual manner, they are making history for the coming generations.

In his chapter on relationships between Black males and Black females, Braithwaite identifies factors that influence the quality of interaction between males and their families. Among the factors discussed are the following: (1) the male sex role, (2) sexual behavior, (3) the scarcity of eligible Black men, (4) the women's liberation movement, and (5) class and family background. After examining data from a national survey of over 600,000 Black people, Braithwaite makes some specific suggestions for improving relationships between Black males and females.

In any discussion of family dynamics in Black communities, some consideration must be given to the interactions between parents and their children. Allen examines family relationships in the two two-parent, teen-aged-son family. Focusing on parent-son, especially father-son, relations, the author uses Black and white families in his study. Although Allen finds some racial differences, he notes that there are cross-racial and cross-sectional similarities. Looking more specifically at a younger population, that is, preschool children, McAdoo explores verbal and nonverbal interaction between middle-class fathers and their offspring. Negative (or restrictive)and nurturing behavior are identified and total interactions evaluated with respect to these criteria. McAdoo finds that a large majority (76 percent) of both types of interaction are nurturing, and that fathers had positive interactions with their children. In the final chapter in this section, Hendricks reports on a study of unwed Black adolescent fathers in terms of their relationships with their children's mothers and their attitudes toward fatherhood. He concludes that they maintain friendly relations with their children's mothers, and that such services as training in parenting would be useful to these adolescent fathers.

# 3

## BLACK MALE AND FEMALE RELATIONSHIPS
### An Afrocentric Context

Molefi K. Asante

Relationships have been and will continue to be a significant concept in any discussion of the social interaction between males and females. Numerous articles and books dealing with the troubled "relationship" between Black females and males have begun to appear. While these studies seem to have proliferated in the recent past, they are nonetheless the continuation of a long history of concern that began with the imposition of slavery. This chapter examines the possibility of conceptualizing a type of relationship that would add to the quality of Black male and female interaction. Such a conceptualization would deal with relationships as opposed to affairs. Affairs are temporary and transitory; relationships transcend time and are based upon shared values and objectives. The assumption upon which this conceptualization rests is that our relationship problems are indicative of cultural disintegration or, more accurately, our lack of cultural integration. Ultimate victory on the personal level, which is sure to come, must be based upon cultural reconstruction. Edward Wilmot Blyden once remarked that there was not an African in the Americas who was on the practical road to sanity. Of course, Blyden was trying to generate interest in settlements in Africa, rather than perfect the union between men and women. Yet, without actually returning to Africa, the closest that African Americans can come to sanity in their relationships with one another is through an Afrocentric awakening rooted in both the African and the American history of our people.

In Africa, the rites of passage from childhood to adulthood were clear, if complex. A boy knew that he had to kill a lion, endure ritual scarification, or live in a forest for a period of time as a symbol of crossing over to manhood. A breakdown in these rites of passage for boys and girls was more detrimental than was any other breakdown of a cultural institution for us. Our value revival must adequately address this question if we are to achieve the healthy relationships we so desperately need. Questions surrounding the rites of passage are, "When is a man accountable?" and "To whom is he accountable?"

Writers frequently claim that the church is the most important institution within the Black community in America (Lincoln, 1974; Mitchell, 1970). If it is true that the church's influence is pervasive, it follows that more than any other institution it affects the relationship between men and women. Because of its symbolism, ensconed in mystery and sanctified by our historical allegiance, the church is the single most tragic influence on Black male-female relationships.

There are several reasons the church must be considered a conspirator against the relationships Black males have with Black females. First, the church has institutionalized the worship of the white male. In this worship are the seeds of hero worship that retard Black male sanity and substitute a kind of super agent to deal with our problems. The extent of this psychological terror has been explored by an increasing cadre of young scholars (Karenga, 1978; Richards, 1980; Semaj, 1980; Baldwin, 1980). What these writers have concluded is that symbols hold relationships together as they hold societies together. When Black men, women and children worship the image of a white person (whether that image was created by the Europeans and has nothing to do with spirit, as some claim, is beside the point), they are in effect denying their own godliness. Second, the church defines a sexist role for males, making it easier for them to subjugate women. Rather than promote the shared relationship that must accompany any Afrocentric reconstruction, the church retains the servile notion of master and slave for man and woman. Women are to obey men; men do not have to obey women. Third, the church enthrones duty above love in regard to relationships: Men and women must remain together as the result of a sense of duty long after the effective ending of the relationship. This teaches hypocrisy and encourages infidelity. Finally, the church substitutes rites of passage from the experience of others for Blacks' own historically derived passage rites. Thus, we find the children of Black couples wanting to seem as pure as the little blonde angels they hear about in the churches, see in the books, or are taught to respect by their parents' deference to anything that is white. Inasmuch as the church exercises such a dominant role in our lives, it is necessary for us to understand the basis of our struggle to capture our rites from the church. What is called for is a conceptual model of relationship that can explain not only Jemima, Beulah, Sapphire, and Geraldine, but Nehanda, Harriet Tubman, Yaa Asantewaa, and the Nzingha as well. When this is done, men will possess a deeper understanding of women and vice versa. The quality of our relationships will then be directly related to the quality of our philosophical value base.

Normally, such discussions as these are cast in the light of traditional Judeo—Christian philosophy with its attendant concerns with questions of hierarchy, linear control, vertical-horizontal conflicts, the use and misuse of persons, and material rewards of the relationship between a man and a woman. I want to challenge you to think in a different way, to perceive the difficulty that we all profess exists between us as one of philosophical fragmentation, value dislocation, and spiritual destitution based on our acceptance of the incorrect premise of relationships. There is no more perfect way for us to develop our relationships than that derived from our own historical experience. All religious philosophies are nothing more than the deification of someone's nationalism. Our problem in relationships is symptomatic of our fragmented views about our history, mythology, motifs, and creative ethos. Therefore, what I propose is an Afrocentric philosophy of relationship. By seeking to minimize the contradictions in our own relationships through an Afrocentric world view, we participate in the general rise of our people.

*The Way* (Asante, 1978) teaches that man and woman are equally the source of our strength and indeed our genius. Because of this, it is possible to discuss the nature and place of relationships within an Afrocentric philosophy. There are four aspects of Afrocentric relationships: *sacrifice, inspiration, vision,* and *victory.* In each of these aspects, we see elements of mutual respect and sharing. Sacrifice means that each partner is willing to give up certain aspects of himself or herself for the advancement of the people. In effect, the relationship is taken out of the individual context and placed into the collective context, thus becoming a part of the generative will of the people. "What can this relationship bring to the people?" rather than "What can it bring to me?" becomes the crucial question. If the relationship, not connection, is strong and powerful for the people, then it should be beneficial for the participant. Every man should want his lady to be Isis, Harriet, or Yaa Asantewaa, and every women should want a Turner, Malcolm, Elijah Muhammad, King, or Garvey. The truth of the matter is that whatever is necessary for the collective will of the people must be done. A man and a woman willing to sacrifice the things of society will find a full life in Afrocentricity. It means that sometimes you cannot be involved in the elementary existential manifestations of a decadent world view. Afrocentricity is not opposed to fun; it is rather the creation of a new era in excitement and joy. Our creative wills in music, art, poetry, dance, and literature, and our productive capacities in science, technology, and industry, constitute the fun for us. A woman's time to create and a man's time to produce must be looked upon as contributing to the collective will. But like all sacrifices, Afrocentric sacrifice never really leaves us less. What seems to be a sacrifice always increases our happiness and joy. Although there is danger that some people will try to "pimp" from the sacrifice of another, it must be understood that the only successful relationship is Afrocentric.

Material considerations alone do not make a relationship; spiritually, that is, collective cognitive imperatives, make relationships (Karenga, 1978). A few more flowers, a few more gifts, a ring, or an expensive trip do not make a relationship. Karenga (1978) is correct to view such material considerations as merely the "cash connection." Understand that the person who pimps from the sacrifice of another will not be able to withstand the battle fire. Ultimately, the test of sacrifice is the willingness to be Afrocentric everywhere and at all costs.

The Afrocentric relationship is a spiritual force with all the spirituality of the world; therefore, it is universal in itself. Our contribution to the nature of the male-female relationship must grow as does everything we do, from our experience as a people. The repository of that experience multiplies daily.

The Afrocentric relationship is also inspiritional. You are stimulated by your interactions with your partner, not just physically, but emotionally, psychologically, and intellectually as well. Our history teaches us that when this is not the case, relationships falter. If one person is always giving and another is always receiving, the relationship is not satisfying to the Afrocentric person. There is no inspiration for building the collective will. In thought and action, the man and woman in a relationship must be attuned to the primary objective of all Afrocentric unions: the productive and creative maintenance of the collective cognitive imperative.

Now, I have mentioned this collective cognitive imperative several times; what does it mean? It is the overwhelming power of a group of people thinking in the same direction. It is not unity in the traditional sense of a group of people coming together to achieve a single purpose; it is a full spiritual and intellectual commitment to a vision which constitutes the collective cognitive imperative. When we have a man and a woman as the smallest unit of society committed to the Afrocentric world view, we have one link in the spiritual chain. That link determines the future of the collective cognitive imperative by being an exact indication of the status of our will. Inspiration does not come from the sky; it comes from active throught and interaction. The collective will of African people is in you, not outside of you.

When the ancient African priests in Egypt, the Yoruba priests in Nigeria, or the Macumba priestess of Brazil spoke or were possessed, their power was created by the generative will of mind. You can do the same thing if you are in contact with your god-force. However, this is no easy task and that is precisely why DuBois (1961) said only 10 percent would suffice. Give us 250,000 conscious and willful Afrocentricists and a revolution will take place in our attitudes and behavior toward each other. The inspired man and woman or the man who inspires his lady and the lady who inspires her man must believe in the appointed destiny of the people. It is a destiny appointed by us and consummated in our dynamic thrust toward the future. Each couple's inspiration must be to convert others to Afrocentricity. Thus, it is not so much the giving of 250,000 as it is the making of 250,000.

Total conversion of the current population to Afrocentricity is not necessary to improve the relationships we have between the sexes. What is necessary is the persistent pressure of the Afrocentricists on other couples to create in art, literature, science, music, and so forth, in order to counteract the reign of intellectual deviation among our creative people. Couples must inspire each other toward correct and righteous Afrocentricity. If she or he does not, then this is sufficient reason to raise serious questions about the practicability of the union. People do change; elements of future or potential change should be clearly discernible before you enter the relationship.

Do the people dream of what can be and how it can be done? A visionary aspect must exist in the relationship. The ability to plan for the future on the basis of a religious commitment to the Afrocentric world view is the criterion of vision. Nothing can substitute for the visionary experience; it is the galvanizing element that keeps the relationship on track. To be able to ask, "Do you see?" and to be assured that your partner does see the same vision that you see provides a sense of communion. Commitment to a fundamental vision, a profound project, a spiritual quest, is the kind of commitment that demonstrates vision. Relationships based on Afrocentric vision are never boring, never without vitality. A visionary aspect to a relationship establishes a purpose outside of and beyond the daily considerations of living. The man and woman who dream together constitute the most advanced unit of an Afrocentric society.

What we must see in our visions are the victories of Afrocentricity. Its enlightened shadow must be made to cast itself upon all who interact with the couple. As visionaries, they must work for the creation of schools, factories, laboratories, institutes, and centers. Visionaries do not simply work for others, they extend what they find. Anyone can walk into a store and start selling books, but to make the store something different from that which you found when you started working there is the key to your vision. Anyone can teach, but not everyone can build a curriculum or a school. The visionaries say we shall do such and such and believe that it will be done because all things are possible. Afrocentricity should not be contradictory to your vision in a relationship. You should not have to be compartmentalized and say, "I'll do this and that there." Your whole center determines your effective vision and your vision relates, in turn, to your center. Thus, they become one. Sometimes a brother or sister gives the impression that he or she shall have to find time to be Afrocentric or to have a vision. This is a deviation. It is true that couples often engage in this compartmentalization, which dictates that events, affections, situations, and activities are based on their personal isolation, and this is a dangerous and fractionalizing practice.

Perhaps most significant of all is the fact that Afrocentric love is victorious. A celebration of ourselves, our aspirations, and our achievements accompanies the victorious aspect of a relationship. It is a relationship of joy, of power, of peace, of overcoming; it does not speak of failure or losses, of suffering, or of oppression. Victory means that you have won, not that you are expecting to win. Afrocentric relationships are victorious by their nature. Being Afrocentric is being victorious. When a woman finds a man who has achieved Afrocentricity, she has found a victor. The same is true for the man. Thus, both of them can create on the basis of their victory. Certain expressions, such as "we can't," "you ought not," "it is impossible," and "we're not equipped to," are anathema to the victorious relationship. We say more exactly, which means more Afrocentrically, "we can do it" (Asante, 1980).

Victory is important because it bestows a sense of importance on the relationship and those participating in it. The women can be Isis, Nzingha, Yaa Asantewaa, and Harriet; they are all in the Afrocentric history and are products of interactions with the ancestors in our history. Ours is a victorious history regardless of how you look at it. In fact, it is the longest-running history on the face of the earth, having been violated seriously and at length only three times—namely, during the Greek penetration of Eastern Africa in 332 B.C., the Arab penetration of Eastern Africa in 640 A.D., and the European exploitation in the fifteenth century. The latter violation covered the whole continent, East, West, and South Africa. European footnotes to our history can cause us to lose sight of our victorious nature. Couples must underscore their participation in the great drama of our history by demonstrating a love that can transcend the mundane activities of a relationship. Love is victory. But understand that the true Afrocentric love is found only in the context of the profound cause; otherwise, it degenerates into a spectacle of buying and selling. What is one more diamond ring if there is no sense of destiny, no togetherness in a victorious union as an expression of the relationship? The answer is clearly nothing more than the meaningless plan of rituals established to support the cash, flesh, or dependent connection

(Karenga, 1978). To get beyond this, we must seriously rise up in victory for Afrocentricity. This will reconstruct our families, reorganize our values, and protect our culture. The crisis in priority has produced the crisis in relationships.

Never before in the history of the world has a people been so completely severed from their collective cognitive imperative. Such splintering has been the downfall of numerous nations and peoples; it has rendered us dull to the shock treatments of capitalist society as it tries to resurrect a corpse. Without a collective will, our people often enter relationships for all the wrong reasons. Caught up in the collective will of Hollywood, we fall victim too easily to an alien notion of what love is and how to achieve it. In a victorious union, we celebrate our Afrocentricity and grow into it each day. When we have achieved sacrifice, inspiration, vision, and victory, we realize that we have accomplished all the elements of an Afrocentric relationship. From this fountain flows all the good that we do for each other and for our people. This good is never unconnected with the life of the people, because to be together as one is to be together as one with others as well as with another. Our Afrocentricity expands in proportion to our involvement with the spiritual and intellectual forces within our own history. When a man and a woman become related in a physical, emotional, and spiritual manner, they are making history for the coming generations. Every act must be made with an "ourstorical" sense. When you introduce yourself to your lover, when you agree on things to do, when you work together on projects for the people, it must be with an Afrocentric base. Only this base allows you the kind of true identity with the past and future that each of us seeks. When the union of man and woman is victorious, nothing can separate you from the love of the people; you are one with each other and, consequently, you are one with the people. It is an impossibility to be one with each other Afrocentrically and not be one with the people. The one who claims to love you but does not love the people is attempting to deceive you. This occurs most often when individuals have deceived themselves into believing that they can separate their love for you from their love for the people and still remain Afrocentric. This is not possible.

In order to get the brother she thought she wanted, a sister went through numerous outer changes of sartorial fashions, hairstyles, and manners of speech. After he had begun relating to her, she ceased her external changes and the relationship went from bad to worse. She accused him of not being interested in her for herself but because of her fashions and styles. In this case, both the brother and the sister had made some gross errors of judgment, errors that could not have been made if they had been Afrocentric. Indeed, the sister felt that the brother would naturally respond to her display of outward symbols of Afrocentricity; she was correct in the assumption because all people automatically respond to the elements of spirit in our heritage. However, the brother, not being Afrocentric, although aware of the outer changes and possibilities, was seduced by superficialities. Neither was satisfied because neither came from the center, which starts with the people as all-encompassing and all-embracing. The people are the source and inspiration for all that the couple does in word or deed. If they decide to build a factory, buy a building, or create a play, then that sense of action must be rooted in the principles of collective economics and unity.

The Afrocentric drive to create must always be based on a deep collective commitment to excellence. Thus, Afrocentricity detests the conspiracy of unproductivity and generates the ability to handle problems by the will of our genius. When someone says, "Watu weusi ought to have a school," or "We ought to create a museum," or "We need to build a shoe factory," he has set the task for himself. You are the one who must do what you propose. If you say, "Why don't we establish?" you have stated the responsibility for bringing the idea into being. Only then can we have the collective consciousness necessary to carry on the reconstruction of the world.

## REFERENCES

Asante, M. K. *The way.* Buffalo, NY: Amulefi, 1978.

Asante, M. K. *Afrocentricity: The theory of social change.* Buffalo, NY: Amulefi, 1980.

Baldwin, J. The psychology of oppression. In M. K. Asante & A. S. Vandi (Eds.), *Contemporary Black thought: Alternative analyses in social and behavioral science.* Beverly Hills, CA: Sage Publications, 1980.

DuBois, W. *The souls of Black folk.* New York: Fawcett World Library, 1961.

Karenga, M. *Beyond connections.* Los Angeles: Kawaida, 1978.

Lincoln, C. *The Black experience in religion.* New York: Anchor, 1974.

Mitchell, H. *Black preaching.* Philadelphia: Lippincott, 1970.

Richards, D. European mythology: The ideology of progress. In M. K. Asante & A. S. Vandi et al. (Eds.), *Contemporary Black thought: Alternative analyses in social and behavioral science.* Beverly Hills, CA: Sage Publications, 1980.

Semaj, L. *Cultural sciences.* Ithaca, NY: Cornell University African Research Center, 1980.

# 4

## INTERPERSONAL RELATIONS BETWEEN BLACK MALES AND BLACK FEMALES

Ronald L. Braithwaite

Building and sustaining a relationship between men and women has historically been characterized as a quid pro quo process. Reciprocity is a prerequisite if genuine and meaningful relationships between Black women and Black men are to flourish. However, these linkages are often stymied by multiple social forces that serve to reinforce alienation between the sexes. Both Black women and Black men have been victimized by the whims of the dominant culture to the extent that they participate in self-defeating behaviors that are destructive to the formation of healthy relationships and unification within Black families.

Slavery and neocolonialism as experienced by Blacks have taken a heavy toll on the prospect for unification between Black men and Black women. The traditional distinction of sex role differences was obscured by the manipulation of the slave master. The persistence of the basic slave social order—which has sustained the Black man in a subservient and dependent role while fostering the domination of the woman— has inhibited more natural patterns of role definition. Moreover, the absence of real masculine prerogatives for the Black man has obscured his role and the role of his counterpart.

AUTHOR'S NOTE: The author acknowledges the research assistance of Eartha Sanders and Marolyn Parker of the Institute for Urban Affairs and Research, Howard University.

Akbar (1976), a noted Black psychologist, advances that the pejorative quality of sexism has made the contrast of femininity even to more abhorrent to the Black woman. Consequently, he reports the alternation of opposites, which should be personified in male and female relations, is disordered and results in role confusion.

The economic and status pressures of contemporary American compound the likelihood of forming and maintaining positive and healthy relationships between Black men and Black women. Moreover, issues of male scarcity, self-disclosure, racism, sexism, and myths about masculine and feminine roles all serve as forces that influence the quality of interaction between Black men and Black women. This chapter discusses some of these factors, and essentially summarizes the literature that reflects the thinking of contemporary scholars. In addition, the results of the Essence Quality of Life Survey (Wells, 1980), which queried an extraordinarily large sample of Black women (6157), serve as the empirical base for a significant part of this discussion.

The significance of Black male and female relationships has been discussed by social scientists (Staples, 1978; Cox, 1964; Noble, 1978; Jackson, 1978; Karenga, 1979; Scott, 1976; Hare, 1979), psychologists (Akbar, 1976; Tucker, 1979; Wells, 1980), novelists (Wallace, 1979; Jordan, 1977), political scientists (Wilcox, 1979; Gary, 1981), and psychiatrists (Welsing, 1974; Poussaint, 1979; Grier & Cobbs, 1968). These authors have indeed covered the gamut of perspectives regarding the dynamics operative within Black male and Black female relationships. The treatment of the subject has ranged from an Afrocentric model (Asante, 1980; Akbar, 1976; Karenga, 1978) to a popularist model (Wallace, 1979). There are no easy solutions to the problem of a weakening bond between Black men and Black women, and none have been proposed by contemporary authors. However, these weak relationships are at epidemic proportions, and deserve attention by all Black men and Black, women who are desirous of healthy and loving relationships with significant others of the opposite sex.

Toffler's (1970) nationally acclaimed book, *Future Shock*, forecast that the future of societal relationships will be characterized predominantly by temporary intercourses. He believes that nothing is permanent and that people negotiate the terms of a relationship. Negotiating the terms of a relationship at a micro or dyad level is positive, and may well enhance the degree of mutual understanding between pairs. However, when one considers a race of oppressed people establishing temporary relationships, a debilitating effect upon the family structure weakens the probability of building a unified political bond for the collective well-being of that race. The Black community is in need of models that depict the positive aspects of the Black diaspora. This does not mean that interpersonal problems should be dismissed as unimportant, but that healthy Black relationships do exist and should be emulated.

This chapter is most pertinent to Black men and women between the ages of 22 and 45 years, for it is within this age range that the conflict and turmoil between the sexes seems most acute. Moreover, courtship and dating, marriage, and professional relationships between Black women and men are of significant importance during this age range. Beginning with the question of sex ratios, a research review of the salient factors that impact on these relationships will be summarized within the context of interactions between unmarried Blacks.

## SCARCITY OF BLACK MEN

The increasing scarcity of Black men can be attributed to several factors: (1) There are higher infant mortality rates among Black male babies in contrast to Black female babies (Scott, 1976). In 1977, the National Center for Health Statistics reported that there were 275,556 live births for Black males as compared to 268,665 live births for Black females. The mortality rate for Black male infants in 1977 was 25.9, while it was 21.3 for Black females. (2) There is a shorter life expectancy for Black males. Life expectancy rates of Black males are shorter than those of Black females, white females, and white males; for Black men, Black women, white men, and white women the life expectancy is 64.6, 73.1, 70,0 and 77.7 years, respectively (U.S. Department of Commerce, 1980). (3) Accidents and homicides contribute to the decimation of Black men. (4) War casualities have been high among Black males. (5) The number of Black males in prisons far outstrips that of any other ethnic group. (6) Drug addiction is a contributing factor to the shortage of Black males (Jackson, 1978). Staples (1978) reports that there is only one acceptable Black male for every five Black females when you exclude married, imprisoned, and homosexual Black males. U.S. Bureau of the Census (1977) data indicate that there were 732,000 more Black females than there were Black males within the 22-to-24-year-old age group during 1977.

The statistics make evident the grave consequences for the Black family and particularly for Black male and Black female relationships. First, the insufficient supply of Black men pits Black women against each other in competition for the attention of this scarce resource. Second, some Black men are aware of the imbalance and will play their upper hand by requiring Black women to accept them on their terms. If Black women fail to comply, interracial courtship is another option increasingly available to those who are so inclined. The Black woman sees this as a personal rejection of her own desirability.

Scott (1976) has discussed the male shortage problem from a sociological perspective and advances that a modified polygamous climate is currently in vogue among Black Americans. His research is based on interviews with 22 Black women, each of whom has been sharing at least one man during the past five years. His study was designed to ascertain how the low sex ratio and the intense competition for the scarce available men were being addressed by single adult female heads of households in coping with their sex needs, companionship needs, and material needs. Among the 22 case studies, mate-sharing was typical. Scott (1976: 14) reports that

> the low sex ratio sets up a great demand for the scarce desirable males, namely emotionally stable and employed males. In most urban communities, women outnumber men so greatly that single women feel little hesitation about trying to attract the husbands of other women and establishing social-sexual and even conjugal-type relationships with them. These women, more often than not, will have children out of wedlock rather than accept the option of being barren simply for the lack of legal marriage.

Sharing mates became a practice that these women accepted, although most of them reported negative feelings about having to share. Most of these women anticipated that their men would ultimately choose them over the "other woman". It is interesting to note that six of the twenty-two women in this case study (Scott, 1976) did share themselves concurrently, and they maintained that women should also have a "spare". This type of family arrangement within the Black community, Scott (1976) says, will increase in the future if one-parent families continue to increase. He claims that it is too early to evaluate whether the overall effects will be positive or negative. Currently, these family arrangements have low visibility by virtue of the laws, welfare regulations, and dominant societal mores.

## MALE SEX-ROLE IDENTITY

There are several paradoxes concerning the interests, attitudes, and traits men are expected to exhibit vis-à-vis their role in society. The individual-level, sex-role identity perspective contends that persons develop their sex roles by identifying with and imitating the parent of the same sex and, to a lesser extent, with other same-sex adults (Pleck, 1976). Males are more likely than are females to experience the complete absence of the same-sex parent (Herzog and Sudia, 1971). Consequently, males are predicted to have greater difficulty in attaining their sex-role identity and to exhibit more insecurity in their sex-role identity than do females (Pleck, 1976). The status of Black men as a racial minority is an additional dimension in their attainment of sex-role identity. Sociocultural forces have presented complex problems for Black males. Institutional and overt discrimination and negative stereotyping confront Black men at all levels.

Black male youths are exposed to multiple socializing agents that determine their male identity. Several different value orientations and roles are projected to them. The thesis that persons develop their sex roles by identifying with or imitating the parent of the same sex supports the unproven theory that the male role is not sufficiently conveyed to Black youth due to an absent or weak father figure. Further, there is the supposition that in matricentric households, there are no male role models available that male children can mimic (Staples, 1978). However, Stack's (1974) research on matricentric households notes that there are almost always male relatives, in-laws, and boyfriends in such homes. Male children have constant contact with these men on a long-term basis; thus modeling ensues.

Black men assume the roles of lover, sexual partner/husband, and father. A racist conception depicts the Black male as preoccupied with his role as a lover and sexual partner. This charge of hypersexuality ignores the normative sexual socialization patterns of Black men (Hammond and Ladner, 1969). At an early age, males are exposed to a more permissive sexual ethos resulting in a less rigid sex role. Since the restraints on the Black, female's sexual expression have not been as rigid as those of her white counterpart, a greater opportunity for sexual contacts has been provided the Black male. While less conservative sexual standards exist for Black men, discretion in sexual affairs and sexual exclusivity in a relationship investment is expected of Black women (Johnson, 1978).

## MALES AND SELF-DISCLOSURE

Jourard (1971) has explored the lethal aspects of the male role, and advances that the socially defined male role requires men to appear tough, objective, striving, achieving, unsentimental, and emotionally unexpressive. If behind his persona a man is tender, if he weeps, for instance, he will likely be viewed as unmanly by others. The contradiction between the way Black men are expected to present themselves in public and their real emotional feelings is a key to understanding the malaise of being a Black male in America. Moreover, the tendency of males to mask their true feelings makes it difficult for Black men to achieve insight into and empathy with Black women.

To the extent that women request expressions of intimate and personal emotions in exchange for their availability as social or sexual partners, the nonexpressive male may find himself in a difficult situation. If he is to execute properly his role as a Black man by associating with women who demonstrate their attraction to him, he must be fairly successful at something he has been explicitly trained not to do, i.e., expressing emotions of gentleness, tenderness, and verbal affection toward women.

The verbal facility among Black males makes it easier for them to create an initial impression of genuine feelings, and thus they readily enter relationships with women. However, as the relationship continues and the woman becomes more familiar with his ways, it becomes increasingly difficult for the Black male to camouflage his absence of genuine feelings for his partner. The male must constantly "fake it" and express sentiments he really does not feel, thus continuously running the risk that his "cover" will be "blown" and the relationship terminated. Hence, this problem is not one of entering relationships with women, but of sustaining them.

Black men, however, still evaluate each other and are evaluated by women largely by the degree to which they approximate the ideal masculine model. Whereas men have a tendency to respond to women on the basis of physical appearance, the typical woman's attraction to a man is often founded on his status, income, and power. Women have typically married men whom they (a) could look up to; (b) view as ambitious, self-contained, and self-controlled; and (c) believe are success-oriented (Jourard, 1971).

Tucker (1978) indicates that success with women is important to many men because they are engaged in covert competition with other men. They believe that through success they will avoid ridicule and will be considered "hip." In the process, a woman becomes a target, and the game becomes an end in itself rather than a means to an end. In this situation, Black men feel that they must not let their emotions leave them vulnerable. To invest emotional energy raises the risk of failure. Women can help immensely by letting men know that they measure manhood not in terms of "cool" but in terms of responsiveness, support, care, and honesty. Black men need to be encouraged to struggle and to deal with their emotions rather than to conceal them. They need assurance that women do not associate "gentleness and kindness" with "weakness" and that they find a man more attractive when he shares his feelings with them. Black men may complain about women who force them to deal with issues, but ultimately they respect them much more than they do meek, compliant women who make no demands (Tucker, 1979).

Mutual stroking is hard, even in committed relationships, and Black men rarely say I love you, which is what women want to hear (Hare, 1979). In a survey of Black males, Gary et al. (1981) conducted a survey of 142 subjects in which 112 responded to a question regarding problems with showing love to their mate or spouse. They found that 21 (9 percent) indicated that sharing love was a problem, while 90 (81 percent) indicated that it was not a problem for them. Learning to say "I love you" and mean it is hard for Black men because it is interpreted as being vulnerable, and they have been taught to fight that, and to show few emotions. Black men seem callous, but maybe only due to ignorance. Black men must have proof that love is not fatal, that the act of loving makes you better, not weaker. Not being able to love is like not really living.

## SEXISM AND WOMEN'S LIBERATION

Staples (1979) asserts that sexism does exist among Black males, and that it is a force that corrupts and limits all the relationships Black men and Black women have with themselves and with each other. In his opinion, it is a positive development that the criticism of sexism among Black people has become an issue. However, the issue threatens the Black community with an assault on the male population. Staples further explains that female equality involves not only personal relationships, but also political and economic relationships. Many of the inequalities perceived in male and female relationships must be remedied through a reeducation of men and women and changes in sex-role socialization. For Black women, involvement in a feminist movement entails a tripartite battle against sexism, racism, and capitalism. Racism and capitalism are forces that have subjected Black women to political and economic subordination. Staples alerts us to the divisive effects of feminism in an oppressed community such as Black America.

Different opinions exist concerning the feasibility of Black feminism. In support of feminism, Lorde (1979) explains that Black women bear the brunt of sexism; therefore, it is in their interest to abolish it. Moreover, it is the responsibility of Black women to decide whether or not sexism in the Black community is pathological. In the opinion of Lorde, "creative relationships of which Staples speaks are to the benefit of Black males, considering the sex ratio of males and females." Salaam (1979) argues that the struggle against sexism is not a threat to Black masculinity. The forces that attack Black women individually, institutionally, and ideologically also assault Black men.

Many Black men and Black women have spoken out against feminism (LaRue, 1970; Duberman, 1975). The arguments they advanced are that (1) Black people as a race need to be liberated from racism; (2) the feminist notion creates negative competition between the Black male and female for economic security; (3) white women hoard the benefits of the struggle from Black women; and (4) this movement facilitates increased tension in the already strained interpersonal atmosphere in which Black men and women interact. In effect, women's liberation impacts negatively on the Black liberation movement and on Black male and female relationships.

The women's liberation movement has engendered a growing distrust between Black men and women that is tearing marriages apart and fracturing personal relationships. The Black male feels it is he who has been oppressed and has suffered the most, and that the liberation of Black women will come as a part of the Black liberation movement, not the feminist movement. The writings of Black feminists such as Michelle Wallace (1979) and June Jordan (1977), productions like Shange's (1977) *For Colored Girls* (a play with poetry and prose delivered by seven young Black women, describing their trials and tribulations, primarily with their men), and Lonnie Coleman's (1973), *Beulah Land* Illustrate the complications of interpersonal relationships between Black males and females. Karenga (1979) argues that one does not have to be as nauseatingly negative as are Wallace and Shange to admit that there are substantive problems concerning relationships between Black males and Black females.

Unfortunately, there is a growing body of Black women who deny that Black men are the main targets of white oppression and who contrarily blame Black men—the victims—for their own victimization. The white women's liberation movement and efforts supportive of the Equal Rights Amendment are currently supported by a small segment of Black women to justify their fundamental unwillingness to identify their interests as integral to the Black family and community first, foremost, and always (Wilcox, 1979). Many Black women seem to be assigning to Black men a power to oppress women commensurate with that of white men, the historical oppressor. Wilcox (1979) argues that if white women were serious about their expressed intentions, they should be trying to destroy rather than evaluate the concept of white supremacy. Racism and sexism are inextricably linked to each other. Both manifest deleterious effects (economic, psychological, and social) on Black people. Building a separatist Black women's movement, wherein Black females collaborate with white females against the needs of their own people, is antithetical to the interests of the Black race.

# MODES OF CONNECTING

Black men and Black women engage in relationships that are not always in their mutual best interest. Karenga (1979) describes four modes through which Black males and Black females come together. They are (1) the cash connection; (2) the flesh connection; (3) the force connection; and (4) the dependency connection. All of these modes of connecting are related to a realization that Black-on-Black exploitation is prevalent in the Black community. Male and female relationships are so natural that they do not have to be learned, and are viewed as a sine qua non; hence, people without them feel deformed and deficient. Karenga (1979) says "a connection is a short-term or tentative association which is utilitarian and alienated and designed primarily for the mutual misuse of each other's body. On the other hand, a quality relationship is a stable association defined by its positive sharing, its mutual investment in each other's psychological well-being and development."

The "cash connection" is motivated by a presence of financial resources by at least one of the dyad members. Women are sparring with other women over available men with money, and men are sparring with each other over available women with money. In short, men and women are looking at one another as potential "marks" in a petty confidence game. Women and men who have a steady job, their own apartment or house, and an automobile make very attractive potential marks. Conjugal relationships are initiated between a "mate and a mark," resulting in an emotional dependency on the part of the mark as his or her fiscal resources are siphoned away. This monetary connection is typically the root of much evil within male and female relationships, culminating in conflicts over money.

The underlying assumption of the "cash connection" is that everything has a price and that money can solve all problems. One would think, however, that these notions, which are so vulgar in conception and brutal in practice, would be rejected by well-intentioned people. Yet, mothers continue to tell their daughters to seek out a mate who can "take care" of them, as if they were disabled or required to produce a dowry. Such an exchange of sex for economic security under the guise of marriage truly diminishes the chances for a quality relationship.

The "flesh connection" is rooted in the new morality which is characteristic of contemporary society and is based predominantly on the pursuit of sex. This linkage focuses on the body and all the perverse things one can do with all selected parts of it. This connection typifies the sex machine phenomenon of society and is a shift from a conservative to a more liberal value orientation. The source and essence of the flesh connection is a sexual commodity. While the "force connection" is predicated on the violent nature of society, it typically involves the "macho" mentality of men taking what they are compelled to take as a result of an illusion of ownership.

The "dependency connection" results from engaging in one or all of the three previously mentioned connections. In this context the dependent nature of this situation plays havoc with the woman's psyche and whe will not leave her man even under the worse conditions, including physical abuse. Some women learn to like the sadistic treatment. If he has to beat her to keep her, certainly he does not need her nor she him, for she has no sense of worth or identity outside the deformation and oppression she suffers. She may even justify and rationalize the abuse to her associates, thus adopting a true slave mentality.

## VIEWS OF BLACK WOMEN

A contemporary view of the perceptions of Black women is documented in the Essence Quality of Life Survey of 1980, which addressed a wide range of topics that are important to the psychosocial well-being, survival, and growth of Afro-Americans. While this research represents the views primarily of Black females (97.4 percent), the findings tend to support many of the popular notions about male and female interaction. The results of the study suggest that Black people basically love one another, yet the respondents expressed mixed opinions regarding whether Afro-Americans are becoming more unified. Of the approximately 72 percent of the 6157 respondents, (4433) perceived that Black men and women were in competition with each other; 52 percent (3211) disagreed with the statement, "Black men are supportive of Black women"; and only 37 percent of the women (2279) indicated that Black men are supportive of Black women. On the other hand, survey respondents reported that Black women are developing stronger, more positive relationships with each other (Wells, 1980).

Of all the respondents, 95 percent (5849) reported that Black women are subjected to both racism and sexism, and 67 percent (4225) agreed that, in general, racism tends to be more severe for Black men than it is for Black women. There were 82 percent (5049) agreeing that Black women encounter sexist attitudes and behavior as much from Black men as they do from white men. However, 63 percent (3879) expressed the opinion that Black women are discriminated against primarily due to their race and not as a result of their sex. This finding is indicative of an ideological dilemma confronting many Black women who have contemplated involvement with the women's liberation movement: 67 percent of the respondents (4125) felt that feminist issues are relevant to Black women; 37 percent (2279) disagreed with the statement, "My interest as a Black person takes precedence over my interest

TABLE 4.1

If you could start all over today and choose
the ideal style of living, which of the
following alternatives would you choose?

| Style of Living | n | Percentage |
| --- | --- | --- |
| Single/no dependents | 1013 | 16.4 |
| Head/one-parent household | 247 | 4.0 |
| Living with opposit sex; no legal marriage | 351 | 5.7 |
| Living in traditional union with children | 3580 | 58.1 |
| Living in traditional union without children | 543 | 8.8 |
| Living in nontraditional union | 49 | .8 |
| Married with extramarital affair | 73 | 1.2 |
| Other | 301 | 4.9 |
| | n = 6157 | 100.0 |

SOURCE: Leroy Wells, Jr., *Essence's quality of life survey results,* Vol. 1. Adapted by permission of the author.

as a woman"; and while 49 percent (3017) agreed with the statement, 14 percent (8621) took a neutral stance.

A measure of the conflict between men and women when sexism is contrasted with racism was depicted in the response to the statement, "Sex discrimination will persist long after race discrimination is eliminated": 52 percent (3211) agreed, while 21 percent (1293) took a neutral position or were unsure; but 27 percent (1663) rejected this hypothetical question, thereby demonstrating an awareness of the political-economic dynamics between racism and sexism. When asked if "Black women are discriminated against primarily because of their sex, not their race", 69 percent (4248) disagreed, 10.4 percent (640) were unsure, and 21 percent (1293) agreed.

The responses to several questions concerning the relationship Black females have with significant others were quite revealing. For example, 33 percent of the respondents indicated that they were "dissatisfied" with the relationships with their lover(s), while 60 percent were "satisfied". For the married woman, 48 percent were "satisfied" with their relationships with their spouses; however, 33 percent selected a neutral position, suggesting a satisfaction dilemma. Approximately 20 percent were dissatisfied with their husbands. In general, 87 percent of the respondents were dissatisfied with how Blacks treat each other. Table 4.1 depicts how Black women responded to the question, "If you could start all over today and choose the ideal style of living, which of the following alternatives would you choose?"

The results suggest that most of these women are still desirous of becoming part of the traditional family mode, despite the high improbability of their doing so, particularly for females over 25 years of age and those who are college-educated (Staples, 1973). Within this survey, 50 percent of the respondents were over 27 years of age and 44.3 percent were college graduates, while 39 percent had some college or had graduated from a two-year college.

Fifty-six percent of the respondents (3448) agreed that "interracial marriages will become more accepted in the 1980s," and 23 percent (1416) agreed that "race is not an important factor in the selection of a marriage partner." Seventy percent (4310) disagreed with the latter statement, while 7.3 percent (450) were neutral or uncommitted on the topic. Approximately 25 percent of the Black women (1539) said that Black men prefer white women, while 56 percent (3448) disagreed with that perception and 20 percent (1231) were neutral on the subject. When the same question was reversed, only 4.8 percent of the respondents (276) agreed that Black women prefer white men, while a resounding 86 percent (5295) disagreed with this premise; 9.5 percent (585) took a neutral position on this issue.

The Essence Quality of Life Survey results raise more questions than answers about the future of relationship-building between Black females and Black males. Strengthening the bond between the two has significant implications for the stability of Black family amidst the myriad of social forces. Evidence of disproportionate sex ratios, male sex-role ambiguity, low self-disclosure of males, and issues related to sexism and women's liberation all function to obscure the positive aspects of relationships between Black men and Black women. Moreover, the modes of connecting as described by Karenga (1979) suggest that the Black community needs to identify with proactive models for facilitating genuine and sustained bonding between the sexes. The mutual investment in each other's psychological and spiritual well-being is the desired outcome. Reviewing the perceptions of contemporary authors provides an enlightening breath of fresh air and, it is hoped, will encourage more dialogue between social scientists and lay persons concerning the realities of Black men and Black women entering and sustaining relationships based on principals of (a) Black unity, (b) self-determination, (c) cooperative economics, and (d) self-respect.

## SUMMARY RECOMMENDATIONS

The quality of Black male and Black female relations may determine the growth or destruction of Black people. An in-depth understanding of the nature and conditions that affect relations between Black males and Black females is essential for the continued survival and growth of Black people. Black behavioral scientists' research on relations between Black males and females should be given more empirical and theoretical priority. As a contribution to such aims, the following recommendations are advanced:

(1) that social science investigators begin to raise researchable questions exploring the nature of the context in which Black male and Black female relationships are embedded;

(2) that demographers be challenged to focus greater attention on the scarcity of Black males as a national phenomenon having potentially grave consequences for the race and having deleterious effects on Black women;

(3) that Black men and Black women address unsatisfactory interpersonal relationships by participating in personal growth and human relations group sessions;

(4) that universities develop and include a course on male and female relationships as a part of their general education and continuing education curriculum; and

(5) that Black national organizations place on their program agenda the issue of strategies for strengthening relationships between Black women and Black men.

While it is indeed true that the quality of Black male and Black female relationships is impacted by a host of societal factors, the survival of these relationships must depend increasingly upon the concept of self-reliance. Black people must continue to search their souls for the workable solutions to their interpersonal conflicts.

## REFERENCES

Akbar, N. Rhythmic patterns in African personality. In L. King et al. (Ed.) *African philosophy: Assumption and paradigms for research on Black persons.* Los Angeles: Fanon Center, 1976.

Asante, M. *Afrocentricity: The theory of social change.* Buffalo, NY: Amulefi, 1980.

Coleman, L. *Beulah land.* Garden City, NY: Doubleday, 1973.

Cox, O. *Caste, class and race.* New York: Modern Reader Paperbacks, 1964.

Duberman, L. *Gender and sex in society.* New York: Praeger, 1975.

Gary, L. Personal communication, January 10, 1981.

Gary, L., et al. *Helpseeking among Afro-American men: Preliminary results.* Unpublished manuscript, Institute for Urban Affairs and Research, Howard University, 1981.

Grier, W., & Cobbs, P. *Black rage.* New York: Basic Books, 1968.

Hammond, B., & Ladner, J. Socialization into sexual behavior in a Negro slum ghetto. In

C. Broderick & J. Bernard (Eds.), *The individuals and society*. Baltimore: John Hopkins University Press, 1969.

Hare, J. Black male-female relationships. *Sepia,* November 1979, p. 82.

Herzog, Ed. and Sudia, C. *Boys in fatherless families* (DHEW Publication No. OCD 72-33). Washington, DC: Government Printing Office, 1971.

Jackson, J. But where are the men? In R. Staples (Ed.), *The Black family: Essays and studies*. Belmont, CA: Wadsworth, 1978.

Johnson, L. Sexual behavior of southern blacks. In R. Staples (Ed.), *The Black family: Essays and studies* (2nd ed.). Belmont, CA: Wadsworth, 1978.

Jordan, J. *Things that I do in the dark*. New York: Random House, 1977.

Jourard, S. *The transparent self.* New York: Van Nostrand, 1971.

Karenga, M. *Beyond connection: Liberation in love and struggle*. New Orleans, LA: Ahidiana, 1978.

Karenga, R. On Wallace's myths: Wading thru troubled waters. *The Black Scholar,* 1979, *10*(8, 9), 36-39.

LaRue, L. Black liberation and women's lib. *Transactions,* 1970, *8*(1), 59-63.

Lorde, A. Feminism and black liberation. *The Black Scholar,* 1979, *10*(8, 9), 17-20.

National Center for Health Statistics. *Vital statistics of the United States*. Washington, DC: Department of Health and Human Resources, 1977. (Unpublished data).

A new black struggle. *Newsweek,* August 27, 1979, pp. 58-60.

Noble, J. *Beautiful, also, are the souls of my Black sisters: A history of Black women in America*. Englewood Cliffs, NJ: Prentice-Hall, 1978.

Pleck, J. The male sex role: Definitions, problems, and sources of change. *Journal of Social Issues,* 1976, *32*(3), 155-164.

Poussaint, A. White manipulation and black oppression. *The Black Scholar,* 1979, *10*(8, 9), 52-55.

Salaam, K. Revolutionary struggle/revolutionary love. *The Black Scholar,* 1979, *10*(8,9), 20-24.

Scott, J. Polygamy: A futuristic family arrangement for African-Americans. *Black Books Bulletin,* 1976, 13-19.

Shange, N. *For colored girls*. New York: Emerson Hall, 1977.

Stack, C. *All our kin*. New York: Harper & Row, 1974.

Staples, R. *The Black woman in America*. Chicago: Nelson-Hall, 1973.

Staples, R. Masculinity and race: The dual dilemma of Black men. *Journal of Social Issues,* 1978, *34*(1), 169-183.

Staples, R. A rejoinder: Black feminism and the cult of masculinity: The danger within. *The Black Scholar,* 1979, *10*(8, 9), 63-67.

Toffler, A. *Future shock*. New York: Random House, 1970.

Tucker, R. Why do Black men hide their feelings? *Essence,* September, 1978, p. 4.

Tucker, R. Therapy to quell the rage: Love, sex and Black Macho. *The Washington Post,* November 3, 1979.

U.S. Bureau of the Census. *Current Population Surveys*. Washington: DC: Department of Commerce, 1977.

U.S. Department of Commerce. *Social indicators III*. Washington, DC: Government Printing Office, 1980.

Wallace, M. *Black macho and the myth of the superwoman*. New York: Dial Press, 1979.

War between the sexes. *Ebony,* June 1979, pp. 33-39.

Wells, L. *Essence's Quality of Life Survey results* (Vol. I). College Park: University of Maryland, 1980. (Unpublished data).

Welsing, F. The cress theory of color confrontation and racism. *The Black Scholar,* 1974, 5, 32-40.

Wilcox, P. Is there life for Black leaders after ERA? *Black Male/Female Relationships,* 1979, 2(1), 53-55.

Wilkinson, D. The stigmatization process of the Black male's identity. In D. Wilkinson and R. Taylor (Ed.), *The Black male in America.* Chicago: Nelson-Hall, 1977.

# 5

## MOMS, DADS, AND BOYS
### Race and Sex Differences in the Socialization of Male Children

Walter R. Allen

This chapter is based on a study of family interpersonal dynamics and adolescent male socialization outcomes in a sample of Black and white middle-class families in Chicago, Illinois. The rationales for undertaking this research were numerous. The principal goals were (1) to challenge pathological conceptions of Black family life and Black child socialization; (2) to explore the family life of middle-class Black Americans; (3) to shed light on the family roles of Black men; (4) to adopt an integrative view of Black child socialization outcomes; and (5) to accomplish these goals in the context of a comparative perspective by race, sex, and social class status of parents (and sons). I will elaborate briefly on these stated goals:

(1) The overwhelming thrust of research on Black families and their members has tended to stress pathological interpretations. For documentation, see Allen (1978a, 1978b), Billingsley (1968), and Peters (1978). This occurs despite the fact that the reality of Black family life suggests otherwise. In addition, the research of scholars such as Hill (1971), Ladner (1971), Nobles (1978), Scanzoni (1971), and Stack (1974) shows that Black families are resilient, adaptable units capable of fulfilling their members' needs under the most extreme conditions. Nevertheless, negative perspectives

**99**

seem to dominate the research literature on Black families. This study represents a direct challenge to such negative views of Black family life.

(2) When this study was conceived, the family life of middle-class Blacks had been largely neglected. Recently, scholars such as Landry and Jendrek (1978) and McAdoo (1978) have sought to expand our understanding of middle-class Black family life. Such research stands in sharp contrast to the bulk of research on Black family life. In the past, the tendency has been to focus on lower-class, inner-city Black families, usually as contrasted with middle-class, white suburban families. Moreover, stable, low-income, inner-city Black families have tended to be ignored. This study hopes to illustrate that diversity by class, observable among Black families, is the same type of diversity by class that is evident in white families.

(3) As many astute evaluations of family research have noted, male family roles have historically been neglected and deemphasized. What has gone under the guise of family studies has, in fact, been the study of women and children in families (Hochschild, 1973). Paradoxically, many negative conclusions about Black fathers' role performances have been drawn (Allen, 1978a, 1978b). Often such conclusions were based on aggregate data that revealed at best only the broad outlines or structures of Black family life (e.g., statistics on father absence). For the most part, these data revealed little about the actual underlying processes. Hence, another intent of this research is to ascertain the true nature of Black fathers' role performances by studying fathers present in the home.

(4) Rarely do social and behavioral scientists study Black child socialization outcomes in the context of an integrated model. Instead, individual characteristics (e.g., class, race, and sex) are correlated with observed outcomes presumed to result from socialization (e.g., scores, behaviors, and responses). The assumption is that if the correlation is established, the true nature of the relationship between these factors is also established. In reality, socialization outcomes are tied to family social and economic characteristics by a myriad of intervening processes across the general realm of values (produced by socioeconomic circumstances), child-rearing practices (related to socioeconomic status and values), and parent-child interpersonal relations (outgrowth of socioeconomic status, values, and child-rearing practices). This research uses a social structure and personality perspective (Elder, 1973) in an attempt to develop a dynamic, integrated view of child socialization processes in Black families.

(5) Finally, this study seeks to accomplish its goals in the context of a comparative framework. Elsewhere (Allen, 1978a), there have been identified three prominent ideological approaches to the study of Black families: the cultural-deviant, the cultural-equivalent, and the cultural-variant perspectives. Briefly, the *cultural-deviant* perspective is one that approaches Black families

as pathological deviations from normative white families. The *cultural-equivalent* perspective, on the other hand, views Black families as comparable to white families and seeks cross-race similarities. The *cultural-variant* perspective, used here, treats Black families as distinct cultural forms, legitimate insofar as they overlap *or* depart from conventional white family patterns and processes. Thus, this study employs a comparative-culture view that incorporates parent/sex comparisons while holding class more or less constant. In essence, this study seeks to explore race and sex variations in parent child-rearing goals (values), parent child-rearing practices, and parent interpersonal relations with the son and goal outcomes. More specifically, it examines the comparative role performances of Black fathers (relative to their spouses and white fathers) in relation to the comparative socialization outcomes for Black sons (relative to their white peers).

## DATA AND METHODS OF STUDY

Data for this study come from a 1974 survey of Chicago, Illinois, male adolescents and their families. A stratified-cluster sample of 100 two-parent families with sons aged 14-18 in the home, was drawn using the following procedures:

(1) 1970 census data were used to stratify city tracts by race, income level, and educational attainment.

(2) This information (supplemented by visual examination of neighborhoods and questioning of informants knowledgeable about the composition of communities in the city) was then used to select tracts falling into one of four major groups: Black or white, either working-class (lower-middle-class) or middle-class neighborhoods.

(3) Thirty blocks were then selected from each of the four tract groups using a probability of selection proportional to size of cluster sampling plan (Kish, 1965).

(4) A randomized quota sampling plan was used at the block level to identify specific households that qualified for inclusion in the study. (See Allen, 1978a, for more details on the sampling plan.)

In each household, interviewers sought to complete two-hour *separate* interviews with the concerned family members. Of the 360 respondents originally sought (father, mother, and son in each family), 245, or 68 percent, were obtained. For these analyses, the sample breaks down as follows: Black fathers (18), mothers (32), and sons (27); white fathers (35), mothers (45), and sons (45).

# FINDINGS

In our discussion of findings, we first compared parent and family socio-economic characteristics. We then moved to a comparison of parent child-bearing goals. Next, differences in parent child-rearing practices were probed. From there, we moved to a consideration and comparison of parent-son interpersonal relations. Finally, we concluded with a comparison of son socialization outcomes. Contingency table analyses, the primary mode for presentation and analysis of relationships in the data by race, sex, and other pertinent variables, are summarized.

# PARENT AND FAMILY SOCIOECONOMIC CHARACTERISTICS

Results from our selective comparisons of the Black and white families in this sample show them to be comparable in terms of indicators of socio-economic status level. Whites, significantly more so than Blacks, had long histories in their present neighborhoods and owned or were buying their homes. The fact that over two-thirds of the Black families were long-term residents of their present neighborhoods (six or more years) and that nearly three-quarters of them owned or were buying their homes helps to temper the statistically significant race differences on these items. Both groups were quite established in their neighborhoods. The only difference was that whites were somewhat more established than Blacks. Comparisons of parents by education, occupation, and income yielded similar results.

On average, white status was higher than that of Blacks across these respective dimensions. However, only in the cases of women's educational attainments and men's occupational status were these advantages for whites statistically significant.

# PARENT CHILD-REARING GOALS

A revised version of Kohn's (1969) index of parental values for children was used to measure parent child-rearing goals. Parents were given a list of twenty child-rearing goals and asked (1) to rate each as not at all important, somewhat important, important, or very important, and (2) to rank the five *most* important and the five *least* important goals on the list. The twenty child-rearing goals listed were:

- popular with other children
- hardworking and ambitious
- polite and well-mannered
- affectionate
- obeys parents well
- independent
- dependable, reliable
- takes life seriously
- good athlete
- religious
- able to defend self
- happy
- good student
- honest
- considerate of others
- neat and clean
- able to handle responsibility
- respectable
- self-concern
- curious

Although this measurement strategy relies on verbal report rather than observation of actual behavior, there is considerable justification for its use in drawing inferences about actual child-rearing goals.

Before showing parents the list of twenty child-rearing goals, interviewers asked them to identify the goals stressed in their own child-rearing approaches. Honesty was the most frequently mentioned parental child-rearing goal, irrespective of race or sex. Blacks and whites differed, however, on the second most common response. Blacks most frequently mentioned the more traditional goal of obedience and whites the more developmental goal of good academic performance. While growth in independence was a frequently reported maternal goal, few fathers attributed any major importance to it.

Parent rankings of the five *most* and the five *least* important goals from the list of twenty were striking for the unanimity shown between spouses on most important goals and between races on least important goals. Black parents rated ambition and obedience as the more important of all important goals, while white parents assigned these spots to honesty and happiness. Parents of both races concurred in assigning the lesser importance of all unimportant goals to popularity and athletic ability. However, while white parents considered seriousness as the next least important of unimportant goals, Black parents opted for self-concern.

Parent ratings of the importance assigned in their own child-rearing to the twenty child-rearing goals specified revealed several interesting patterns. Black fathers, for instance, were much more likely than other parents to rate the specified goals as having great importance. For seventeen of the twenty goals specified, half or more of the Black fathers rated them as very important. By contrast, only ten goals by white fathers, twelve by Black mothers, and nine by white mothers were reported as having been very important to half or more of the respondents. Fathers and Blacks also tended to claim that the specified goals had slightly more importance in their child-rearing than did mothers and whites. Statistical tests revealed significant paternal differences only for the goal of neatness, on which Black fathers placed more stress than did white fathers ($X^2$ = 3.4, s = .07). Black fathers also expressed more concern for seriousness as a desirable goal ($X^2$ = 2.2, s = .14).

## PARENT CHILD-REARING PRACTICES

Data on five types of parent child-rearing practices were obtained from interviews with husbands and wives. The following open-ended questions were used:

(1) *Parent attitudes toward child-rearing experts* were measured by asking the parent, "When you were raising [child's name] did you ever read any books or magazines about child care and how best to raise children?" and "Do you think child-rearing 'experts' really know things about raising children that most mothers or fathers don't?"

(2) *Husband involvement in child-rearing and child care* was measured by asking the wife, "Compared to the help other husbands give their wives with caring for their children, how much help would you say your husband gave you in caring for [son's name] when he was growing up?" (This was scored along a five-item response scale from "a lot more help than most husbands" to "a lot less help than most husbands.")

(3) *Sources of parent child-rearing advice* were measured by asking each parent the following seven-part question, "Over the years, how much helpful advice regarding how best to raise children have you gotten from: your

husband (wife)? your children's teachers? your mother? your relatives (other than mother)? your friends? doctors, social workers, or people like that?" (Each question had a four-item response scale ranging from "none" to "a great deal.") Parents were then asked, "Which of these people has given you the most helpful advice about how best to raise children?"

(4) *Parent independence expectations.* An index was constructed by averaging parent responses to the following questions: "At what age did you expect [son's name] to be able to bathe and dress himself? know his way around the neighborhood so that he could play where he wanted to without getting lost? be willing to try things on his own without depending upon you to help? be able to clean up after himself? make his own friends among children his age?"

(5) *Parent patterns of reward and punishment.* Parent methods and frequency of punishment in child-rearing were measured through responses to the following: "I'd like for you to tell me how often you used each of these methods of punishment: scolding or yelling; spanking or slapping; sending child to room; taking away privileges and talking things over with [son's name] when he was eight years old?" "When [son's name] was around 12 years old, how often did you punish him by *each method of punishment?*" "How often do you use *each method of punishment* as a way of punishing [son's name] now that he is older?" (Each question had a six-item response scale: "never," "at least once a month," "two or three times per month," "at least once a week," and "nearly every day.") Punishment indices were constructed by taking the mean reported parent frequency of use at three different age points for each of the five punishment methods. Parents were also asked, "When [son's name] was 8 years old (12 years old, now), how often did he do things that you found it necessary to punish him for?" (A six-item response scale, as above, was used. Later it was collapsed to three items.)

Parental method and frequency of reward in child-rearing was measured by responses to the following: "I'd like for you to tell me how often you used each of these methods of reward: kissing and hugging; giving him a gift or special privilege; praising him and not making a big deal out of it when he was eight years old and his behavior pleased you?" "When [son's name] was around 12 years old, how often did you reward him by *each method of reward?*" "How often do you use *each method of reward* as a way of rewarding [son's name] now?" (A response scale ranging from "never" to "nearly every day" was used.) Reward indices were constructed by taking the mean reported parent frequency of use at three different age points for each of the five reward methods.

In this sample, Black fathers were the least likely of all parents to have read magazines or books in search of advice on child care and child-rearing:

78 percent of Black fathers reportedly did not read any type of child care and training publications while their sons were growing up. At the other extreme, white mothers reported that 73 percent of their number consulted child care books or magazines while rearing their sons. Generally, greater proportions of mothers than of fathers reported having read child care publications. Parent reliance on child care publications is indicative, to some extent, of overall parent evaluations of "child-rearing experts." We note, therefore, that over three-quarters of Black fathers believed parents knew as much about child-rearing as "experts" do. By the same token, white mothers expressed greatest confidence in the knowledge of these experts. Significantly, only 2 of the total of 140 parents believed unequivocally that experts knew more about child-rearing than parents did. Statistical tests of race and sex differences in evaluation of experts were significant only for Black mothers versus fathers ($X^2$ 2.7, s = .10).

Black wives rated husband involvement in child care and child-rearing slightly higher than did white wives ($X^2$ = 3.4, s = .15). A fifth of the white wives claimed their husbands gave less than ordinary assistance, while only 6 percent of Black wives made such claims. Further, a sizable 63 percent of Black mothers versus 47 percent of white mothers reported that their husbands had given more help than average in rearing the son.

Parents in the sample claimed to have received advice on child-rearing from a variety of sources. When asked to identify the person(s) who had given the most helpful advice, however, white parents and Black fathers commonly cited the spouse (60 percent or higher). Black mothers broke the pattern somewhat by citing their own mothers (41 percent), followed by husbands (33 percent) as the sources of consistently helpful child-rearing advice. On the average, larger percentages of Blacks than of whites, and of mothers than of fathers, reported having received "some" or "a great deal" of helpful child-rearing advice from the various sources cited. In each instance, husbands were prone to rely more heavily on wives for advice than the reverse. Statistical tests revealed no significant race differences in sources of advice for fathers. Black mothers, by contrast, relied much more on advice from "other relatives" and "friends" than did their white counterparts ($X^2$ = 2.1, s = .15, and $X^2$ = 4.4, s = .04, respectively).

Race and sex differences in parent independence age expectations are striking. Fathers and Blacks tended to expect independence in the son's behavior at a much older age than did mothers and whites. In this sample of parents, white mothers claimed to make the earliest demands for independence, followed by white fathers, Black mothers, and Black fathers.

It seems that fathers punished sons considerably more often than mothers did at each of the three periods of childhood specified (Blacks $X^2$ = 45, s < .05). There was also a pronounced tendency for more white than Black parents (2 to 1) to claim that they had never or almost never punished the son. Several other interesting general patterns emerged when we looked at the specific punishment practices of these parents. For example, the majority of parents (34 percent or more for each race-sex subgroup) reported infrequent (once a month or less) use of discussion, the most indirect of all strategies, in their child-rearing approaches. On the other hand, a sizable majority (57 percent or more for each race-sex subgroup) reported frequent (once a week or more) use of the most direct punishment, spanking. Few statistically significant race differences in preferences for specific punishment were found. In the realm of sex differences, fathers reported significantly more frequent use than did mothers of *all* the various punishment strategies. (All chi-square values for father-mother comparisons were significant at the .01 level or beyond.)

Interestingly, a majority of parents reported that it was not their practice to take special notice of good behavior by the son. Similarly, the majority of parents said that they rarely complimented or praised the son as a reward. Of all parents, mothers in general and white mothers in particular seemed to dispense the most rewards to sons. At the other extreme, white fathers proved least likely to reward their sons.

Several statistically significant differences in parents' use of the specific reward techniques were found. Black mothers and white fathers, for instance, were more likely than their spouses to ignore good behavior by the son ($X^2 = 17.2$, $s < .01$, and $X^2 = 21.3$, $s < .001$, respectively). Mothers in both races were much more likely to praise the son as a reward than were fathers (Blacks $X^2 = 17$, $s < .01$; whites $X^2 = 19$, $s < .001$). White mothers and Black fathers also used verbal rewards ($X^2 = 8$, $s < .10$) more frequently than did their racial counterparts. Material rewards were given to the son significantly more often by Black fathers than mothers ($X^2 = 18$, $s < .01$) and more by white mothers than fathers ($X^2 = 25$, $s < .001$). Predictably, given the traditional roles assigned to parents by sex, fathers were significantly less likely than mothers to reward the son during his childhood by kissing or hugging (Blacks $X^2 = 21$; whites $X^2 = 30$; both $s < .001$).

## PARENT-CHILD RELATIONSHIPS

Several measures were used to assess the nature of parent-son supportive, interpersonal relationships. To estimate the extent of shared activities between parent(s) and son, the son was asked, "When you were growing up how many things did you and your mother (father) do together to have fun?" (This was coded from none = 1 to lots of things = 5.) Parent-son effect was measured by the question, "In comparison to other teenagers and their relationships with their parents, how close do you feel you are to your parents?" (This was coded from much closer than most teenagers = 1 to much less close than most teenagers = 5.) Strength of adolescent identification (emotional bond) with the respective parents was tapped by asking him: "Which parent do you feel you have the most in common with in terms of interests and personality?" (This was coded from father much more = 1 to mother much more = 5.) Parental approval and acceptance of the son for whom he is, was measured by asking the adolescent, "how much would you say the following people approve of the kind of person that you are *now*: your father? your mother? (This was coded from approves very much = 1 to disapproves very much = 4.)

Parental control of the son was measured along two dimensions: control of his social relationships and control of his decision-making process. In the first instance, the adolescent was asked, "How many of your friends does your father (mother) know?" (This was coded from all = 1 to almost none = 4.) In the second instance, sons were asked, "In general, how are most decisions made between you and your mother (father)?" (This was coded from she/he decides what I should do = 1 to I can do what I want to, regardless of what she/he thinks = 5.)

Several interesting race and sex differences in parental interpersonal relationships with sons were observed. For instance, Black mothers and white fathers, according to the adolescents, shared significantly more activities with sons than did white mothers and Black fathers. (Respectively, these values were $X^2 = 14$, $s < .001$, and $X^2 = 5$, $s < .10$.) When compared with their spouses, white fathers were reported to have spent sizably more shared activity time with the son as he was growing up. Black mothers and fathers apparently spent about the same amount of time in shared activities with the son.

Pronounced, though not significant, race differences were also reflected in the son's reported emotional closeness to parents. While 60 percent of Black adolescents claimed above-average closeness with parents, only 47 percent of white adolescents did. More strikingly, while white sons believed themselves to have the most in common with their fathers, just the reverse was true for Black sons. Blacks' sons were significantly more likely than whites' sons to identify more closely with the mother rather than the father ($X^2 = 12$, $s < .02$). Interesting race and sex differences also emerged when parental approval and acceptance of the son was compared. Black mothers were reported by their sons as significantly more approving and, by inference, supportive than were white mothers ($X^2 = 10$, $s < .02$). In general, sons viewed Black parents and mothers as more approving than white parents and fathers.

Parents in this sample, according to sons' reports, exercised considerable control over the adolescent social relationships and decision-making processes. White mothers kept significantly closer tabs on their sons' friendships than was true for Black mothers ($X^2 = 7$, $s < .06$). Similarly, mothers were significantly more aware than fathers of who their sons' friends were (whites $X^2 = 52$, $s < .001$; Blacks $X^2 = 42$, $s < .001$). White fathers knew more about their sons' friends than Black fathers (69 percent versus 48 percent knew most or all), although the differences were not statistically significant. When parental control over son's decision-making was compared, no major differences between fathers were revealed. In both races, however, fathers were significantly more authoritarian than mothers (Blacks $X^2 = 28$, $s < .001$; whites $X^2 = 18$, $s < .01$). White mothers also exerted much less control than Black mothers over their sons' decision-making ($X^2 = 11$, $s = .03$).

## SON SOCIALIZATION OUTCOMES

Parents' current satisfaction with overall adolescent socialization outcomes was measured by asking, "If you could change the following activities of [son's name], which of these activities would you have him do as he does now?" (This was scaled from much less = 1 to much more = 5.) The expected response was, "I wish my son would do this activity." Parent responses to questions about sons' activities were grouped so as to indicate basic satisfaction (code = 3), slight dissatisfaction (code = 2 or 4), or great dissatisfaction (code = 1 or 5). Examples of the 25 sons' activities about which parents were queried include getting good grades in school, taking advice from older people, showing affection toward their fathers, worrying about what goes on in the world, making plans for the future, and wanting to be liked by young people their age.

Several questions about aspirations, self-conceptions, values, and attitudes were put to sons in order to determine socialization outcomes. Educational expectations were measured by asking, "Considering your abilities, grades, financial situation, and other factors, how far do you *actually* expect to go in school?" (This was measured by a six-item scale that ranged from some high school to completion of graduate or professional school after the B.A.)

Occupational expectations were measured by asking, "Considering your abilities, financial situation, and other factors, what occupation or type of occupation do you think you will *actually* choose once you are older?" (This was scaled from 0 to 100 along the Duncan SEI occupational prestige index.) Adolescent self-esteem was measured by an index that averaged sons' responses to the following statements: (1) "I certainly feel useless at times," (2) "On the whole, I am satisfied with myself," (3) "All in all, I am inclined to feel that I am a failure," (4) "I am able to do things as well as most other people," and (5) "I feel I do not have much to be proud of." (Each of these was measured by using a four-point scale from "strongly disagree" to "strongly agree." Questions 2 and 4 were reverse-coded.) The academic self-concept index represented the son's average response to the question, "How do you rate your ability in the following school subjects compared with others in your class at school?: English and reading, social studies, science, and mathematics." (Each of these was measured by using a five-point scale ranging from "among the worst" to "among the best.") Achievement values were measured by an index of adolescent agreement with the following statements: (1) "Whatever a person does, he should try to do it better than anyone else." (2) "A man's job should come first, although it may require his spending less time with his wife and children." (3) "The more education a person has, the better able he is to really enjoy and appreciate life." (4) "Generally, in making important decisions, a person should decide what is best for him even if it goes against what his parents and friends want him to do." (Each of these was measured by using a four-point scale from "strongly agree" to "strongly disagree.") The adolescent's sense of control over his own life was measured by an index of mean agreement with the statements, (1) "People like me don't have much of a chance to be successful in life," (2) "Good luck is more important than hard work for success," and (3) "Everytime I try to get ahead, something or someone stops me." (Each of these was measured by using a four-point scale from "strongly agree" to "strongly disagree.")

Several differences were found in the parents' overall levels of satisfaction with the socialization outcomes in the form of the sons' personalities and behaviors. Black parents expressed considerably greater desire for changes in the son's activities. These parents were significantly more likely than white parents to wish that the son would change his activities, by doing either more or less of an activity. Black fathers were also significantly less satisfied with the socialization outcomes, as reflected in their reported satisfaction with sons' activities. This was particularly true when they were compared with Black mothers. Interestingly, no significant differences in general satisfaction with the son were revealed between white spouses. In considering these findings, it was important to note that rarely did parents of either sex express extreme dissatisfaction with the socialization outcomes reflected in their sons' behavior and personalities. The 20 percent of Black fathers was the highest proportion of expressed major dissatisfaction with socialization of outcomes of all race-sex parent subgroups.

Numerous Black-white differences were found in socialization outcomes as measured by sons' attitudes and expectations concerning the future. White sons reported significantly higher occupational expectations, generally expecting to move into higher compensation, status, and demand occupations than their Black counterparts. In this sense, the occupational expectations reported by Black and white sons tended to mirror occupational disparities by race in the contemporary labor force. White sons also sensed themselves to be in greater control of their lives. Again, this race difference reflected in microcosm the self-evident differences prevalent throughout the society in Blacks' versus whites' personal control over their life and environment. Interestingly, of the two racial groups, Black sons valued achievement more highly and stated higher educational attainment expectations. On the other hand, Black sons' self-esteem and academic self-concept levels were lower.

## DISCUSSION

This study of child socialization patterns provides interesting insights into several dimensions of Black male family roles and relationships. We find, for example, little evidence to support prevalent pathological conceptions of Black males *vis-à-vis* their families. The Black fathers here are shown to be highly involved in the rearing of their sons. Moreover, the Black parents studied here are evidently producing well-adjusted, positively motivated sons. As one reviews the findings from this study and compares Black fathers with their spouses and with their white counterparts or compares Black sons to white sons, one wonders how Black male family roles could have been so grossly misreported in the past. Certainly, there were several points of differentiation in these race and sex comparisons. Just as certainly, the extent of such differences did not theoretically or empirically justify the all-too-prevalent negative evaluations of Black males' family relationships. Where, then, does the rationale for such pathological conceptions of Black male family roles reside?

To the extent that researchers continue to approach Black families and Black family members as deviations from the white norm, they will continue to misunderstand the essential character of Black family life. Black families represent a distinct cultural form in this society and, as such, the definitions, roles, and responsibilities of their members differ from those of whites. The distinctiveness of the Black family's cultural form resides in the unique cultural, historical, social, economic, and political circumstances that shape (and continue to shape) their experiences as people. In recognizing this fundamental fact, we move closer to comprehending the complexity represented by Black family life in the United States.

Placed in the experiential context of Blackness, these findings, relative to Black males in family settings, become quite revealing. For instance, we see in the reported child-rearing goals of Black parents reflections of the reality that their sons are being socialized to confront. These Black parents recognize that their sons' future success, indeed their survival, hinges on their abilities to be alternately and selectively assertive and acquiescent. As such, the implied contradiction in Black parental ratings of ambition and obedience as their top child-rearing goals is placed in its proper perspective. Quite simply, Black people (and particularly Black men) at all levels of this society periodically encounter "attempts to keep them in their place." Any but the most negligent Black parents, therefore, necessarily incorporate this reality of race discrimination into achievement aspirations in the socialization of their children.

Still another instance where the Black experiential context resolves conflictual interpretations occurs with respect to the relative importance of Black mothers and fathers in the socialization process. Clear evidence of the mother's more central role is provided by the son's greater identification with her, their warmer interpersonal relationship, and her closer control of his social life. Indeed, similar findings have been interpreted in past studies as evidence of a "Black matriarchy." However, we see that the Black fathers in this study are not peripheral to the socialization process. On the contrary, Black fathers retain warm interpersonal relations with their sons and are active in the child-rearing process. The point is that these Black families represent a distribution of parental child-rearing responsibilities different from that of the modal white family. Mothers are the central adult figures in their sons' lives. Fathers, on the other hand, are active on both the instrumental and the expressive planes, and there is generally a greater flexibility in the assignment of parental responsibilities. Without doubt, these characteristics derive from the unique cultural orientations, histories, and socioeconomic circumstances of Black families in this society.

In numerous other instances, findings from this study are placed in sharper relief by a consideration of the Black experience and related factors. It is not necessary, however, to belabor this point through a long series of examples. One recognizes by now that to the extent Black male family roles and relationships are evaluated out of context, gross misinterpretations are likely to result. Among the many recommendations derived from this study and aimed at influencing future studies of Black male family roles and relationships are the following:

(1) The need exists for comprehensive studies of Black family life using a variety of alternative theoretical frameworks and methodological approaches. Above all else, such studies should stress the humanistic, respectful treatment of Black families as legitimate cultural forms.

(2) Students of Black family life will need to avoid reductionism in the form of overly deterministic perspectives. Determinism, whether it be based on biological, psychological, cultural, social, or economic premises, misrepresents the Black experience. Throughout U.S. history, Black institutions and people have been characterized by a remarkable adaptability that ultimately permitted the persistent pursuit of consistent goals despite uncertainty and resistance. Ours has been the task of constructing and altering the Black reality within the boundaries imposed by this society. The result of these historical processes has been to produce a diversity in Black experiences and outcomes that is too often ignored. Black men are as distinct from one another as they are alike. Thus, they cannot be fully understood apart from the recognition of this diversity.

(3) Considering the issue of diversity among Black men, this study argues that there is a necessity for research focused specifically on Black male family roles and responsibilities. How are these roles defined across class, region, and age groups? How does family status and the individual responsibilities of Black male roles vary across these same contexts? What are some factors that commonly retard and facilitate appropriate family role performance(s) by Black men? In short, we need to consider the family lives of Black males as problematic and eminently worthy of serious investigation.

# REFERENCES

Allen, W. Black family research in the United States: A review, assessment and extension. *Journal of Comparative Family Studies,* 1978, *9,* 167-189. (a)

Allen, W. The search for applicable theories of Black family life. *Journal of Marriage and the Family,* 1978, *40*(1), 117-129. (b)

Billingsley, A. *Black families in white America.* Englewood Cliffs, NJ: Prentice-Hall, 1968.

Elder, G. On linking social structure and personality. *American Behavioral Scientist,* 1973, *16,* 785-800.

Hill, R. *The strengths of Black families.* New York: Emerson Hall, 1971.

Hochschild, A. A review of sex role research. *American Journal of Sociology,* 1973, *78,* 1011-1029.

Kish, L. *Survey sampling.* New York: John Wiley, 1965.

Kohn, M. *Class and conformity.* Homewood, IL: Dorsey, 1969.

Ladner, J. *Tomorrow's tomorrow: The Black woman.* Garden City, NY: Doubleday, 1971.

Landry, B., & Jendrek, M. The employment of wives in middle-class Black families. *Journal of Marriage and the Family,* 1978, *40,* 787-798.

McAdoo, H. Factors related to stability in upwardly mobile Black families. *Journal of Marriage and the Family,* 1978, *40,* 761-768.

Nobles, W. Toward an empirical and theoretical framework for defining Black families. *Journal of Marriage and the Family,* 1978, *40,* 679-691.

Peters, M. Notes from the guest editor. Special issue: Black families. *Journal of Marriage and the Family*, 1978, *40*, 655-661.

Scanzoni, J. *The Black family in modern society*. Boston: Allyn & Bacon, 1971.

Stack, C. *All our kin: Strategies for survival in a Black community*. New York: Harper & Row, 1974.

Staples, R. Towards a sociology of the Black family: A decade of theory and research. *Journal of Marriage and the Family*, 1971, *33*, 19-38.

# 6

## BLACK FATHER AND CHILD INTERACTIONS

John L. McAdoo

Very few studies have focused on father-child interaction, socialization, and coping strategies in Black families. Social scientists have generally studied the structure of the most economically deficient, socially vulnerable, problematic Black family and inferred negative interaction patterns from that structural viewpoint. These vulnerable Black families have usually been compared to economically stable white middle-income families. No studies were found that examined the interaction patterns within middle-income Black families.

The role of the Black father in his child's development process is portrayed in the scientific literature as that of an invisible man, who has no power in the family and is assumed not to have any active interest or role in the socialization of his children (J. McAdoo, 1976). Except for a few studies related to white father-child interaction, almost no studies have related patterns of Black father-child interaction. Interaction studies dealing with Black families usually have focused on patterns of mother-child interaction and inferred father's socialization patterns from the mother's reports of their attitudes. Many of these studies of mother-child interaction have attempted to compare middle- and upper-class white families with lower-class Black families and

AUTHOR'S NOTE: This research is part of a larger project that is supported by the National Institute of Mental Health, Grant 1 RO1 MH 25838-01.

have tended to use a cultural deficiency model in attempting to explain their findings.

The purposes of this study were (1) to determine the patterns of verbal interaction that take place between the Black father and his child, (2) to determine the types of nonverbal interaction that take place between the Black father and his child, and (3) to explore the fathers' attitudes toward child-rearing. The goal was to observe the process of interaction that takes place between a Black father and his preschool child, using methodologies developed by observing other ethnic-group fathers.

# REVIEW OF THE LITERATURE

## TYPES OF INTERACTION

*Nurturance.* Verbal nurturance was defined as the expression of warmth and positive feelings toward the attitudes and behavior of the child. An example of verbal nurturance might be the father telling his child that he enjoyed the child's part in the school play and really likes the way he plays with his younger brother.

Several researchers (Radin, 1972, 1975; Baumrind, 1971) have suggested that maternal warmth (nurturance) facilitates the child's, particularly the female child's, identification with the mother. Radin (1972) has suggested that paternal nurturance facilitates the male child's identification with his father. Identification with either parent should lead to an incorporation of the parent's ideas, attitudes, beliefs, and feelings about the child. The parent communicates to the child a positive acceptance of the child as a person. Nurturance is one of the patterns of interaction that is important in the development of social competence in preschool children.

Nurturance (warmth) is used more by parents who recognize and respond to their child's needs, who communicate acceptance, and who are available for interaction, than it is by parents who are inaccessible and insensitive. Warmth is seen as characteristic of both male and female parent roles and is usually expressed as praise or approval through nonverbal interactions, including patting, touching, stroking, hugging, kissing, and playful activities (Newman & Newman, 1978).

*Restrictiveness.* Verbal restrictiveness is defined as the opposite of nurturant interaction, and is described as coldness and the expression of negative feelings toward the child's attitudes and behavior. An example of restrictiveness would be the father ordering the child, without any explanation, to turn off a favorite television program.

Parental restrictiveness does not facilitate positive communication and identification between the child and his parents (Radin, 1972). Restrictive behaviors are those behaviors that are not warm, loving, and supportive of the child. Nonsupporting behaviors are usually described as criticism or expressed disapproval and may also include grabbing, pushing, or forbidding the child's participation in some event or activity without explanation. It may be viewed as a negative reaction by the parent to the child's attitudes, behaviors, and beliefs. Nonsupport may also lead the parent to deal with the symptoms of the problem and not the needs of the child, or to control his or her own behavior, eliminating the usual patterns of identification and communication to the child. Parental restrictiveness can lead children to develop a negative image of themselves and their worth as human beings, as well as negative feelings about those around them.

*Parenting Styles.* Baumrind (1971), Biller (1969), and Radin (1972) focused on the impact of the parent-child interaction on the child. Baumrind examined types of parenting and their effects on cognitive and moral development; Radin was concerned with its impact on cognitive development; and Biller focused on the impact of paternal nurturance on sex-role formation and cognitive development in the child. The present author has found no study of Black middle-class parents interacting with their preschool children.

Baumrind (1971) observed the relationship between three types of parenting styles—authoritarian, authoritative, and permissive—and competence in preschool children. She found that authoritative parents prompted purposive and dominant behavior in boys and girls. Authoritative control was associated with the development of social responsibility in boys and with achievement (but not friendly, cooperative behavior) in girls. Authoritarian child-rearing practices were associated with either markedly high or markedly low overall competence in preschool children. Children from permissive homes exhibited similar levels of cooperation as the children of authoritarian parents.

Radin (1972) also studied patterns of interaction between white middle- and working-class parents and their children. Three verbal interaction patterns were identified in her group of mothers: nurturant, restrictive, and nonnurturant. She studied the relationship between these patterns and interaction, and the child's cognitive growth one year later. Radin found that children of verbally nurturant mothers did well in school, while children of restrictive mothers did poorly on cognitive tasks in kindergarten.

Most of the observational studies (Radin, 1972; Baumrind, 1971) tended to use verbal interaction patterns to measure paternal warmth and restrictiveness; however, no systematic attempt was made to measure these on a nonverbal level. McAdoo, McAdoo, and Teresa (1976), using the verbal interaction categories of Radin's work, developed a nonverbal interaction scale for this study.

The nonverbal interaction scale focused on tone of voice, physical interaction, meeting implicit and explicit needs, and neutral nonverbal interactions.

With the exception of neutral, we were interested in learning whether the nonverbal interactions were positive or negative. The types of physical interactions included touching, pointing, hugging, holding, and restraining. Meeting explicit needs was defined as physically responding to a request by the child. For example, David asks his father to hold him and the father responds by holding the child. Meeting implicit needs occurred when the father observed the child and decided he or she needed something. For example, Mary is wandering aimlessly around the room and the father gives her some crayons and paper. Another example of implicit needs might be that Julia, while playing in the room, suddenly sits down and crosses her legs. The father gets up and carries her to the bathroom.

In summary, most of the interaction studies between parent and child did not focus on the patterns of interaction, but attempted to correlate these patterns with the child's cognitive, moral, or sex-role development. The studies looked only at verbal interaction and did not focus on the Black family. While these studies are of great importance in terms of shedding light on white families, we need to obtain a better understanding of the interaction processes in Black families and of the role the Black father plays in the socialization process of his children.

This study asks three important questions: (1) How does the Black father interact with his child? (2) What is his attitude toward child-rearing? and (3) Does he interact differently with his sons and daughters?

## METHOD

### SAMPLE

The sample consisted of 40 Black fathers and their preschool children, evenly divided between girls and boys aged 4-6 years, living in a suburban town within the Baltimore-Washington, D. C., metropolitan area. This town offered the researcher an excellent opportunity to study intact, middle-class Black families living in the same neighborhood and having children who attended the same schools. The fathers were randomly selected from a pool of fathers who volunteered to take part in the project. They were located by advertisement in nursery schools, local church bulletins, and door-to-door canvassing.

All the fathers were found to be in Type I or Type II of the Hollingshead-Redlich Socioeconomic Status scale. Forty-six percent of the fathers were found to be upper-middle-class and 54 percent were found to be lower-middle-class. When asked to rate themselves, 76 percent of the fathers stated that they were middle-class, while 24 percent rated themselves as working-class. Of those fathers who reported on the occupational status of their own

## TABLE 6.1
### Description of the Total Sample

| Group | f | Percentage |
|---|---|---|
| Sex of child | | |
| Boys | 20 | 50 |
| Girls | 20 | 50 |
| Total | 40 | 100 |
| SES, of father | | |
| Class I, upper class | 18 | 46 |
| Class II, middle class | 22 | 54 |
| Total | 40 | 100 |
| SES, self-rating | | |
| Middle-class | 29 | 76 |
| Working class | 9 | 24 |
| Total | 38 | 100 |
| Mobility Pattern | | |
| Born middle-class | 4 | 13 |
| Born working-class | 27 | 87 |
| Total | 31 | 100 |
| Education | | |
| Graduate/professional degree | 16 | 40 |
| College degree | 17 | 43 |
| Some college | 7 | 17 |
| Total | 40 | 100 |
| Occupation | | |
| Executive, professional | 7 | 20 |
| Manager | 25 | 69 |
| Administrative, semiprofessional | 4 | 11 |
| Total | 36 | 100 |
| Religion | | |
| Protestant | 34 | 92 |
| Catholic | 3 | 8 |
| Total | 37 | 100 |

fathers, 27, or 87 percent, reported their fathers were working-class (see Table 6.1).

About 40 percent of the fathers reported having received education beyond the B.A., and having undergone professional training. Forty-three percent of the fathers reported earning a B.A., while 17 percent reported having college credits that amounted to less than the B.A. (see Table 6.1).

In response to questions related to their occupational status, the majority of these fathers (69 percent) reported that they worked in middle-manage-ment positions in government and private industry. A few of the fathers (20 percent) reported that they were employed in high-level government and private-industry positions. The remainder of the fathers (11 percent) reported that they were employed in semiprofessional or lower-level government positions. The overwhelming majority of the fathers in this sample (92 percent) belonged to the Protestant faith (see Table 6.1).

## INSTRUMENT

*Verbal Interaction.* Verbal interaction may be defined as a verbal communication between parent and child related to an attitude, event, or behavior that has meaning and consequence for both of them. A modified version of the Radin (1975) Cognitive Home Environment Scale (CHES) was used. This semi-structured questionnaire gathered information on the father's perceptions about his attitude and role in socializing his child. Some of the questions centered on the degree of help the father gave in school learning tasks. The father was asked, "Did you teach your child to read, spell, or count?" He was also asked about the number and types of books and magazines currently in the home and the amount of time the child spends reading them. Other questions related to whether or not the child had a library card and the number of times he went to the library.

In addition, the questionnaire elicited information about the father's attitudes toward child-rearing. There were questions about his expectations of the child's behavior, his role in the decision-making process, and the types of the child's behavior of which he most approved. Since the Black father's attitudes toward child-rearing were considered to be the most important part of the CHES, we are reporting on those results. The CHES was used to observe the verbal interaction that took place between the father and his child. All responses, as well as any verbal communication that occurred between the parent and child, were tape-recorded.

In addition to the father's child-rearing attitudes, there were variables related to verbal nurturance and verbal restrictiveness that were collected from the taped interview. Several subcategories were devised to make up the verbal nurturance variable. They were reinforcing, influencing, and limitsetting behavior strategies; responding to explicit needs; responding to implicit needs; and expressing warmth and initiating motivating behaviors. The subcategories constituting the verbal restrictive variable included ordering without explanation, threatening and other adverse verbal stimuli, and physically stopping undesirable behavior.

*Nonverbal Interaction.* For the purposes of this study, nonverbal interaction may be defined as any act or behavior by a parent or child that is used to communicate feelings and meanings about an occurring event or behavior.

These feelings or meanings may be positive, negative, or neutral. This study was interested in generating information-learning about the types and amount of nonverbal behavior. A timed grid was built into the questionnaire at three predetermined points to gather information about tone of voice, physical contact, meeting explicit and implicit needs, and neutral behavior. The neutral category was used for those acts or behaviors that did not fall into any of the other four categories.

For each nonverbal category of behavior there were subcategories. For example, tone of voice may be described as positive, negative, or neutral. Physical touch also had subcategories, such as touching, holding, hugging, restraining, and spanking. The parent was described as meeting explicit needs when he responded to a request to be held or to do something for the child. The father was described as meeting implicit needs when the behavior of the child indicated that he or she had such a need. For example, in one interview, the child moved about, doing things that distracted the father's attention from the interview. The father stopped the process and picked up the child.

## DATA COLLECTION

Two data collection procedures were used in this study: (1) the modified version of the CHES (Radin and Sonquist, 1968), which was used to collect information about the father's child-rearing attitudes and to collect verbal interaction data; and (2) the McAdoo et al. (1976) nonverbal interaction rating scale.

*Verbal Interaction* Four Black male interviewers were trained over a three-week period to observe and record parent-child interactions in the parents' own homes. There were two interviews. The first interview involved the whole family in a discussion of the aims of the project in order to gain the father's permission, to gather some socioeconomic data, and to help the child become familiar with and relaxed around the interviewer.

The second interview also took place in the home, with only the father and the child present. The Radin and Sonquist (1968) CHES was administered to the fathers, and their responses to the CHES questions were tape-recorded. At the end of the interview, the child was given a puzzle to complete and the interviewer was able to observe the verbal interaction patterns that took place between the father and his child. Fathers were asked to keep the child in the room throughout the hour-and-a-half to two-hour interview on child-rearing attitudes in order to play puzzles at the end. The child was expected to get restless during this time, allowing us an opportunity to see how the parent would control the child's behavior.

Following this interview, the tapes were given to two trained verbal coders, who reviewed each tape and divided it into four 15-minute segments. The two consecutive 15-minute periods with the most verbal interactions were coded. The average intercoder reliability was .92. The verbal interactions were scored according to seven factors: (1) reinforcing, (2) responding to implicit needs, (3) relating to explicit needs, (4) initiating motivating behaviors, (5) expressing warmth, (6) influencing and limit-setting categories, and (7) restricting behaviors (Radin, 1972).

Nurturant behavior, for example, involved any positive parental response after the child's behavior, such as saying "good," or expressing appreciation; asking the child what he wanted; and setting a limit, but providing an explanation for the limit. Restrictive behavior, for example, would be ordering the child to do something without explanation; scolding, name-calling, sarcasm, yelling, and so forth. One point was given for each verbal nurturant and verbal restrictive interaction. A total interaction score was found by summing the nurturance and restrictive scores. The total was then divided into the nurturance and restrictive scores to obtain proportional scores.

*Nonverbal Interaction.* The interviewers coded nonverbal behavior on a timed grid placed after the first ten, middle ten, and final ten questions. The interviewer recorded nonverbal interactions at 15-second intervals, a maximum of two minutes per question during the first, middle, and last ten questions on the questionnaire. There were five categories of nonverbal behavior: tone of voice, physical touch, meeting implicit needs, meeting explicit needs, and no interaction. Within these five categories were measures of degrees, that is, positive tone of voice, negative tone of voice, and neutral tone of voice.

Following the interviews, the scores on the number of nonverbal interactions were obtained by counting the number of 15-second intervals in which nonverbal interactions occurred between father and child. A proportional score was obtained by dividing the frequency of interaction by the maximum number of 15-second intervals possible in which nonverbal interaction could have occurred.

The interviewers were trained over a three-week period using role-playing techniques and the coding of an actual interview presented on video cassette. The coders achieved an average intercoder reliability of .85.


# RESULTS

The overwhelming verbal interaction type found in this study was nurturance. Sixty-seven percent of the fathers exhibited behaviors toward their

TABLE 6.2
Means and Standard Deviations of
the Black Fathers' Verbal and Nonverbal
Interactions with Their Children

| Variable | n | M | SD |
|---|---|---|---|
| Verbal Interactions | | | |
| Nurturance | 40 | .76 | .20 |
| Restrictiveness | | .25 | .20 |
| Child Initiates | | .31 | .21 |
| Nonverbal Interactions* | | | |
| Positive | | .04 | .03 |
| Negative | | .02 | .02 |
| Noninteractions | | .94 | .02 |

* Fathers on a nonverbal level were equally positive with their sons and daughters.

TABLE 6.3
Means, Standard Deviations, and t Tests
of Black Fathers' Verbal and Nonverbal
Interactions with Their Daughters and Sons

| Variable | | n | M | SD | df | t | p |
|---|---|---|---|---|---|---|---|
| Verbal interactions | | | | | | | |
| Nurturance | Daughter | 20 | .747 | .22 | 38 | - .29 | ns |
| | Son | | .765 | .17 | | - .02 | ns |
| Restrictiveness | Daughter | | .254 | .22 | | - .02 | ns |
| | Son | | .255 | .19 | | | |
| Child initiates | Daughter | | .313 | .20 | | .16 | ns |
| | Son | | .302 | .23 | | | |
| Total interactions | Daughter | | 27.4 | 21.2 | | -1.75 | ns |
| | Son | | 39.8 | 23.6 | | | |
| Nonverbal interactions | | | | | | | |
| Positive | Daughter | 20 | .022 | .02 | 38 | - .59 | ns |
| | Son | | .029 | .08 | | | |
| Negative | Daughter | | .015 | .04 | | - .16 | ns |
| | Son | | .017 | .02 | | | |
| Noninteractions | Daughter | | .722 | .14 | | -1.99 | .05 |
| | Son | | .798 | .10 | | | |
| Total ratio interactions | Daughter | | .319 | .18 | | 2.32 | .03 |
| | Son | | .208 | .11 | | | |

TABLE 6.4
Intercorrelations of Black Fathers' Verbal
and Nonverbal Interactions

| Fathers | | | | |
|---|---|---|---|---|
| Verbal | | | | |
| Nurturant | | | | |
| Restrictive | -.950*** | | | |
| Child initiates | -.633*** | .571*** | | |
| Nonverbal | | | | |
| Positive | .033 | .115 | | |
| Negative | -.455*** | .477*** | .060 | .160 |
| | N | R | C | POS |

*p < .05    **p < .01    ***p < .001

children that could be identified as warm and loving, supportive, and meeting implicit and explicit needs of their children, while at the same time setting limits on the child's behavior with some explanation. Twenty-five percent of the fathers were found to be restrictive and exhibited such behaviors as commanding without explanation, threatening, and taking sharp verbal control of their children's behavior. Almost one-third of the time the child initiated the interaction, making requests of the father or using acting out behaviors designed to attract attention (see Table 6.2 ).

Fathers were equally positive toward their sons and daughters. No sex differences were found in their restrictive interaction patterns toward their children. The boys and the girls in this sample equally initiated the contact with their fathers (see Table 6.3),

Fathers in this context were nurturant or restrictive in verbal communication with their children. Those fathers who were very warm and loving toward their children seldom used restrictive measures in controlling their children's behavior. Children of these fathers seldom initiated conversation. They were content to sit and observe or to go about the activities they chose for themselves during this period (see Table 6.4).

Highly demanding fathers, on the other hand, seldom showed warmth and loving behavior toward their children. Like the restrictive fathers in Radin's (1972) study, they tended to ignore their children's explicit and implicit needs and make commands when the children's behavior irritated them. Children of these fathers initiated significantly more requests for attention to leave the room than did children of the more nurturant fathers. The more the child made demands that his/her needs be met, the more the father gave restrictive responses (see Table 6.4).

## NONVERBAL INTERACTION

The Black father's communication of his feelings and meanings in reaction to the child's verbal requests and behavior on a nonverbal level took place in less than 25 percent of the time selected to observe the behavior. We were not able to determine the type of gesturing, touching, caressing, holding, and restraining nonverbal behaviors most used by fathers in controlling the children's behavior. The results were collapsed across the above categories and we are reporting the number of positive and negative nonverbal interactions (see Table 6.2).

Table 6.2 notes the total proportion of positive and negative interactions. Fathers were equally positive toward their sons and daughters. No sex differences were found in their negative nonverbal interactions with their children. The fathers of girls related significantly more on a nonverbal level than did fathers of boys (see Table 6.3).

Nurturant fathers, who were verbally warm in this study, used a very low amount of negative nonverbal behavior in interacting with their children. Verbally restrictive fathers, however, were more likely to use negative gestures, grab, cut their eyes at, or physically punish the child for unacceptable behavior. Not only would a verbally restrictive father tell the child to get off the furniture, but he would also get up and restrain the child from further furniture-climbing (see Table 6.4).

### CHILD-REARING ATTITUDES

The CHES (Radin & Sonquist, 1968) contained a number of questions related to child-rearing practices. Like fathers in other studies (Blood and Wolfe, 1960), more than two-thirds (70 percent) of these fathers felt that they were equally involved with the mother in the family decision-making process; only 11 percent reported that they made all the child-rearing decisions; and 19 percent of the fathers noted that the mother made all the major child-rearing decisions (see Table 6.5).

In response to the question of whether their children's needs come before their own, 28 percent of the fathers responded affirmatively. Only four fathers (12 percent) said their own needs come before their children's, and two fathers said that whether or not their children's needs come first depends on the situation (see Table 6.5).

We asked questions related to the kinds of behaviors in which fathers liked to see their children engaged. More than half of the fathers (54 percent) responded that they felt good about and approved of their children exhibiting independent and assertive behavior around the home and in the community. Ten fathers (27 percent) reported that they wanted their child to exhibit good behavior and good personal hygiene. An equal number of fathers

TABLE 6.5
Frequency Distribution and Percentages of Black Fathers' Responses
to Questions Relating to Child-Rearing

|  | f | Percentage |
|---|---|---|
| **Who makes the major child-rearing decisions?** | | |
| Father | 4 | (11) |
| Mother | 7 | (19) |
| Both | 26 | (70) |
| Total | 37 | |
| **Do the child's needs come first?** | | |
| Yes | 28 | (82) |
| No | 4 | (12) |
| Sometimes | 2 | (6) |
| Total | 34 | |
| **What things child does that you approve of?** | | |
| Independent/assertive behavior | 20 | (54) |
| Good behavior/personal hygiene | 10 | (27) |
| Being affectionate | 1 | (3) |
| Household chores | 1 | (3) |
| Everything | 5 | (14) |
| Total | 37 | |
| **How do you show approval?** | | |
| Tell the child | 25 | (66) |
| Smiling, hugging, etc. | 9 | (24) |
| Allowing action to occur/does not show approval | 4 | (10) |
| Total | 38 | |
| **Are you raising your child as you were raised?** | | |
| Yes | 5 | (13) |
| No | 32 | (84) |
| Partially | 1 | (3) |
| Total | 38 | |
| **How much education do you expect your child to recieve?** | | |
| Graduate or professional training | 6 | (18) |
| College graduate | 18 | (55) |
| Partial college | 3 | (9) |
| High school graduate | 6 | (18) |
| Total | 33 | |

approved of affectionate behavior and doing household chores on time. Five
fathers (14 percent) noted they approved of everything their children do.

Two-thirds of the fathers (66 percent) responded they would verbally
praise and compliment their children as a reward for doing things that they
approved. Nine fathers (24 percent) reported that they would also smile, hug,

TABLE 6.6
Frequency Distribution and Percentages of Fathers' Responses
to Questions Related to Their Strictness

| | f | Percentage |
|---|---|---|
| How strict are you? | | |
| Very Strict | 6 | (16) |
| Moderately strict | 19 | (51) |
| Not strict at all | 10 | (27) |
| Total | 35 | |
| Should child obey right away? | | |
| Child should obey immediately | 21 | (54) |
| Obey but need not be immediately | 10 | (26) |
| Depends on situation | 8 | (20) |
| Total | 39 | |
| How much disorderly behavior allowed? | | |
| A great deal/some | 8 | (22) |
| Very little | 10 | (27) |
| None | 19 | (51) |
| Total | 37 | |
| How much problem with child's temper display? | | |
| No problem | 14 | (37) |
| Slight problem | 19 | (50) |
| Some problem/a big problem | 5 | (14) |
| Total | 38 | |

and positively embrace their children to show their approval. However, four (10 percent) claimed that they did not show approval, but would let the children continue in their behaviors when the children were doing things they felt were acceptable (see Table 6.5).

In response to a question regarding the differences between their own and their parents' child-rearing practices, 84 percent of the fathers claimed to be rearing their children differently from their parents. Another 3 percent claimed to be rearing their children partially differenly from their parents, and 13 percent felt they were doing exactly as their fathers had done in rearing their children. The majority of these fathers felt that they were less strict with their children than their own fathers had been (see Table 6.5).

Table 6.6 presents the fathers' responses to questions related to their perceived strictness and control of their children. The majority of these fathers (51 percent) reported that they were moderately strict. Some fathers (27 percent) noted that they were not strict in expectations of their children's behavior, while a few fathers (16 percent) admitted to being very strict with their children.

More than 50 percent of the fathers felt that their children should obey their commands right away. Twenty-six percent of the fathers agreed that the children should obey their commands, but that immediate obedience was not necessary. Eight fathers (20 percent) reported that whether or not the child obeyed immediately depended on the situation (see Table 6.6).

In their own homes, 51 percent of the fathers claimed that they did not allow any disorderly behavior. Almost 30 percent would allow very little disorderly behavior to occur before they actively set limits. However, 19 (50 percent) of the fathers claimed to have a slight problem with their children's tempers. Another five fathers (12.5 percent) claimed to have from "some" to a big problem controlling their children's tempers, while only 14 fathers (37 percent) reported having no problem with their children's tempers (see Table 6.6).

## DISCUSSION

We have attempted to answer three important questions: First, the Black fathers in this study were quite similar in their verbal interaction patterns to the white fathers in Radin's (1972) study. While the total amount of verbal contact with their children was lower, the majority of the Black fathers' verbal responses to the children were equally nurturant, warm, firm, and loving as those of the white fathers.

Second, few differences in interaction patterns were found to exist between fathers of boys and fathers of girls. However, the fathers interacted on a verbal level slightly more often with boys and on a nonverbal level more often with their daughters.

Third, while the fathers in this sample saw themselves as strict, their overall interaction patterns and attitudes suggest that they really are authoritative in their child-rearing behavior (Baumrind, 1971). They were firm in their expectations, made them clear to their children, explained behaviors that were punishable, and were warm toward their children.

There were some other implications of the interaction findings that needed to be better understood. The restrictive fathers in this study paid attention only to behavior that required negative and restrictive control, ignoring the children's good behavior. In turn, the children initiated more demands for attention, which caused the fathers to increase their verbal and nonverbal restrictiveness to control the child's behavior. Over an extended period of time, this negative cycle of behavior could lead to a child's having a poor image of himself and becoming a behavior problem at home.

Another implication is that of double jeopardy. The child may be positively reinforced for the same negative behavior in the school. Thus, if teachers and peers pay attention only to negative behavior, we could have the home and the school cooperating in negative socialization practices—a vicious cycle could develop. Negative socialization at home, reinforced by school, could lead to stereotypic behavior on the child's part and to his accepting negative role models as positive reinforcers. This may explain how deviant, delinquent, pimp and prostitute, thief and murderer become perceived by the child as people to emulate. If these characters are also glorified on television, the child growing up in double jeopardy may have no place to turn.

Finally, we want to reiterate that these middle-income Black fathers exhibited the same range of attitudes, behaviors, and beliefs as did fathers from other ethnic groups in our American culture. They tended to be warm and loving toward their children. They tended to be more egalitarian in their decision-making regarding child-rearing practices than did other ethnic groups. However, as H. McAdoo (1976) has stated, these differences are disappearing.

These findings are suggestive to the Black mental health practitioner. If we wish to help the Black male survive within the family structure, we need to help him, particularly the overrestrictive Black male, to find ways to be more nurturant toward himself, his wife, and his children. This may mean parenting-education programs. It may mean developing strategies to help the middle-class Black father deal with the external stress—economic, political, and social—that may be sapping his energies to deal with the developmental processes of his child in a positive manner. Toward that end, we may also need to develop programs to strengthen his kin network, community support, and social and religious systems to help him mediate economic, social, and psychological pressures.

We social scientists must seek to understand the context in which the Black father is functioning, observe the patterns of family interaction that take place, and stop blaming the victim. Social scientists, in their attempts to understand the Black father and his role and function within the family, will need to go beyond popular and self-serving stereotypes and ethnocentric biases embedded in the literature about the Black father and his child. While this study is not meant to be generalized to all Black fathers, it is certainly suggestive that Black fathers do exhibit the same amounts of variability in interactions that are found in other ethnic groups, given their socioeconomic status differences.

# REFERENCES

Baumrind, D. Current patterns of parental authority. *Developmental Psychology Monographs,* 1971, *4*(1, Pt. 2).

Blood, R., & Wolfe, D. *Husbands and wives.* New York: Free Press, 1960.

Biller, H. Father absence, maternal encouragement, and sex role development in kindergarten age boys. *Child Development,* 1969, *40,* 539-546.

McAdoo, H. *The development of self concept and race attitudes of young Black children over time.* Paper presented at the conference on Empirical Research in Black Psychology III, Ithaca, New York, Cornell University, 1976.

McAdoo, J. *The relationship between Black father-child interaction and self esteem in preschool children.* Paper presented at the conference on Empirical Research in Black Psychology III, Ithaca, New York, Cornell University, 1976.

McAdoo, J., McAdoo, H., & Teresa, H. The development of nonverbal categories in current child interaction patterns. Unpublished position paper, 1976.

Newman, G., & Newman, P. *Infancy and childhood development and its contents.* New York: John Wiley, 1978.

Radin, N. Father-child interaction and the intellectual function of four-year-old boys. *Development Psychology,* 1972, *6,* 353-361.

Radin, N. *Observed paternal behavior with preschool children: Final Report.* Bethesda, MD: National Institute of Child Health and Human development, 1975.

Radin, N., & Sonquist, H. *The Gale preschool programs: Final report.* Ypsilanti Michigan: Ypsilanti Public School, 1968.

# 7

## BLACK UNWED
## ADOLESCENT FATHERS

Leo E. Hendricks

There is a dearth of information on the unwed adolescent male partner of the teen or preteen woman who becomes pregnant. There is even less information on his attitude toward fatherhood and his relationship with the mother of his first child. Moreover, much of the information that has been documented on unmarried adolescent fathers has concerned white adolescents (Vincent, 1960; Pannor, 1971; Robbins & Lynn, 1973). This is surprising since a disproportionate number of teenage pregnancies have involved young Black women (Ventura, 1977; Zelnik, 1979). Thus, it seemed appropriate to conduct an exploratory study to identify and describe the perceptions of a select population of Black unwed adolescent fathers toward fatherhood and their relationships with the mothers of their first children. The purpose of this study was to document information that will be helpful to social service agencies in meeting the needs of adolescent parents, both male and female.

## METHOD OF PROCEDURES

Twenty Black unwed adolescent fathers were identified and selected with the help of the social service staff of the Margaret Hudson Program (MHP) and unwed teenage mothers registered with the program. Begun in Sep-

## TABLE 7.1
### Select Study Characteristics and Descriptive Statistics
### of the Twenty Unwed Adolescent Fathers

| Characteristic | Descriptive Statistics | | |
| --- | --- | --- | --- |
| | Median | Mean | SD |
| Family size[a] | 5.0 | 5.0 | 3.7 |
| Age of unwed father[b] at first sexual intercourse with a girl | 13.2 | 12.8 | 2.4 |
| Age of unwed father[c] at birth of his first child | 18.0 | 17.8 | 1.4 |

a. Family size as used here refers to the number of children in the family of origin of the unwed adolescent father.

b. Age of first intercourse with a girl ranged from 8 to 16 years.

c. Age at birth of first child ranged from 15 to 20 years.

tember, 1969, this program is a comprehensive service project for school-aged parents in Tulsa, Oklahoma. Participation in the study was voluntary; however, the subjects selected for the study were paid $10 as an incentive for participation. The respondents were selected through a convenience sample and do not necessarily constitute a representative sample of Black unwed adolescent fathers in Tulsa or in other sections of the country.

Data was collected from the young fathers in face-to-face private interviews through the use of an interview schedule. Age, family size, and educational status were among the social and demographic information collected from the study population. Closed-ended as well as open-ended questions were employed to obtain information from the unmarried adolescent fathers concerning their perceptions of selected aspects of both fatherhood and their relationships with the mothers of their first children.

## FINDINGS

With regard to who he is, the unmarried adolescent fathers of the current study present an interesting mixture of sociodemographic characteristics (see Tables 7.1 and 7.2). For example, their mean age at first sexual intercourse with a girl was 12.8 years, and on the average they became fathers for the first time at age 17.8 years. Further, these young fathers were likely to come from families with at least five children; in fact, 60 percent of the unwed adolescent fathers were members of families with five or more children. Despite being from such large families, these adolescent fathers were likely to come from families with their fathers present in the home (65 percent). Even

TABLE 7.2
Percentage Distribution of Select Sociodemographic
Traits of the 20 Unwed Adolescent Fathers

| Trait | n | Percentage |
|---|---|---|
| Years of school completed | | |
| less than 12 | ·5 | 25 |
| 12 or more | 15 | 75 |
| Employment Status | | |
| Employed | 12 | 60 |
| Not Employed | 8 | 40 |
| Presence of father in home | | |
| Present | 13 | 65 |
| Not present | 7 | 35 |
| Active church member | | |
| Yes | 8 | 40 |
| No | 12 | 60 |
| Sisters who are unwed mothers | | |
| Yes | 8 | 40 |
| No | 12 | 60 |
| Brothers who are unwed fathers | | |
| Yes | 7 | 35 |
| No | 13 | 65 |

so, there was a hint of a family trend toward unwed parenthood, as 40 percent of these young fathers had sisters who were unwed mothers and 35 percent had brothers who were also unwed fathers. Of the subjects themselves, 25 percent were born out of wedlock; and one subject was in doubt as to whether he was born in or out of wedlock. A majority of these fathers (60 percent) were not likely to be active church members. Most (60 percent) were employed, and the majority of the unmarried adolescent fathers had completed twelve or more years of school.

The findings pertaining to what the unwed adolescent father is like were mixed and contradictory. For example, when these fathers were growing up, most of them (70 percent) reported that they were closer to their mothers and most (80 percent) that their relations with their families were happy. Moreover, most of these fathers (90 percent) indicated that they got a lot of fun out of life. Even more striking were the findings suggesting that these fathers felt that their destiny was controlled not by chance, fate, or other people, but by themselves (see Table 7.3). Despite these findings, a majority of the young fathers (60 percent) stated that they felt useless at times. Additionally, a sizable majority (80 percent) indicated that, when they were

TABLE 7.3
Measurement of Internal and External Locus of Control
of the 20 Unwed Adolescent Fathers

| Internal Locus of Control | | | External Locus of Control | | |
|---|---|---|---|---|---|
| Do you feel that what happens to you is your own doing? | | | Do you feel that you can do very little to change your life? | | |
| | n | % | | n | % |
| Yes | 16 | 80 | Yes | 5 | 25 |
| No | 4 | 20 | No | 15 | 75 |
| When you make plans, do you feel that you're almost certain that you can make them work? | | | Do you feel that it is mostly luck if one succeeds or gets ahead? | | |
| | n | % | | n | % |
| Yes | 17 | 85 | Yes | 2 | 10 |
| No | 3 | 15 | No | 18 | 90 |

growing up, they felt that they would have liked to move away from home. These negatives notwithstanding, most of these unmarried adolescent fathers either liked school somewhat (35 percent) or liked school very much (60 percent); and most (85 percent) got along with their teachers at school.

## ATTITUDES TOWARD FATHERHOOD

Five questions were used to elicit knowledge on the young fathers' attitudes toward parenthood. Since it is commonly thought that adolescent fatherhood is a mistake, the young fathers were asked to resopond to the question, "Right before your first child was born, how ready did you feel to be a parent?" Most of the fathers responded that they were either "very ready" (30 percent) or "somewhat ready" (35 percent); the remainder of the young fathers reported that they were either "somewhat unready" (20 percent) or "very unready" (15 percent). These responses were compared to those given for the question, "Knowing what you know now and looking back, how ready would you say you really were at that time?" These comparisons are presented in Table 7.4. The proportion of fathers who felt "very unready" did not change. However, the frequency of those who felt that they were either "very ready" or "somewhat ready" to be a father decreased from 65 percent to 55 percent, while those who felt that they were

## TABLE 7.4
### Unwed Adolescent Fathers' Perception of Readiness
### for Parenthood Before and After Birth of Child

| Perceived Readiness | Before Birth | | After Birth | |
|---|---|---|---|---|
| | n | % | n | % |
| Very ready | 6 | 30 | 5 | 25 |
| Somewhat ready | 7 | 35 | 6 | 30 |
| Somewhat unready | 4 | 20 | 6 | 30 |
| Very unready | 3 | 15 | 3 | 15 |

either "very unready" or "somewhat unready" increased from 35 percent to 45 percent. On the surface, these and other findings reported here suggest that these adolescent fathers' perceptions of their readiness to become a parent might have been unrealistic.

Some credibility is given to the notion that the adolescent fathers' perceptions of their readiness to become a parent were unrealistic insofar as 55 percent of the fathers said they believed that their experience as an unwed father would change their life in a positive way. Additionally, 70 percent of the adolescent fathers saw nothing wrong in having a child out of wedlock. Contrary to what these adolescent fathers think, it has been pointed out that teenage parents—both male and female—suffer financial, social, psychological, and educational setbacks from which they virtually never recover (Card & Wise, 1978). Regardless of how the unmarried adolescent fathers perceived fatherhood, all were concerned about their children's futures.

Due to the interest in discovering whether unwed adolescent fathers would be interested in attending a parenting agency for teenagers, the young fathers in this study were asked, "If the Margaret Hudson Program offered services to the unwed fathers, would you be interested in receiving such services?" Ninety-five percent of the fathers gave a positive response to this question. The primary reasons for seeking services offered for adolescent fathers were to obtain information on parenting, sex education, and job training and job placement. Other reasons the adolescent fathers' sought parenting services designed for them are given in Table 7.5. The one father who indicated that he would not attend services offered for unwed fathers stated that "it would not be any use for me to attend." Despite this minor opposition, the implication of these findings is clear; that is, more parenting agencies for teenagers need to provide services for young unmarried fathers.

## TABLE 7.5
### Representative Range of Reasons Given by Unwed Adolescent Fathers for Wanting to Attend a Parenting Agency for Teenagers

| REASONS |
| --- |
| "I want to learn how to raise my child the best way I can." |
| "To learn about parenting—it will be good for me and her." |
| "I would want information that would help me become a better father." |
| "Sex education." |
| "I would like to know what happens during pregnancy." |
| "...learn what life is about; learn about kids." |
| "Because I may learn something about my child or how to prevent something." |
| "Job training...job placement." |
| "Because I need to get finished with school." |
| "Would learn more about fatherhood." |
| "Child development." |

## TABLE 7.6
### Unwed Adolescent Fathers' Perceptions of the Relationship Between Them and the Mothers of Their First Children

| Character of Relationship | Before Pregnancy | | After Pregnancy | |
| --- | --- | --- | --- | --- |
| | n | % | n | % |
| Love | 15 | 75 | 16 | 80 |
| Friendship | 3 | 15 | 3 | 15 |
| Casual | 2 | 10 | 1 | 5 |
| Hostile | 0 | 0 | 0 | 0 |

## RELATIONSHIP BETWEEN ADOLESCENT FATHERS AND MOTHERS OF THEIR FIRST CHILDREN

Seven questions were used to describe various aspects of the relationship between the unwed adolescent fathers and the mothers of their first children. Table 7.6 indicates that, both prior to and after the pregnancy of the mothers of their first children, the majority of the unwed adolescent fathers perceived their relationship with the mothers to be one of love. Similarly, Table 7.7 indicates that the majority of the young fathers in this study said they

TABLE 7.7

Unwed Adolescent Fathers' Perceptions of How They Believed
Mothers of Their First Children Regarded Their Relationships

| Character of Relationship | Before Pregnancy | | After Pregnancy | |
|---|---|---|---|---|
| | n | % | n | % |
| Love | 19 | 95 | 18 | 90 |
| Friendship | 1 | 5 | 1 | 5 |
| Casual | 0 | 0 | 1 | 5 |
| Hostile | 0 | 0 | 0 | 0 |

believed that the mothers of their first children felt that the relationship between the two of them was one of love. As used here, love refers to feeling passion, devotion, or tenderness for someone. These findings would suggest that the relationship between these unmarried parents is a meaningful one. This suggestion is given support by previous findings reported by Pannor et al. (1965) and Sauber and Rubinstein (1965).

Further support for the notion that the relationship between the adolescent parents is a meaningful one may be noted in that 85 percent of the adolescent fathers in this study responded in the negative to the question: "Do you see serious problems in the current relationship between you and the mother of your first child?" Of the fathers who gave positive answers to this question, in their own words they described their problems as: "Child support; she doesn't want me to see the baby." "Lack of understanding, communication, and disagreeing in general." "Being young and other fellows trying to talk to her; and arguments around things that the baby does."

Finally, and with regard to sexual relations between the young fathers and the mothers of their first children, 70 percent of the adolescent fathers had sexual intercourse with the mothers of their first children with full knowledge of the potential outcome, that is, pregnancy. This, too, would suggest that their relationships may have been more than casual.

## DISCUSSION

Before considering what implications may be derived from this study, consideration must be given to the limitations of this exploratory investigation that relate to the usefulness of the findings. The first point is that questions forming the interview schedule used in this study may have been worded in such a way as to elicit socially desirable answers from the subjects.

A second point is the small number of respondents. Several identified trends may have had more strength had the study population been larger. The small number of subjects decreased the potential influence of the actual findings on the knowledge base about unmarried adolescent fathers, especially with regard to the various ages of adolescents. As Chilman (1975) has pointed out, it makes a difference whether the adolescent is aged 12, 13, 14, 15, and so on. The point to remember here is that the findings from this report must be regarded as tentative.

The main implication to emerge from this study relates to the findings that 95 percent of the young fathers expressed a high degree of readiness to attend a teenage parenting agency if it offered services for unwed adolescent fathers. Therefore, agencies and institutions serving family planning needs should provide services for unwed adolescent fathers as well as for unwed adolescent mothers. If agencies and institutions would provide such services to unmarried adolescent fathers, it would mean a vital source of community social support for them.

## REFERENCES

Card, J., & Wise, L. Teenage mothers and teenage fathers: The impact of early child-bearing on the parents' personal and professional lives. *Family Planning Perspectives,* 1978, *10,* 199-205.

Chilman, C. Adolescent sexuality in a changing American society: Social and psychological perspectives. (DHEW Publication No. NIH 79-1426). Washington DC: U. S. Department of Health, Education and Welfare, Public Health Service, National Institutes of Health, 1975.

Pannor, R. *The unmarried father.* New York: Springer, 1971.

Pannor, R., et al. The unmarried father: Demonstration and evaluation of an assertive casework approach. In *Illegitimacy: Data and findings for prevention, treatment and policy formulation.* New York, National Council on Illegitimacy, 1965.

Robbins, M., & Lynn, D. The unwed fathers: Generation recidivism and attitudes about intercourse in California Youth Authority wards. *Journal of Sex Research,* 1973, *9,* 334-341.

Sauber, M., & Rubinstein, E. *Experiences of the unwed mother as a parent.* New York: Community Council of Greater New York, 1965.

Ventura, S. Teenage childbearing: United States, 1966-1975. *Monthly Vital Statistics Report: Natality Statistics from the National Center for Health Statistics,* 1977, *26*(5, Supplement, September 8), 1977.

Vincent, C. The unmarried fathers and the mores: Sexual exploiter as an ex post facto level. *American Sociological Review,* 1960, *25,* 40-46.

Zelnik, M., et al. Probabilities of intercourse and conception among U. S. teenage women, 1971 and 1976. *Family Planning Perspectives,* 1979 (May/June), 177-183.

# PART III
# PSYCHOLOGICAL AND SOCIAL
# COPING PATTERNS

In this section, consideration is given to how Black men adjust or adapt to the pressures from the various social institutions. Taylor analyzes the application of various concepts of stress to the modes of adaptation among Black males. In this essay, the author covers a broad range of concerns and identifies some of the critical issues for future research in the area. Moreover, Taylor maintains that adaptations to stressful situations are a developmental process involving a complex interaction between the individual and his environment. He notes that systematic stigmatization has been experienced primarily by Black males. Finally, the author describes how the socioeconomic status of Black men serves as an antecedent to stress, and how some men are able to use external and internal resources to mediate the impact of stressful situations.

Hall explores specific support systems available to Black men. He stresses that the initial and most basic system—the family—remains perhaps the most influential. As the maturation process progresses, other groups—peer groups—become the focus of the man's coping patterns. The author feels that expression of emotion in sports, arts, and recreation alleviates some tension caused by the system and the problems it creates. His conclusion, however, is that the most effective support system is internal.

Harper indicates that one coping mechanism used by Black men in struggling with the major institutions of our society is alcohol. The author concludes that while the rate of heavy drinking for Black males is approximately the same as that for white males, the former are more adversely affected by drinking problems than are white males. He states that heavy drinking in some Black communities has become a status symbol, and lists six ways that this behavior contributes to self-destruction among Black men. Resistance to help by the men and lack of peer pressure to change their behavior contribute to the perpetuation of this problem. The author concludes that more explanation of and research into this area is needed.

Using demographic methods, Davis details the patterns of suicide among Black men. He maintains that the group aged 18-29 years seems to be most vulnerable. For example, he shows that during a 30-year period, 1947-1977, suicide rates among Black males in the 20-24 age group increased 195 percent, and among those Black males aged 25-29 years the suicide rate increased 250 percent. He indicates that outside influences affect men in various ways, thereby causing the large fluctuation in suicide rates. Davis believes that the increase in suicide rates among Black men is strongly related to the isolation of these men from social support systems within Black communities, at either the family, group, communal, or institutional levels.

# 8

## PSYCHOLOGICAL MODES OF ADAPTATION

Ronald L. Taylor

Despite recent arguments to the contrary (for example, Wilson, 1978), racism has been and continues to be a central feature of the American social dynamic. In its mode of operation, racism involves a psychopolitical process of stigmatization, that is, a configuration of aggressive and debasing behaviors, practices, and dogmas by which to defame or discredit both the character and the identity of its victims (Wilkinson & Taylor, 1977). While racial oppression is an experience shared by all Black Americans, the process of systematic stigmatization has been experienced primarily by Black males (Hernton, 1965; Staples, 1978; Genovese, 1974). As Wilkinson and Taylor (1977: 154) have noted, "restricted opportunities and life chances, along with historically systematized discrediting, have had a profound effect on the Black male's self conceptions, his psychology, his relationship with Black women, his relationship with other Black men ... and his interactions with whites of both sexes." In sum, a variety of social forces conspire to impair effective role enactment and coherent identity among Black males in American society.

In their treatment of the Black community, various writers have called attention to the adaptive values and mechanisms that have evolved in order to blunt the potentially disabling impact of a stigmatized status (for example, Blassingame, 1972; Hill, 1973; Gutman, 1976). Yet, beyond the easy generalization and rhetorical assertion, few empirical studies currently exist on the basis of which definitive conclusions can be made regarding the character and quality of psychosocial modes of adaptation to stigmatization among Black males.

To be sure, epidemiologic reports on the incidence and prevalence of serious mental or emotional disorders are indirect and extreme indicators of psychosocial response. However, these data provide little insight into the less extreme resolutions that are presumably devised by the majority of Black males to manage a stigmatized identity. Indeed, the challenge of future research is to delineate the processes through which Black males achieve and maintain mental health in spite of conditions inimical to its development. What is required is a theoretical framework that takes account of the multiple possibilities for individual adaptations within the parameters imposed by the conditions of social life. Such a theoretical formulation is offered in the literature on social stress. When it is observed that stress is a fundamental aspect of all adaptive reactions (Selye, 1956), then the relevance of this perspective becomes apparent. The value of this perspective for the study of modes of adaptation among Black males lies in its potential to specify more precisely the independent and generalized effects of stress in evoking certain types of behavioral responses. Psychosocial modes of adaptation among Black males will be treated in the following discussion only in broad outline; it is intended to be suggestive rather than definitive, and seeks to identify some of the crucial issues for future research in this broad area.

## STRESS AND THE GENERALIZED ADAPTIVE PROCESS

While the sources and consequences of social stress have received considerable attention in recent years (see Lazarus, 1966; Appley & Trumbull, 1967; Levine & Scotch, 1970; McGrath, 1970), the literature is marked by much confusion and controversy. Much of the confusion is a result of the failure to agree on the definition of "stress." Different investigators have used the term to refer to divergent procresses and dimensions. In reviewing the history of research in the field, Mason (1975: 29) observes:

> Whatever the soundness of logic may be in the various approaches to defining "stress," ... the general picture in the field can still only be described as one of confusion. The disenchantment felt by many scientists with the stress field is certainly understandable when one views two decades in which the term "stress" has been used variously to refer to "stimulus" by some workers, "response" by some workers,

"interaction" by others, and more comprehensive combinations of the above factors by still other workers. Some authorities in the field are rather doubtful that this confusion over terminology is correctable in the near future.

Given the discontinuity in basic theoretical and operational constructs, and the widely divergent interests of specialists working in the field, some researchers have proposed that "stress" be employed as a generic term to refer to a complex of interrelated phenomena. Thus, Lazarus (1966: 27) states:

> It seems wise to use "stress" as a generic term for the whole area of problems that includes the stimuli producing stress reactions, the reactions themselves, and the various intervening processes. Thus, we can speak of the field of stress, and mean the physiological, sociological, and psychological phenomena and their respective concepts. It could then include research and theory on group or individual disaster, physiological assault or tissues and the effects of this assault, disturbances or facilitation of adaptive functioning produced by conditions of deprivation, thwarting or the prospectus of this, and the field of negatively toned emotions such as fear, anger, hopelessness, and guilt. Stress is not any one of these things; nor is it stimulus, response, or intervening variable, but rather a collective term for an area of study.

However researchers have elected to define the term, research in the field is plagued by methodological inadequacies. Common problems include (1) the failure to separate independent measures of stress from purported outcomes (Levine & Scotch, 1970); (2) the tendency to treat stress as a "quantum" rather than a continuous variable (Wild & Hanes, 1976); (3) an inability to distinguish between types of stress (for example, episodic as contrasted with chronic) and their order of magnitude, and; (4) the use of highly questionable referents for the term. As a consequence, problems emerge in interpreting the results and implications of many studies, and vitiate the value of the concept as a guide to further research (Levine & Scotch, 1970).

Although a systematic theory of stress is yet to be developed—one that delineates its antecedent conditions, mediating factors, and response patterns or processes—some initial efforts along these lines have been made. Dohrenwend (1961) has formulated a model of stress based on the paradigm developed by Seyle (1956) from his studies of the effects of stressful stimuli on laboratory animals. Dohrenwend has identified four basic sets of factors involved in stressful situations: (1) antecedent stressors or agents that induce an imbalance in the routine state of the individual; (2) conditioning or mediating factors that increase or decrease the impact of stress; (3) the adaptive syndrome, which involves the individual's attempt to cope with the stressor, and; (4) the individual's response, which may be either adaptive or maladaptive. In his work, Dohrenwend has emphasized the role of mediating factors in the adaptive process. These mediating factors are of two types: those that determine the amount of *external* constraint associated with stress, and those that determine the amount of *internal* constraint. The former consists of such material and social resources as money, social support from family and friends, and access to services, information, or knowledge; the latter include characteristics of the individual such as intellectual ability, values, beliefs, and motives. These external and internal constraints define the environment within which the individual is capable of response, and are presumed to have a constraining influence on the individual's future responses to stress. From his paradigm, Dohrenwend derives a number of propositions concerning factors that determine the intensity and duration of stress. In his model, stress is defined as an intervening state between antecedent constraints and consequent efforts to reduce the constraints. Viewed in these terms, adaptations to stress are regarded as having "a number of baseline social psychological manifestations which form syndromes that are distinct and different from each other, both for different persons in the same general situations, and for the same person in different situations" (Dohrenwend, 1961: 300).

Other researchers have sought to distinguish between "stress" viewed as an external force, and the resulting intrapsychic "strain" it produces. Kahn et al. (1970) have used an "engineering analogy" in their definition of stress. As conceived by the engineer, stress is "the application of an external force, while the strain it produces must be reckoned with in terms of the substance to which it is applied. Hence, the stress-strain effect is a relationship between an entity and its environment" (McGrath, 1970: 14). This formulation enables the investigator to distinguish between demands or pressures exerted directly by the environmental stimuli, and perceived intrapsychic effects of a given type of stimulus. The distinction also draws attention to two important problems in the field. The first concerns the issue of the order of magnitude environmental stimuli should be assigned relative to their effects in evoking certain behavioral responses. In this regard, Kahn et al. (1970) observe that the environment places more or less urgent demands on the individual, and that some of these demands may be denied or go unperceived by the individual but evoke an observable behavioral response nonetheless (for example, stress and psychosomatic disorders). Thus, pressure exerted directly by environmental stimuli is referred to as "stress."

The second issue concerns the differential responses of individuals to similar environmental demands, and the nature of the underlying processes involved. In accounting for differences in individual responses to similar environmental demands, Kahn et al. call attention to differential perceptual abilities as these are influenced by individual attitudes, values, and beliefs; the capacity of the individual to use external resources at his or her disposal at a given time; and the influence of past experience and training—all of which have provided the individual with ongoing defensive strategies and coping skills. These elements, taken together, determine the degree of perceived environmental demand by the individual and are referred to collectively by Kahn et al. as "strain." The importance of this formulation lies in its emphasis on the perceptual aspects of the adjustive process, including the role of the environment as an important force with unperceived consequences for the individual, and its recognition of the individual as an active agent and synthesizer of environmental demands.

In their efforts to develop a more dynamic conceptual model of stress-response processes, Wild and Hanes (1976) have synthesized much of the thinking and research in the area and formulated a "developmental perspective" in which they attempt to specify the important feedback mechanism operating at several levels of response to stressful events. In their model, stress is viewed as a complex interactive process between the individual and the environment. It is the result not only of the "direct effects of particularly noxious stimuli upon the individual, but also of an interaction between possibly less noxious environmental stimuli and past failures of the organism to deal successfully with these stimuli, resulting in a positive feedback spiral of increasing tension and strain" (Wild & Hanes, 1976: 320). Emphasizing the perceptual dimensions of individual responses to stressful events, the authors postulate a triphasic order of response, referred to respectively as first-, second- and third-order responses. First-order response refers to the initial perception and evaluation of the stressor event itself. Second-order responses include the perception evaluation, and decision and/or adjustment within the context of various internal and external mediating factors insofar as these may be relevant to the stressor stimulus. Third-order responses refer to the perception and evaluation of possible incongruities resulting from external pressures to respond to the stress stimulus in one fashion and the internal pressures to behave in a different and possibly conflicting manner. Where second-order responses prove insufficient to reducing the tension occasioned by stress, the energies of the individual may be transferred to a third level of response oriented more directly to the initial stressor stimulus. Such responses may be cognitive, behavioral, physiological, affective, or some combination of these. Behavioral responses are regarded as instrumental insofar as they represent attempts by the individual to deal directly with the stressor stimulus and have been referred to as "coping" (Mechanic, 1962). On the other hand, cognitive and affective responses are regarded as "palliative" modes of action, the goal of which is to relieve the emotional impact of stress through the activation of defense mechanisms such as denial and displacement. According to Wild and Hanes (1976) third-order responses may have a direct feedback effect on external and internal mediating factors by defining the parameters of future responses. In sum, this view holds that response to stress is a cumulative and dynamic process involving multiple levels of response, and the maladaptation is best understood as "the dynamic result of a process of continuing response, feedback and amplification of past responses and events" (Wild & Hanes, 1976: 331).

Several conclusions can be drawn from the foregoing discussion. Stress, as a social psychological phenomenon, may be viewed as a function of perceived or anticipated threat and frustration. The threat may derive from the physical or social environment, and may involve anticipated harm to the individual's physical or psychological self, or threats to interpersonal relations (McGrath, 1970). Similarly, frustration may result from thwarted opportunities to achieve some valued goal, and may refer to an ongoing event or a situation that has already occurred (Monat & Lazarus, 1977). This distinction calls attention to the fact that each of these experiences requires a different mode of response: the anticipated threat requiring preventive actions, the frustration requiring some form of compensatory behavior.

The effects of stress stimuli are mediated through cognitive or subjective processes that may be affected by a number of external and internal phenomena, including material and social resources, physiological predispositions, and personality characteristics. In addition, responses to stress may also vary as a function of new experiences and training; accordingly, considerable interindividual differences in perception and response to stress may be observed. Finally, adaptation to stress is best understood as a developmental process involving a complex interaction between the individual and the environment, with important feedback effects on the individual's future responses to stress.

With these observations in mind, we turn to consider their implications for the study of psychosocial modes of adaptation among Black males.


## BLACK MALES, SOCIAL STRESS, AND PSYCHOSOCIAL ADAPTATIONS

The observation that stressful situations are more frequent and more severe for Blacks than they are for their white counterparts seems obvious if not indubitable. Such conditions as poverty, joblessness, and broken families are undoubtedly among the major factors contributing to high levels of stress, and are highly correlated with a range of physical, emotional, and behavioral problems among Blacks, both male and female. Yet, there is reason to believe that certain characteristics associated with the male role renders it inherently problematic if not lethal (Jourard, 1971; Pleck, 1976). It is argued that, in contrast to the requirements of the female role, the requirements of the male role turn male maturation into an achievement, an accomplishment purchased at considerable psychic cost. Some of the consequences of this orientation are noted by Harrison (1978: 78).

> Anxiety about failure to achieve may result in compensatory behaviors designed to show outward conformity to the role. Compensatory behaviors involve risk taking of various kinds which may lead to accidents, exhibition of violence, excessive consumption of alcohol and smoking. Reciprocally, anxiety about failure to achieve male role requisites may result in denial of dimensions of human experience more stereotypically associated with women's role.

These consequences may apply with special force to Black males, many of whom have suffered an impairment of their capacities for effective role enactment as a result of their stigmatized status.

Accordingly, the nature of the Black male's relationship to the social order becomes an essential consideration in any effort to assay the sources and consequences of stress in his life. This relationship is determined largely by his socioeconomic position and ethnic membership, and may have independent and generalized effects in evoking certain reactions to stress. Thus, we focus on social status and racial membership as important antecedent stressors for Black males. In addition, internal and external mediating factors that may be seen to increase or decrease the impact of these antecedent stressors, and that in turn affect the individual's response to stress, will also be discussed.

Dohrenwend and Dohrenwend's (1969) distinction between "achievement-related" and "security-related" stress is useful in considering the role of class and race as important sources of social stress. Achievement-related events refer to pressure exerted on the individual to change customary modes of activity or conduct to a new set of higher-status activities, and include such events as finishing school, obtaining one's first job, marriage, job promotion, and the birth of the first child. Security-related stress refers to pressures exerted on the individual to adjust to a new set of lower-status activities or conditions, and include failure to complete school, inability to obtain the first adult job, divorce, job loss, illness, and injury. In these terms, and on the basis of a variety of empirical data, security-related stress is far more common among Black males of low socioeconomic status than it is among their white counterparts or Black males of higher status.

Census data reveal that low-income Black males, on the average, more frequently suffer chronic health problems, disabilities, activity restrictions, and work limitations than their white counterparts do. These limitations directly affect the participation of low-income Black males in the labor force and their ability to work and earn an income (U. S. Bureau of the Census,

1973). Moreover, low-income status implies limited funds for an adequate diet, proper hygiene, and a healthy living environment, all of which may exacerbate the health problems of these Black males. Indeed, as Levitan et al. (1975) have shown, much of the difference between Blacks and whites in terms of work limitations and activity restrictions is a function of income. Although the data are more equivocal and contradictory, the incidence of certain mental or emotional disorders also appears to be greater among low-income Black males than it is among their white counterparts (See & Miller, 1973; Cannon & Locke, 1977).

The security of low-income Black males may be threatened not only by illness or injury, but also by loss of employment. Due to their greater concentration in occupations where unemployment tends to be high, Black males are more likely than are other groups to have their income and employment interrupted by forced idleness for prolonged periods of time (U. S. Department of Labor, 1971). Moreover, the considerably higher rate of unemployment among Black youth suggests that young Black males experience more difficulty finding gainful employment than do their white counterparts. The implication of this fact is that many young Black males find themselves isolated from the mainstream of economic activity and faced with the prospect of long-term unemployment (National Urban League, 1978). Similarly, the inverse relationship between social class and the rate of marital disruption through divorce or separation indicates that low-income Black males experience greater difficulty and, consequently, greater stress, in maintaining their marriages than do their white counterparts (Scanzoni, 1971; Rainwater, 1970)—for low income, and intermittent employment and unemployment, together with other factors, may combine to undermine the stability of the family even when the marriage is not dissolved. While it may be assumed that Black males of low socioeconomic status experience many of the pressures associated with achievement-related stress as defined by Dohrenwned, on balance the evidence suggests that, given the disadvantages of their status, these Black males are likely to be confronted with situations in which security-related events are more likely to outnumber achievement-related events and are therefore more likely to demand their attention.

Presumably, Black males of high socioeconomic status are less pressured by security-related concerns than are Black males of lower socioeconomic status. By definition, middle-income status implies relatively high income, low unemployment, high educational attainment, and marital stability. In contrast to their low-income counterparts, middle- and upper-income Black males experience fewer of the health-related problems or activity restrictions reported for the former. Moreover, while Black adult males have experienced the sharpest increase in joblessness in recent years (National Urban League, 1978), the incidence and duration of unemployment is considerably lower among Black males employed in high-status occupations.

Similar differentials between low- and upper-income Black males are observed in the rates of marital breakdown by reason of divorce or separation. Although the incidence of divorce and separation has continued to rise among Blacks of all socioeconomic levels during the last decade (U. S. Bureau of the Census, 1980), marital instability is a less frequent occurrence among middle- and upper-income Blacks than it is among low-income Blacks. Additionally, when compared to males from impoverished backgrounds, Black males from affluent backgrounds more frequently graduate from high school and attend college (Levitan et al., 1975) and, thus, are more likely to be employed in high-status occupations. On the other hand, middle-income Black males may experience higher rates of other stressors than do low-income Black males. Job promotions, responsibilities associated with professional or community organizations, extensive travel connected with employment, and other radical changes from the usual pattern of life, are almost exclusively middle-income stressors and are likely to be outside the experience of most low-income Black males (Dohrenwend, 1969).

While current data do not permit a definitive judgment as to the relative frequency and severity of security-related, compared to achievement-related, stressors among Black males of high- and low-status positions, the respective advantages and disadvantages often associated with these positions imply that there are also differences in the nature of sociocultural problems experienced by Black males occupying these positions. In any case, the distinction between these two positions draws attention to major categories of stressful events that may affect Black males of different socioeconomic backgrounds differentially.

Just as Black males may differ in the degree to which they are exposed to major categories of stress, they may also differ in the relative capacity to utilize certain external and internal resources that mediate the impact of stressful situations. As noted earlier, external and internal resources define the environment within which the individual is capable of responding to stressors and, therefore, exert a constraining influence on individual behavior.

With respect to external resources, Black males of low socioeconomic status appear to be relatively handicapped in terms of their ability to cope with stressful events through the manipulation of objective conditions. Low income, together with other circumstances, makes them less able than are Blacks of higher income to command essential goods and services (Dohrenwend, 1969). For instance, although expanded federal assistance has improved the quality and availability of health services to the medically indigent in recent years, these services remain fragmented and less adequate than are those available to middle-income Blacks (Levitan et al., 1975). Moreover, census data indicate that low-income Blacks spend far less of their income on medical services and insurance premiums than do their white counterparts or middle-income Black families, the consequence of which is that they have less protection against the risks of illness (U. S. Bureau of the Census, 1974). Similarly, low-income Blacks are more often forced to live in crowded conditions, and experience more restrictions in their choice of housing, than do Blacks of higher status (Farley, 1970).

Insofar as access to information relevant to the resolution of a variety of personal problems is determined by socioeconomic position (Berger & Luckman, 1967), Black males of low socioeconomic status appear to be at a relative disadvantage. For example, compared to other groups, Black workers in general, and Blacks of low occupational status in particular, tend to have less access to informal networks of job contacts through which employment is typically secured, and more frequently rely on formal agencies (for example, schools, employment agencies, and training programs) and walk-in searches (Anderson & Sawhill, 1980). In addition, low-income Blacks tend to be less aware of the existence of the variety of local, social, legal, and political services or knowledgeable personnel that might assist them in resolving personal problems (Suttles, 1968). On the other hand, there is evidence that low-income Blacks have more extrafamilial sources of social support, and are more likely to join and participate more actively in social and religious organizations in comparison to their white counterparts (Marx, 1967; Hannerz, 1969; Suttles, 1968; Stack, 1974). Yet low-income Black males may receive less psychological support from their spouses than do their middle-income counterparts (Rainwater, 1965; Stack, 1974; Hannerz, 1969).

With regard to internal resources for mediating the impact of stressors, the relative differences between Black males of low- and middle-income status are less apparent. Indeed, whether there are fundamental differences in value orientations within the class hierarchy of the larger society is a matter of some controversy (Parkin, 1971; Ryan, 1971). It is argued, on the one hand, that the values underlying major social institutions are shared by members of all social classes, albeit with varying degrees of commitment (Parsons, 1951; Merton, 1957; Mayer, 1955). It is claimed, on the other hand, that values vary sharply between classes so that no unified normative order exists (Hyman, 1953; Miller, 1958). Each of these views has been criticized. As an alternative interpretation, it has been proposed that dominant values are not so much opposed or rejected by the underclass as they are modified to fit their existential condition. Thus, both Rodman's (1963) formulation of the "lower-class value stretch" and Valentine's (1972) characterization of Black collective orientations as products of "biculturation" call attention to the fact that the underclass, both Black and white, subscribe to two distinct levels of normative reference: the dominant value system, and a "negotiated" version of it (Parkin, 1971). Which of these versions the individual actually draws upon will be determined by the particular situation in which that individual finds himself or herself. These observations notwithstanding, it has been noted that a strong orientation toward work and achievement, a belief in the adaptability of family roles, strong kinship bonds, and a strong religious orientation are among the major ingredients of a value perspective shared by Blacks of all social classes (Hill, 1973).

While Blacks may differ little from one another in their basic value orientations, differences in perceived ability to manipulate the objective environment in their own interest have been noted. As a result of their relative deprivation, low-income Blacks tend to express less confidence in their ability to manipulate the social environment than do Blacks of middle-income status. This attitude is reflected in evidence derived from measures of personal efficacy (Gore & Rotter, 1971; Gurin & Epps, 1975) and political alienation (Bullough, 1972). The belief in "external control" (Rotter, 1966)—that is, the individual's expectancy that external forces, over which he or she has little or no control, will determine the rewards received in life—is shown to be consistently related to low occupational and educational aspirations, poor performance in school and on achievement tasks, and overall perception of life chances and opportunities (Gurin & Epps, 1975). More generally, these findings suggest that individuals who lack confidence in their ability to manipulate the environment are less likely than are others to embark on courses of action that will enable them to cope effectively with external stressors.

On balance, Black males of low socioeconomic status appear to be more handicapped relative to internal resources for coping with external stressors than are their Black middle-income counterparts. This apparent disadvantage may be significantly altered or eliminated when other dimensions of personal organization are considered. Individual differences in cognitive and perceptual abilities, early childhood and adult experiences, physiological predisposition, and positive reinforcement derived from successful mastery of past situations giving rise to stress, are collectively or in some combination responsible for what Selye (1956) calls the distinctive way in which each individual "takes to" stressful life occurrences. These factors perforce would qualify any conclusion regarding apparent differences among Black males relative to their abilities to cope with external stress.

Although explicitly formulated to account for differential rates of deviant behavior within the general society, Merton's (1957) classic typology of modes of individual adaptation and social organization offers a preliminary approach in ordering the diverse observations on the dispositional and behavioral tendencies of Black males. Merton relates certain properties of the social structure to personal adaptations and lifestyles, and focuses on the consequences for individual behavior of a disjunction between cultural values and the structural or material means available for their achievement. He argues that the disequilibrium between cultural goals and institutional means engenders structurally induced strain, accompanied by a weakening of individual commitment to prescribed values or the morally prescribed norms for their attainment. Moreover, he assumes that the gap between ends and means and the consequent strain tend to accumulate in the lower social strata, where the belief in the American dream is most frequently observed to be violated by institutional closure. Recognizing that individual reactions to this disparity may take several forms, Merton spells out the logically possible ways in which individuals may adapt to this anomic condition. Hence, he classifies behavior according to the acceptance or rejection of cultural goals and institutional means. Of the five logically possible alternative modes of adaptation identified by Merton, only three will concern us here: innovation, retreatism, and rebellion. *Innovation* is a form of adaptation involving the use of illegitimate means (for example, theft, robbery, or other illegal activities) to achieve normatively prescribed goals, and is considered normal where access to success through conventional means is thwarted. *Retreatism* refers to the abandonment of both the cultural goals and the institutionalized practices by which to achieve them. Having internalized achievement norms, but prevented through structural blockages or internal pressures from achieving personal goals, the individual becomes frustrated and handicapped, and may attempt to cope with the situation through such escape mechanisms as withdrawal, defeatism, and quietism. *Rebellion* refers to a form of adaptation in which there is a withdrawal of allegiance from the social order and a transfer of support to new groups with new sets of goals and practices for attaining them. This mode of response is essentially different from the others in that it involves "efforts to change the existing structure rather than perform accommodative actions within the structure" (Merton, 1957: 140). Merton makes clear that such modes of behavior are not to be regarded as types of personality organization, but do represent, in his view, more or less enduring behavioral responses to specific situations.

What proportion of Black males may be forced to adopt one or more of these coping strategies would appear to depend on the relative absence of other effective means for achieving value goals. However, given their low socioeconomic status and limited opportunities to compete through conventional means, a significant number of Black males might be forced to improvise new or different means through which to crystallize a sense of masculine self-identity (Taylor, 1976). Such improvisations may range from an involvement in illicit activities to an emphasis on hypersexuality and violence (Hare, 1977; Staples, 1978). For some, illicit conduct may offer a viable means of achieving breadwinning competence and, thus, influence their status in the family. For others, hustling, pimping, and related activities are perceived as possible means of status conferral. The psychosocial dynamics involved in such functional adaptations have been detailed in a number of works (for example, Liebow, 1967; Hannerz, 1969; Wilkinson & Taylor, 1977), of which Valentine's (1978) *Hustling and Other Hard Work* is the most recent example. While it is difficult to determine to what extent such modes of response are reflected in crime statistics, the confluence of restricted opportunity and limited personal resources tends to favor a high frequency of innovative and more or less illicit conduct among Black males.

For those unable or unwilling to employ innovative strategies for coping with the frustrations of a stigmatized identity, retreat from normative expectations and demands may be perceived as the only recourse. Thus, relief from the anxieties of striving for valued goals and the consequent feelings of failure, powerlessness, and self-condemnation may be sought in drugs and alcohol, and, in extreme cases, may result in mental illness and suicide. These modes of coping can be regarded as only temporary, however, since they tend to have serious consequences in ordinary situations and are disastrous in situations of severe stress (Dohrenwend & Dohrenwend, 1969). Although reported rates of emotional disorder among Black males are seriously distorted by observational and reporting errors and by response bias, these data do offer some basis for inferring the relative magnitude of the problem. For instance, census data reported for the period 1950-1970 indicate that the rates of hospitalization in mental institutions for nonwhites have been consistently higher than have those for whites, and that the gap was even greater in 1970 than it was in earlier periods (U. S. Bureau of the Census, 1973). According to Cannon and Locke (1977), the admission rates of Blacks to state and county mental hospitals in 1975 were more than double the rates for whites, and the racial disparity was even greater between males and females. Moreover, of the leading diagnoses among persons admitted to state and county mental hospitals in 1975, alcohol disorders and schizophrenia were the most frequently reported diagnoses for males. However, the latter disorder ranked first among Black males, and the rates for both disorders were considerably higher among Black males than they were among white males. Similarly, the rate of suicide among Black males has been shown to be equal to, if not greater than, that of their white cohorts, ranking third among the five leading causes of death for Black males between the ages of 15 and 35 (Dennis, 1977). While alcoholism, drug addiction, and mental disorders are characteristic of a certain segment of the Black population (Staples, 1978), Black males constitute a significant proportion of this population. Nonetheless, retreatism appears to be the least common mode of adaptation among Black males.

In Merton's scheme, rebellion refers to a group rather than an individual mode of response, and involves a repudiation of the normative strictures and goals of the larger society. Drawn together by common circumstances, and by their perception of relative deprivation, lower-class youth in general, and Black youth in particular, may respond by refusing to acknowledge the relevance of societal values and goals to the reality of their own lives and seek instead to create criteria of status by which they can succeed. Cohen (1955) refers to this response as a "reaction-formation" In his view, such youth do not merely reject the dominant value system, "but do so with a vengeance." They display wholesale negativism and malicious behavior of all sorts to demonstrate to others their contempt for the system.

> A tough and bellicose posture, the use of obscene language, participation in illicit sexual activity . . . the deliberate flouting of legality and authority, a generalized disrespect for the sacred symbols of the "square" world . . . all of these may have the primary function of affirming . . . that one is a certain kind of person [Cohen, 1955: 7].

As other writers have observed (for example, Hannerz, 1969; Miller, 1958), the emphasis on "toughness" may be the source of much "instantaneous" violence among young Black males in inner-city communities, and figures largely in their conception of masculinity. Such an extreme disposition finds its most tragic expression in the crime statistics, which show homicide as the leading cause of death among Black males aged 15 to 30 years.

As a theoretical perspective for understanding deviant modes of adaptation to situations of relative deprivation, Merton's typology represents an all-encompassing scheme that accounts for a range of deviant behaviors. However, as a theoretical formulation for analyzing more conventional behaviors, its applicability is severely restricted. Indeed, it has been criticized for its class bias and for ignoring the role of group membership (for example, racial, ethnic, and religious) in influencing individual behavior. Nonetheless, its emphasis on the disjunction between cultural goals and structural or material means, and the consequences of this disparity for individual behavior, appropriately describe the existential condition of a significant proportion of Black males in the United States, and, therefore, lends considerable plausibility to the scheme for analyzing and interpreting Black males' responses to external stress.

## SUMMARY AND CONCLUSIONS

From both a conceptual and a research perspective, we have sought to relate major categories of stressor events to types of adjustive responses for coping or adaptation, given certain internal and external mediating conditions as these apply to Black males of differential socioeconomic status. More specifically, it was noted that stress, as a social psychological phenomenon, is a function of perceived or anticipated threat or frustration, and that the effects of stress are mediated through subjective and external factors which, in turn, have a constraining influence on the individual's future responses to stress. Adaptation to stressful situations was observed to be a developmental process involving a complex interaction between the individual and the environment, and where failure to deal successfully with past situations of stress results in a feedback spiral of increasing tension and strain, that is, to maladaptation.

Applying this model to Black males, we noted that their socioeconomic status and ethnic membership are important antecedent factors of stress. Borrowing Dohrenwend and Dohrenwend's (1969) distinction between security-related and achievement-realted stressors as a means of approaching these issues, we noted that, given the relative disadvantage of their status (for example, low income, high unemployment, poor health care, and marital breakdown), Black males of low socioeconomic status are much more likely to suffer security-related stress than are their middle-income counterparts, whose more favored position increased the likelihood of their betoken exposure to situations more frequently involving achievement-related stress. Differences were also noted in the ability of Black males to utilize certain external and internal resources that serve to mediate the impact of stressful situations. Black males of low socioeconomic status are relatively handicapped in their ability to command material resources for coping with social stress, although apparently not handicapped in terms of their access to sources of social support. With respect to internal resources (that is, values, beliefs, and motivations), the evidence is less clear. Low-status Black males appear to be handicapped only to the degree that they have internalized a generalized sense of external control. While it appears that Black males of low socioeconomic status are disadvantaged relative to Black males of higher status, other dimensions of personal organization than those surveyed here were observed to play an important role in determining individual responses to stressful occurrences. Three modes of individual adaptation to structurally induced stress and strain, drawn from Merton's (1957) typology, were employed in assessing the dispositional and behavioral tendencies of Black males. To the extend that Black males experience structural or internal blockages to the achievement of normatively prescribed role behavior and personal goals, together with the resulting strain, they may respond to such blockages through innovation, retreat, or rebellion.

It is, of course, by no means trivial to ask why some Black males respond to stress in the ways described above; but a more fruitful inquiry might be to ask why so many do not. Although attention has been drawn to the role of community organizations and other extrafamilial sources of social support in mediating the impact of social stress on Black males, the precise contributions of these support systems remain unclear. The formulation presented above offers some clues as to the role of external and internal resources in mediating the impact of external stressors on Black males. In view of the formulation, it might be hypothesized that among Black males under stress, those who have a greater sense of control over occurrences in their lives will cope more effectively with stressful events than will those who feel powerless in the face of external forces. Similarly, Black males who feel a greater commitment to all areas of life—that is, work, family, interpersonal relationships, and self— may, in comparison to those who feel more alienated, perceive a greater purpose in life that serves as a "generalized resistance resource against the impact of stress" (Kobasa, 1979). Future research would do well to focus on the perceptual aspects of stress that bear on how Black males respond to life events.

## REFERENCES

Anderson, B., & Sawhill, I. (Eds.). *Youth employment and public policy*. Englewood Cliffs, NJ: Prentice-Hall, 1980.

Appley, M., & Turmbull, R. (Eds.). *Psychological stress*. New York: Appleton-Century— Crofts, 1967.

Berger, P., & Luckmann, T. *The social construction of reality*. New York: Anchor, 1967.

Blassingame, J. *The slave community*. New York: Oxford University Press, 1972.

Bullough, B. Alienation in the ghetto. In C. Bullock & H. Rogers (Eds.), *Black political attitudes*. Chicago: Markham, 1972.

Cannon, M., & Locke, B. Being Black is detrimental to one's mental health: Myth or reality? *Phylon*, 1977, *33*, 408-428.

Cohen, A. *Delinquent boys*. New York: Free Press, 1955.

Dennis, R. Social stress and mortality among non-white males. *Phylon*, 1977, *38*, 315-328.

Dohrenwend, B. The social-psychological nature of stress: A framework for causal inquiry. *Journal of Abnormal Psychology*, 1961, *62*, 294-302.

Dohrenwend, B. P., & Dohrenwend, B. S. *Social status and psychological disorder: A causal inquiry*. New York: John Wiley, 1969.

Farley, R. The changing distribution of Negroes within metropolitan areas: The emergence of Black suburbs. *American Journal of Sociology*, 1970, *75*, 512-529.

Genovese, E. The slave family, women–a reassessment of matriarchy, emasculation, weakness. *Southern voices*, 1974, *1*, 9-16.

Gore, P., & Rotter, J. A personality correlate of social action. In R. Wilcox (Ed.), *The psychological consequences of being a Black American*. New York: John Wiley, 1971.

Gurin, P., & Epps, E. *Black consciousness, identity and achievement*. New York: John Wiley, 1975.

Gutman, H. *The Black family in slavery and freedom 1750-1925*. New York: Pantheon, 1976.

Hannerz, U. *Soulside*. New York: Columbia University Press, 1969.

Hare, N. The many ways men "pimp" women. *Ebony*, 1977, *33*, 145-151.

Harrison, J. Warning: The male sex role may be dangerous to your health. *Journal of Social Issues*, 1978, *34*, 65-86.

Hernton, C. *Sex and racism in America*. New York: Grove, 1965.

Hill, R. *The strengths of Black families*. New York: Emerson Hall, 1973.

Hyman, H. The value systems of different classes. In R. Bendix & C. Lipset (Eds.), *Class, status and power*. New York: Free Press, 1953.

Jourard, S. *The transparent self*. New York: Van Nostrand, 1971.

Kahn, R. L., et al. Some propositions toward a researchable conceptualization of stress. In J. McGrath (Ed.), *Social and psychological factors in stress*. New York: Holt, Rinehart & Winston, 1970.

Kobasa, S. Stressful life events, personality, and health: An inquiry into hardiness. *Journal of Personality and Social Psychology*, 1979, *37*, 1-11.

Lazarus, R. *Psychological stress and the coping process*. New York: McGraw-Hill, 1966.

Levine, S., & Scotch, N. (Eds.). *Social stress*. Chicago: Aldine, 1970.

Levitan, S., Johnson, W., & Laggart, R. *Still a dream: The changing status of Blacks since 1960*. Cambridge: Harvard University Press, 1975.

Liebow, E. *Tally's corner*. Boston: Little, Brown, 1967.

Marx, G. Religion: Opiate or inspiration or civil rights militancy among Negros? *American Sociological Review*, 1967, *32*, 64-72.

Mason, J. A historical view of the stress field: Part I. *Journal of Human Stress*, 1975, *1*, 6-12.

Mayer, K. *Class and society*. Garden City, NY: Doubleday, 1955.

McGrath, J. (Ed.). *Social and psychological factors in stress*. New York: Holt, Rinehart & Winston, 1970.

Mechanic, D. *Students under stress*. New York: Free Press, 1962.

Merton, R. *Social theory and social structure*. New York: Free Press, 1957.

Miller, W. Lower-class culture as a generating milieu of gang delinquency. *Journal of Social Issues*, 1958, *14*, 5-19.

Monat, A., & Lazarus, R. (Eds.). *Stress and coping*. New York: Columbia University Press, 1977.

National Urban League. *The state of Black America, 1978*. New York: Author, 1978.

Parkin, F. *Class inequality and political order*. New York: Praeger, 1971.

Parsons, T. *The social system*. New York: Free Press, 1951.

Pleck, J. The male sex role: Definitions, problems and sources of change. *Journal of Social Issues*, 1976, *32*(3), 155-163.

Rainwater, L. Crucible of identity: The Negro lower-class family. *Daedalus*, 1965, *95*, 172-216.

Rainwater, L. *Behind ghetto walls*. Chicago: Aldine, 1970.

Rodman, H. The lower-class value stretch. *Social Forces,* 1963, *42,* 205-215.

Rotter, J. Generalized expectancies for internal versus external control of reinforcement. *Psychology Monograph,* 1966, 80, 1-28.

Ryan, W. *Blaming the victim*. New York: Vintage, 1971.

Scanzoni, J. *The Black family in modern society*. Boston, Allyn & Bacon, 1971.

See, J., & Miller, K. Mental health. In K. Miller & R. Dryer (Eds.), *Comparative studies of Blacks and whites in the U. S.* New York: Seminar, 1973.

Selye, J. *The stress of life*. New York: McGraw-Hill, 1956.

Stack, C. *All our kin*. New York: Harper & Row, 1974.

Staples, R. *Introduction to Black sociology*. New York: McGraw-Hill, 1976.

Staples, R. Masculinity and race: The dual dilemma of Black men. *Journal of Social Issues,* 1978, *34,* 169-183.

Suttles, G. *The social order of the slum*. Chicago: University of Chicago Press, 1968.

Taylor, R. Psychosocial development among Black children and youth: A conceptual framework. *Journal of Black Studies,* 1976, *6,* 353-372.

U. S. Bureau of the Census. *Persons with work disabilities* (PC (2)-6C). Washington, DC: Government Printing Office, 1973.

U. S. Bureau of the Census. *The social and economic status of Blacks in the U. S.* Washington, DC: Government printing office, 1974.

U. S. Bureau of the Census. *American families and living arrangements* (Special study, P-23, No. 104). Washington, DC: Government Printing Office, 1980.

U. S. Department of Labor. *Black Americans: A chartbook*. Washington, DC: Government Printing Office, 1971.

Valentine, B. *Hustling and other hard work*. New York: Free Press, 1978.

Valentine, C. *Black studies and anthropology: Scholarly and political interests in Afro-American culture*. Reading, MA: Addison- Wesley, 1972.

Wild, B., & Hanes, C. A dynamic conceptual framework of generalized adaptation to stressful stimuli. *Psychological Reports,* 1976, *38,* 319-334.

Wilkinson, D., & Taylor, R. The stigmatization of the Black male's identity. In D. Wilkinson & R. Taylor (Eds.), *The Black Male*. Chicago: Nelson-Hall, 1977.

Wilson, W. *The declining significance of race*. Chicago: University of Chicago Press, 1978.

# 9

## SUPPORT SYSTEMS AND
## COPING PATTERNS

Leland K. Hall

Over the past several years, a multiplicity of studies and articles have examined Black people in general, usually concentrating on the Black family and Black women. Very little, however, has been written about the Black man. In fact, in most of the earlier studies on Black people, the men have almost always been relegated to a secondary position, considered somewhat like phantoms or villains and alleged to have demonstrated little or no real feelings for their families' well-being. Needless to say, the great majority of these studies were conducted by white academics whose basic goal was to demonstrate that Blacks, for one reason or another, were less capable than the majority population of this society.

The ability of Black people to develop and project a positive image of themselves, as illustrated by these studies, was at most times futile. The investigators usually utilized a negative, deficit model for their studies to prove that Blacks are unable to integrate themselves into the mainstream of this society due to their seemingly negative self-image. Research and studies focused on:

- why Black people feel inferior to whites,
- why Blacks do not have the wherewithal to be self-assured or confident,
- why Black people are so negative about themselves and their culture, and

- why Blacks are nonsupportive of each other.

The basic assumptions inherent in such studies, as mentioned above, permeate this society. The assumption of the published reports and studies is that Black people truly believe they are inferior and have no confidence in themselves and their own. This has to an extent influenced many to believe that the written word is gospel and that Blacks should not respect, trust, or support each other. The majority population of this society has used the Black family, Black women, and the Black community as a laboratory to illustrate their unrelated theses or theories, which have unlimited negative connotations for Black people who have survived in a society that is hostile if not noxious to them.

Just the ability to survive in a society that continues to uncover ways in which Black people can be made to look inadequate and negative is an accomplishment. This demonstrates that the ability of a people to cope amidst such adversity has great merit alone. However, the positive aspects of Black people, Black males particularly, have been denied. The exception is that a very few white academicians and Black scholars have focused on some of the positive values and the real strengths that Black people possess. I do not consider myself either an academician or a scholar, but an average Black man. In this chapter, I will discuss what I feel are some of the formal and informal systems that Black males utilize within the developmental and socialization process to adjust, survive, and thrive within the larger society and within various subcultural and social groups.

## SOCIALIZATION OF BLACK MALES

First, I do not intend to purport that the Black male's developmental process is different from the developmental process of any ethnic group member in this society. Without question, there are some universal elements for all people in this process; however, the experiences of Black men are unique, given their particular cultural variables and norms. A fundamentally unique aspect of the Black male's developmental process is that by being both Black and male he begins with a handicap in this white-oriented society, because he is a threat to those who control this society—to white males, in particular. Thus, the Black man's role in life is to be better than those outside his environment, who make up the rules for the game of life. With such an untenable position, he must have access to various support systems to assist him with learning the rules of the game as well as to have faith and confidence in his ability to survive in this hostile society. At the same time, he must compete with vigor for what he feels is rightfully his.

When a Black male is born into a family, the expectations for him to survive and prosper are great. His presence automatically represents strength, good fortune, and stability—a point seldom made in studies of Black children. The Black man-child is often named after his father or grandfather, or given a name that connotes strength, knowledge, or power (such as Konata, Arabic for "man of high station"). The man-child is exposed to those elements within the family constellation that demonstrate responsibility and forthrightness and are accompanied by the close nurturing relationship of his mother, from whom he takes his first clues as to how he is expected to behave in different life situations. The aspects of his budding life that will be emphasized are contingent, in large part, on the socioeconomic position the family holds within their subculture of this society. (The opportunities for success in life are few, given the limits of the economic position that the man's family may occupy in this society.)

By looking at the Black male's development in a generic way, one realizes that no matter what socioeconomic level he may be part of, he will traverse the different levels of development at about the same time. His Black culture and traditional family rearing have been labeled *matriarchal* (Moynihan, 1965), and obviously, to a great extent, most Black males receive their early socialization via their mother and/or mother surrogates. This part of the male's development is, of course, the first level of a support system in which he learns about himself and the role expectation his subgroup has for him. In addition, he learns what he can expect from others during his time of need for direction. It is within this social network that he begins to deal with determining what his assets and limitations are concerning those who are closest to him. Also, he begins to distinguish how "outsiders" are related to him and what their expectations are for him, relative to the role given to him by the larger network.

The family is where the Black male obtains his initial exposure to an environment of support, love, and affection. It is here that he begins to learn about his basic feelings of belonging and trust. If he is able to show fragility in the light of oppressing odds or occasional doubt about what he should do, and receives support from this intimate inner circle, he will learn to trust the opinions and guidance of those involved with him even after this early stage of his life has passed. He can learn and feel how he is to behave when faced with criticism and ascertain from those close to him a validation of his identity and what he as a person is worth to them. He can be dependent upon and nurtured by this support system and assisted in making the choices that will bring about a full life. These early encounters will structure within him the basis for a long-standing, intimate support system:

> The other people are interested in him in a personalized way. They
> speak his language. They tell him what is expected of him and guide

him in what to do. They watch what he does and they judge his
performance. They let him know how well he has done. They reward
him for success and punish or support and comfort him if he fails.
Above all, they are sensitive to his personal needs which they deem
worthy of respect and satisfaction [Caplan, 1974: 5-6].

## CULTURAL AND SOCIETAL EXPECTATIONS
## OF THE BLACK MALE

The American culture and its subsocieties do not expect the Black male to
exhibit emotions and feelings about his or his family's life situation and the
dire impact that society may have on him when he tries to live up to these
unrealistic expectations. "A man ain't suppose to cry" is one of the cardinal
rules governing the emotions of Black men; they are expected to illustrate
manly strength and confidence. If the emotions of a man are restrained, how
is he to express sadness, pain, loneliness, and isolation? Through the proper
socialization process, Black men learn that activities conducted for recreational purposes can be and are an acceptable outlet for the deep-seated
emotional and visceral feelings that they may have but feel prohibited to
release.

In order to defuse some of the pent-up feelings associated with negative
emotions, the Black male often expresses these feelings of displeasure within
a subgroup that allows him to meet this need to decompress. Often the
avenue for accomplishing this is a common-interest or peer-group association—usually within which he can identify persons who are experiencing
similar problems expressing their true feelings. It is within such groupings that
the Black male can develop self-esteem and confidence outside his earlier
intimate relationship circle. There, behavior that is not always acceptable—
given his role, may be accepted because of the purpose and configuration of
the group.

The time-tried outlets for Black men to alleviate emotional pain and
despair, as well as to express joy, have been play and recreation. (After all, we
are fun-loving people.) When Black males begin to establish ties outside of the
intimate environment, they make linkages with other Black males who have
expressed interest in similar socially accepted activities to gain support and/or
reinforcement to meet their emotional and competitive needs. Via the socialization process of gathering together with the opposite sex—namely,
partying—the youthful and adult Black male has been given the opportunity
to discover whom in his subgroups he can trust and to determine how much,
if any, support he can receive at a time of need. In some instances, he obtains
comfort through whatever company he can acquire.

Operating from a negative position of second-class citizenship in this society, the Black male begins to identify and receive support and, to an extent, protection from within his chosen subgroups. Collectively, the young Black male may express his displeasure through negative aggression, which allows him to obtain some feeling of control, if not a false sense of superiority, by behaving in a manner that brings attention to his need to be identified as an individual as well as a member of a formal or informal group. On the positive side, however, this expression of individuality can be manifested by the fact that he is, for example, a better-than-average dancer at peer parties or larger social affairs. This is also true of the Black male in athletics. His feeling good about himself is really contingent upon the level and degree of support he receives from the subgroup with whom he identifies and from the recognition he receives from groups outside his immediate sphere of influence. In addition, this kind of activity serves the purpose of enabling him to be involved in some action for action's sake. These activities are usually short-range and not goal-oriented. If the Black male's activities are goal-directed, however, they will allow him an opportunity to receive some immediate gratification and a feeling of belonging.

Those Black males who are fortunate enough to possess the physical attributes of athletes will more than likely find themselves in the throes of competing with others in the same condition for some level of recognition if not superiority of performance. It is usually at this stage that the Black male may face crises and need support for dealing with these critical developmental and personal milestones. (Of course, crises emanating from the home, school, and church may also have their impact on the individual regarding his need for support.) During this time in his life, the Black male begins to experience success and failure in his endeavors to prove himself a man. When he begins to feel the sting of failure, it is of the utmost importance that he receive from his peers and subgroup members understanding and support that will assist him with making those adjustments necessary for him again to function adequately in his expanding environment. It is here that the Black male begins to become aware that the larger society's expectation of him is measured by his deficits, his differences, and the fact that he will soon become (if he is not already) a threat to its control over his life.

The cautious teaching and guidance he has received from his parents and immediate family begin to have a lesser effect on him as he matures and ventures out. The protective surroundings of home can no longer shelter him from the pain and trials of becoming a man. The mother and family who may have warned him of social obstacles are no longer as accessible as they may have been in the past, nor does he necessarily want to depend exclusively on this kind of support. Therefore, he is now guided by what he has learned—to depend on himself and the support of the subgroups with which he may now come into contact. One must keep in mind, nonetheless, that the base or core from which the Black male will operate is an unspoken or rarely spoken message that he obtains from his intimate family grouping. This is that "the child must know that the white world is dangerous and . . . if he does not understand its rules, it may kill him" (Grier & Cobb, 1968: 61).

The developmental and learning process can be painful in itself. As crises present themselves throughout a Black male's life, he finds that in moving from one reference or peer group to another, the demands, limitations, and expectations placed on him become more refined as he develops his own identity with a greater dependence upon himself. He begins to sort out those things that are important to him as well as those persons he can depend on in a crisis. His need for support will become more sophisticated but no less important than it was when he was learning about the parameters within which he had to function during his earlier life. He will begin to select those persons on whom he can depend and, based on past experiences, he will seek support from whatever group of persons he feels can give him accurate and definite support when he has need for it or when he is in a crisis. Support can be long-range and continuing (for example, from his family), but other support may be intermittent and short-range (for example, from his various reference groups).

## GROUP IMPACT ON THE
## BLACK MALE

As Black men forge forward in this competitive and hostile society, they are confronted by the fact that they have to work harder and be better than those males who are of the majority. The Black man begins to learn the truth about equality, justice, independence, and fairness as they relate to his chosen area of adult or professional endeavor in life. All of the support he has received during his effort to find his niche in this society—from his family, friends, school, teachers, ministers, and other associates he has encountered through life—has taught him that he must stand up for himself when the chips are down. Although he may have received continuous and intermittent support from his various subgroups during different levels of crisis, it is he who has to make the final choice for solutions, as he becomes older and more responsible.

The various heterogeneous and homogeneous groupings that influenced his identity and role development continue to exist, but to a lesser degree as he develops into a more self-sufficient, reliable individual. Each subgroup's input has supported him as a man-child and youth, but as he grows older and his responsibilities increase the demands placed on him and the pressure to succeed become greater and involve more stress and crisis. His social network expands as he moves further away from his original base, the intimate group, and forms other alliances in order to have his career and emotional needs met. If he is a very responsible person, more responsibility will be placed on him, either to lead to or assist in accomplishing a specific task. Those around him who "know" will be able to ascertain when his abilities to continue to pursue excellence have been hindered by an outside or personal crisis. It is then that he has to realize his own capabilities, limitations, and failures. It is then also that some support system has to be in place so that he can receive some understanding and counseling as to how to proceed:

> Individual response during crisis . . . is influenced by . . . the quality of the emotional support and task-oriented assistance provided by the social network within which that individual grapples with the crisis event [Caplan, 1974: 4].

Although it has existed throughout his life, it is during adulthood that the Black male has a greater need for others to support him as he attempts to master his generic environmental pressures. He begins to realize that in order to persevere, he has to create internal and external means for adhering to the greater society's value system and traditions.

In other words, how does he remain a strong Black male in the eyes of his peers and others when, on the one hand, it is not socially acceptable to express feelings and emotions or to seek help for his problems, and, on the other, his inner strengths are pushed to their limits. He knows that he must move forward and survive or perish for the lack of adequate and appropriate outside support and inner strength. If the Black man is to maintain status and importance in the eyes of his peers and others at times of crisis, where does he find the support to assist him in coping with the accompanying stress and pressures?

## EXISTING SUPPORT SYSTEMS

Black tradesmen and professionals have to an extent been able to find solace, comfort, and support in fraternal organizations and unions. These mechanisms have allowed them some recognition and status while simultaneously allowing them to receive support and reinforcement from the "brothers". Some find peace and support through religious affiliations as individuals, but far too often this occurs only on Sundays. Some obtain a feeling of belonging by visiting the local pub, where other fellows like themselves hide their needs of dependence and their fragility by behaving "macho" around their associates and lady friends. Others either seek comfort and support from friends who understand or suffer alone.

The effect such groups as these have on Black males has been and is positive insofar as they meet the activity and belonging needs of Black men. However, the deep-seated emotional support needs of the Black male many times go unnoticed or are set aside because of the masculine image Black organizations attempt to portray. In fact, these mechanisms are accepted by the Black community as masculine-oriented.

I feel there are at present few effective avenues open to enable the Black male in need of support to cope with his daily life situations. Once a Black male moves (physically) away from his roots and/or his family, he takes upon himself the task of carving out a niche for himself (and his own family) in a hostile society. He is what he has learned and experienced through his involvement with his family, peers, neighbors, and associates. Not often enough do Black males face the fact that they, too, are human and have a need to seek and obtain support and understanding for their own emotional fragility. The pressures and stress related to surviving far too often take their toll on the Black male's physical and psychological well-being. Without true support, these factors can impair if not destroy him.

Black males should be able without criticism to seek out whatever support they deem necessary to assist them with accomplishing their goals in life, and at the same time survive the trials and tribulations that accompany the desire for a better way of life for themselves and their own. As Erickson (1963: 6) says, "mature man needs to be needed and maturity needs guidance as well as encouragement from what has been produced and must be taken care of."

Whether the Black male chooses to pursue a profession in medicine, social work, psychology, manual trades, the clergy, or organized crime, he is still accountable for his actions. In order for him to have greater self-assurance in his actions and his mere existence, he must learn how both to "stand on his own two feet" and to be "interdependent" with those who understand the issues and problems of being a Black male in a society where the competition for survival is bent toward those who make the rules.

As indicated earlier in this chapter, the existence and use of support systems are both continual and intermittent. Those old faithful systems that existed during the early stages of development still exist. There are family and friends who will still listen and assist Black males with sorting out their difficulties. There are Black men with similar problems related to meeting the demands placed on them to succeed and be better than most in life, who share the same experiences of surviving in this noxious and hostile society. There are those they trust who will allow Black men to expose their deep emotional feelings through heart-to-heart discussions about how difficult it is to meet life's demands. There are those who will assist Black men with "letting it all hang out" without producing in them the feeling that they will be embarrassed or criticized for crying or bitching. As for the use of existing formal systems geared to assist Black males in dealing with their innermost problems, very few venture to utilize such mechanisms. Far too often, the Black man feels that if he seeks help from a formal organization or a professional, "he is less than a man" for not being able to solve his own problems. There is a great need at this time for a formal mechanism that allows similar types of Black men to congregate and talk over the problems they feel they cannot mention to most people. However, there is a hesitancy to create or utilize such a mechanism. Black men still feel that they cannot show emotion because it is considered a sign of weakness.

In closing, it can be said that the greatest amount of solace and support that the Black male can depend upon in order to cope with the stress and pressures of the time is still internal. The Black male must first have confidence in himself and his own manhood. He must have strength enough to recognize his shortcomings without seeing them as weaknesses. He must trust and believe in himself before he can really give or receive the support necessary for surviving in this hostile, competitive society. What the years have given him in understanding, knowledge, and skills, no one can take away.

## REFERENCES

Caplan, G. *Support systems and community mental health*. New York: Behavioral Publications, 1974.

Erickson, E. *Childhood and society* (2nd ed.). New York: Norton, 1963.

Grier, W., & Cobb, P. *Black rage*. New York: Basic Books, 1968.

Moynihan, D. The Negro family: The call for national action. Washington, DC: U.S. Department of Labor, 1965.

# 10

## ALCOHOL USE AND ABUSE

Frederick D. Harper

"Alcohol use" connotes the use as opposed to the nonuse of beverage alcohol as well as circumstances surrounding the use of alcohol, whereas "alcohol abuse" specifically refers to the misuse of alcohol in terms of heavy and inappropriate drinking behaviors. Moderate alcohol use has been found to have no harmful effects on health and behavior; however, alcohol abuse has been associated with physical illness, mental disorders, crime, suicides, and accidents, including a number of other personal and social problems and consequences (*Alcohol and Health*, 1971, 1974). Among many Blacks, especially those in urban areas, alcohol abuse has had serious negative consequences. Bourne (1973: 211) ranks alcoholism, a result of alcohol abuse, as "the number one mental health problem, if not the most significant of all health problems, in Black urban communities." Larkins (1965) notes that alcohol use among Blacks can be associated with "explosive issues" that are frequently overlooked or go unrecognized by many Black communities. In general, "the negative consequences of alcohol use by Blacks often exceed those for white Americans in terms of alcohol-related homicides, illnesses, accidents, family conflicts, assaults, and arrests" (Harper, 1976: x). In terms of cumulative negative consequences, alcohol abuse is the number-one health and social problem, historically ignored by Black Americans.

# DRINKING PRACTICES AND
# CONSEQUENCES

For the Black male, especially in urban areas, the abuse of alcohol and its consequences appear more grave when compared to statistics for white men, white women, or Black women. Although Black and white men seem to have similar rates of drinkers, the rate of heavy drinkers for Black men is slightly higher than that for their white counterparts, and exceeds rates of heavy drinking for Black females and white females by an even larger margin (Cahalan & Cisin, 1968; Sterne, 1967). In certain rural towns of the South, heavy drinking by Black men has been reported to be practically "universal," to use Lewis's (1955) term. It is especially prevalent during the nonplanting and nonharvesting seasons, when Black males have more time for drinking (Benjamin, 1976). For example, Benjamin found that Black men of Mississippi often left their wives at home to take care of the baby (or children) while they enjoyed the freedom of drinking "with the boys" in public streets or taverns. Lewis's (1955) study of Kent, a small town in South Carolina, revealed that Black working-class men often drank in public, got in trouble with the law, and used alcohol to facilitate sexual intercourse (i.e., by attempting to intoxicate the female and seduce her).

The literature on drinking among Black male college students and high school youth is practically nil.[1] Maddox and Borinski's (1964) and Maddox and Williams's (1968) studies of Black male college students at traditionally Black colleges in the South indicated strong patterns of heavy weekend drinking. The authors inferred that heavy drinking was employed by the Black male as a means of reducing anxiety, stimulating sexual seduction, and compensating for social inadequacies. The Maddox-led studies are noted here because they are the only studies cited in the literature of Black male-only research samples taken from college populations. However, it must be mentioned that the limitations of these studies loom large, since they represent data collected from an isolated geographic population more than 13 years ago and during the heyday of racial segregation in southern colleges. Maddox and associates' explanations of heavy drinking among Black men may also be challenged by the question of whether Black college men drink heavily for *personal reasons* (anxiety, sexual seduction, feelings of inadequacy), *social reasons* (community encouragement, social expectation, traditions of partying), or a combination of personal and social reasons.

One study of rural high school youth indicates similar rates for Black male and white male drinkers (Globetti, 1970), whereas another study of rural youth found that there was a larger proportion of white than of Black male high school students who drank (Dawkins, 1976). These two studies of rural drinking practices among high school students, carried out in Mississippi and North Carolina respectively, indicate that Black male youth tend to have a similar or lower rate of drinkers when compared to white male youth. With regard to urban Black male youth, no study has been reported in the literature that provides a significant examination of the drinking practices of this population.

Other reports on the drinking practices of Black American males indicate that they often have a preference for Scotch and beer (Scott, 1975),[2] that they tend to get into trouble while under the influence of alcohol (Robins et al., 1968), and that they frequently drink in groups with their male peers (Davis, 1974). In addition, they seem to use creative and imaginative alcohol language (Harper & Hawkins, 1976) and tend to drink most heavily on the weekends.

As to the overall consequences of alcohol abuse, the Black male is probably the most likely candidate to suffer in many different ways from heavy drinking. As a consequence of alcohol abuse, the Black male may become victim to the following:

(1) *Homicide.* In a 1974 study of autopsied homicide victims (Harper, 1976) in the cities of Atlanta, Cleveland, Miami, and Washington, D.C., it was found that the Black male alone accounted for more deaths by homicide (58 percent) than white males, white females, and Black females combined. Moreover, compared to a white male, the Black male was almost three times more likely to die from homicide. Surveying all cases of homicide in the four cities, alcohol was found in the blood of approximately 50 percent of the autopsied bodies. A higher alcohol incidence, however, prevailed for Black male homicide victims (slightly over 60 percent had alcohol in the bloodstream).

(2) *Arrest.* Larkins (1965) was among the first to observe, from historical documents, that the Black male drinking offender had been subject to discrimination in cases of police arrests and court sentences. In support of Larkins' findings, Zax et al. (1964) found that twelve times as many Black men as white men were arrested for drunkenness during the year 1961 in the city of Rochester, New York. These reports suggest that white male police officers may be highly prone to arrest Black male alcohol offenders and that judges are often stiffer in the sentencing of Black males who commit crimes while under the influence of alcohol. It may also be noted that Black males often predispose themselves to the vulnerability of arrest for alcohol-related crimes by drinking on streets and in public places, where they are accessible to the scrutinizing eye and arrest action of roaming police.

(3) *Accidents.* Compared to Black women, a much larger proportion of Black men drive motor vehicles and work on dangerous industrial jobs. These are situations where accidents can easily occur to one under the influence of

alcohol. I have observed numerous Black men in alcoholism-treatment programs wearing evidence of injuries they attest to having received during their drinking careers. For example, one young Black man had half his foot cut off while working with a dangerous grinding machine while drunk. The many alcohol-related automobile or motor vehicular deaths of Black men can be documented in the literature (Harper & Dawkins, 1976) and need not be detailed here. Moreover, the Black male is highly subject to home accidents that occur while under the influence of alcohol.

(4) *Perpetration of Crime.* The very large proportion of Black men who kill other Black men during drinking situations suggests a positive influence of alcohol in aggressive homicidal acts by the perpetrator of the crime. Heavy drinking, and the prevalence of gambling, guns, knives, and acting-out behavior seemingly contribute equally to the consequences of a violent homicidal act. Alcohol can also serve as a catalytic agent in criminal acts by Black males such as violent assault, rape, and vandalism. Many of these crimes include the Black male's violence against "his own woman."

(5) *Assault.* Black males who are drunk or in some way incapacitated by heavy drinking have many times fallen prey to muggers who "lie in wait" especially for such persons on payday. Taxi drivers in the Black community have also been known to "roll" drunken male passengers, relieve them of their wallets, and leave them at their doorsteps or elsewhere at night or early in the morning.

(6) *Illness.* According to the *Textbook of Black-Related Diseases* (Williams, 1975), Black men have been cited as prime candidates for heart disease, hypertension, and cancer of the prostate and esophagus.[3] It has been further noted that the Black male's heavy drinking and tendency not to seek medical help or to get regular physical examinations often aggravate these diseases or conditions and lead to premature death. Furthermore, alcoholism itself as a disease has had grave effects on Black males, more so than on white males, in terms of alcoholic conditions such as delirium tremens and alcoholic hallucinosis as well as deaths from liver disease (Rimmer et al., 1971).

There are numerous other consequences of alcohol abuse and alcoholism that can negatively affect the Black male's personal and social life. These include financial losses and mismanagement, job problems or loss of job, conflicts in interpersonal relationships, family problems, and internal conflict or turmoil.

## CASE EXAMPLES OF ALCOHOL ABUSE BY BLACK MALES

During the last five years, I have traveled to approximately twenty states interviewing counselors, medical doctors, nurses, and psychologists of alcoholism treatment programs as well as talking with Black alcoholics. I have also recorded direct observations of public and private incidents in different communities. It may be worth while to share some of these notes here in further exploring the dynamics, practices, and consequences of alcohol abuse among Black males.

• I have observed Black unemployed and working-class males in different regions of the country who drink primarily in small groups—for example,

(1) in pool halls of Milwaukee where beer is served.
(2) on liquor store lots in the Black community of Atlanta,
(3) at Black football games,
(4) in cars chauffeured by teenage boys in south Florida (the men drink while the boys enjoy driving them around town),
(5) at lots adjacent to shopping centers during early morning in Sacramento,
(6) on vacant lots or at storefronts in rural towns, and
(7) in small taverns of many urban cities such as San Francisco and Chicago.

In Washington, D.C., I have observed groups drinking on the sidewalks of populous streets and on the front steps of homes that line such streets. In the same city, I have also observed individual drinking by Black males who conceal their bottles and cans in brown paper bags as they walk, drive, or wait for a bus.

• Based on professional reports and my own direct observations, it seems that a large proportion of Black middle-class men drink in the privacy of their homes, at parties, at public and private dances or parties, at exclusive private clubs, and at restaurants—many times with or in the presence of females. ("Middle-class," as used here, also includes Black male college students who are more prone to drink at apartment and house parties or at small beer taverns.)

• Counselors in a community treatment program in Florida reported the case of a 70-year-old Black male who would come home drunk at night and beat his wife, who was helplessly confined to a wheelchair. Interestingly, the man told the counselors he did not remember ever beating his wife. They concluded he was probably telling the truth and had been suffering from alcoholic blackouts.

• Counselors from the Midwest, whom I interviewed at a conference, reported that many Black men died in the great Detroit riot and other riots of the 1960s because they had been drinking on the streets. They were too drunk to escape gunfire or to realize the danger of the situation, or so drunk that they challenged police verbally or with their own weapons.

• A surgeon from Virginia reported the case of a young Black man who was brought to the emergency room of a hospital. He had been shot in the stomach by his best friend following a gambling session during which both were drinking. The victim had won his friend's money and refused to give it back upon charges of cheating. The victim, who nearly died, reportedly stated, "He went and got his shotgun; I laughed at him because I didn't think he would shoot his best friend and I still don't believe it happened."

• In Jacksonville, Florida, a young woman was reported to have gone on the blocks to get her husband, who had been drinking heavily with "the boys" at a nearby neighborhood liquor store. After a brief argument centering on the husband's refusal to come home, the husband pulled his knife, stabbed his wife thirty-two times, and threw her dead body on top of a nearby car. (This act characterizes the way Black females are often recipients of violence from Black males whose heavy drinking and anger explode into acting-out aggression.)

• An interview with a Black male alcoholic revealed that he would drink all day with other unemployed men who could not find work because his wife told him each day not to come home if he did not find a day's work. He related that he hated to hear her "nagging," so he would return home late at night after she had gone to sleep.


## BARRIERS TO THE TREATMENT OF BLACK MALE ALCOHOLICS

Although some Black male alcohol abusers are problem drinkers with occasional heavy drinking bouts, others are genuine alcoholics who consistently drink heavily and suffer from all the physical, personal, social, and economic problems associated with the disease of alcoholism. The major barrier to treatment for the Black male is his refusal to accept the concept of alcoholism. Blacks repudiate this term and associate it with whites. A number of Black males who drink a fifth of liquor or a six-pack of beer a day are known to react to the suggestion that they might be alcoholics with the statement, "I am not an alcoholic; I can hold my liquor." In the Black community, heavy drinking is expected and even rewarded for those who drink heavily and maintain their control or "cool." For many Black males, heavy drinking is the norm and is perceived as an attribute of manhood and camaraderie.

Another barrier to the treatment of Black males is the refusal of a great many Black males to accept alcoholism treatment or to seek medical help (Harper, 1979; Williams, 1975). Black alcoholics of different communities have drunk themselves to death over a ten- or twenty-year period of hard drinking and resistance to medical help. Counselors with whom I have talked have cited "the problem of getting Black males into treatment" as their major concern, difficulty, and impasse.

Other barriers to the treatment of Black male alcoholics include a resistance by many to accepting help from Alcoholics Anonymous (AA); the scarcity of alcoholism-treatment programs in Black communities; the lack of education about alcohol as a drug and alcoholism as a disease; the inability to find job placement and sources of income and training for unemployed Black males in treatment; the lack of support and understanding of alcoholism treatment on the part of the Black community (including Black churches); the difficulties in effectively treating Black alcoholics; and the lack of commitment of significant policy makers and service-delivery personnel regarding alcohol treatment (Harper, 1979).

## RECOMMENDATIONS

The following are implications and recommendations in terms of practice, research, decision-making, and mental health:

• Alcohol abuse by Black males compared to Black females is much more serious in regard to prevalence and consequences. Thus, it requires greater effort toward prevention and treatment.

• Black males often drink heavily and inappropriately per situation. Therefore, many Black males need to learn how to drink moderately and in what situations to drink. (Such drinking rules may include no drinking on an empty stomach, avoiding drinking contests, learning to sip slowly and not gulp down alcohol, avoiding drinking while or just before driving, avoiding drinking during situations requiring sober behavior such as work or training, and learning not to use alcohol to solve personal problems or for the purpose of attempting to seduce a female.)

• A survey of the literature (Harper & Dawkins, 1976) indicates there is a great need for empirical research on alcohol use involving middle-class Black males and urban Black male youth. (There are no studies in the literature of significance on these two Black male groups).

• There is also a need to examine social and historical factors associated with alcohol abuse among Black males as well as the effect of alcohol use by Black males on their relationship with their women, children, and families.

• Black institutions, community leaders, and professionals must become aware of the impact of alcohol use/abuse on Black males, and consequently take action to minimize alcohol-related fatalities, illnesses, accidents, social problems, and mental health problems that currently harm and destroy the Black community.

# NOTES

1. There is need for up-to-date national surveys on the drinking behaviors of Blacks, including men, as well as a need for up-to-date surveys of urban drinking patterns. The last national surveys of drinking patterns, which included Black subsamples by sex, were Cahalan and Cisin's "American Drinking Practices..." in *The Quarterly Journal of Studies on Alcohol* (1968), and a report (# 2183) by Harris and Associates for the National Institute on Alcohol Abuse and Alcoholism, titled "American Attitudes Toward Alcohol and Alcoholics" (1971).

2. The Scott (1975) study, appearing in *Black Enterprise,* indicates that Blacks buy 30 percent of the Scotch purchased in the United States, the larger proportion apparently purchased by Black males as opposed to Black females.

3. It might be noted that cancer of the esophagus has been associated with a history of heavy drinking (see *Alcohol and Health,* 1974).

# REFERENCES

*Alcohol and health.* Rockville, MD: National Institute on Alcohol Abuse and Alcoholism, 1971.

*Alcohol and health: New knowledge.* Rockville, MD: National Institute on Alcohol Abuse and Alcoholism, 1974.

Benjamin, R. Rural Black folk and alcohol. In F. D. Harper (Ed.), *Alcohol abuse and Black America.* Alexandria, VA: Douglass Publishers, 1976.

Bourne, P. Alcoholism in the urban population. In P. Bourne & R. Fox (Eds.), *Alcoholism progress in research and treatment.* New York: Academic, 1973.

Cahalan, D., & Cisin, I. American drinking practices: Summary of findings from a national probability sample. *Quarterly Journal of Studies on Alcohol,* 1968, *29,* 130-151.

Davis, F. Alcoholism among American Blacks. *Addictions,* 1974, *3,* 8-16.

Globetti, G. Drinking patterns of Negro and white high school students in two Mississippi communities. *Journal of Negro Education,* 1970, *39,* 60-69.

Harper, F. (Ed.). *Alcohol abuse and Black America.* Alexandria, VA: Douglass Publishers, 1976.

Harper, F. *Alcoholism treatment and Black Americans* (DHEW Publication No. ADM-79-853). Rockville,MD: National Institute on Alcohol Abuse and Alcoholism, 1979.

Harper, F., & Hawkins, M. Alcohol and Blacks: Survey of the periodical literature. *British Journal of Addiction,* 1976, *71,* 327-334. (a)

Harper, F., & Hawkins, M. A glossary of alcohol-related terms used by Black Americans (Appendix A). In F. D. Harper (Ed.), *Alcohol Abuse and Black America.* Alexandria, VA: Douglass Publishers, 1976. (b)

Hawkins, M. Alcohol use among Black and white adolescents. In F. D. Harper (Ed.), *Alcohol Abuse and Black America.* Alexandria, VA: Douglass Publishers, 1976.

Larkins, J. *Alcohol and the Negro: Explosive issues.* Zebulon, NC: Recording Publishing, 1965.

Lewis, H. *Blackways of Kent.* Chapel Hill: University of North Carolina Press, 1955.

Maddox, G., & Borinski, E. Drinking behavior of Negro collegians: A study of selected men. *Quarterly Journal of Studies on Alcohol,* 1964, *25,* 651-668.

Maddox, G., & Williams, J. Drinking behavior of Negro collegians. *Quarterly Journal of Studies on Alcohol,* 1968, *29,* 117-129.

Rimmer, J., et al. Alcoholism, sex, socioeconomic status, and race in two hospital samples. *Quarterly Journal of Studies on Alcohol,* 1971, *32,* 942-952.

Robins, L., et al. Drinking behavior of young urban Negro men. *Quarterly Journal of Studies on Alcohol,* 1968, *29,* 657-684.

Scott, G. Blacks in the liquor industry. *Black Enterprise,* 1975, *6*(48), 33-37.

Sterne, M. Drinking patterns and alcoholism among American Negroes. In D. Pittman (Ed.), *Alcoholism.* New York: Harper & Row, 1967.

Williams, R. (Ed.). *Textbook of Black-related diseases.* New York: McGraw-Hill, 1975.

Zax, M., et al. Public intoxication in Rochester. *Quarterly Journal of Studies on Alcohol,* 1964, *25,* 669-678.

# 11

## A DEMOGRAPHIC ANALYSIS
## OF SUICIDE

Robert Davis

All of the statistical patterns associated with suicide suggest that as urban residents of lower-than-average per-capita income, Blacks should be least likely to commit suicide. To a great extent, this is true. However, Black men of the 18-29 age group do not conform to this pattern. While suicide is not a leading cause of death among Blacks, it is the third leading cause of death among Black males (ranking after accidents and homicides) in the 18-29 age group. Young Black men in this age group are three to four times more likely to commit suicide than are young Black women of the same age (Davis, 1978a, 1978b, 1978c). Young adult Black males accounted for 27 percent of the Black suicides nationally between 1970 and 1975, while young adult Black females accounted for only 8.3 percent (Davis, 1978b).

The rate of suicide among young adult Black men has risen over the past decade to the point where it approximates and sometimes surpasses that of their white male cohorts, which is well above average. The increase has been greatest among Black males aged 20-24 (15 percent) and 25-29 (42 percent) [Davis, 1978b]. A striking increase in the incidence of Black male suicide for

TABLE 11.1
Black Male Suicide Rates (per 100,000 persons)
for Selected Years

| Age/Year | 1947 | 1952 | 1956 | 1962 | 1967 | 1972 | 1977 | Percentage Change, 1947-1977 |
|----------|------|------|------|------|------|------|------|------------------------------|
| 20-24 | 7.3 | 6.4 | 7.9 | 11.8 | 14.3 | 26.0 | 21.5 | 194.5 |
| 25-29 | 8.2 | 11.0 | 11.0 | 10.4 | 18.1 | 23.1 | 28.5 | 247.5 |
| 30-34 | 9.5 | 9.1 | 13.9 | 14.0 | 16.9 | 18.4 | 22.5 | 136.8 |
| 35-39 | 10.3 | 9.5 | 10.1 | 13.5 | 14.0 | 18.5 | 15.8 | 53.4 |
| 40-44 | 11.9 | 7.5 | 10.3 | 11.1 | 15.6 | 13.1 | 13.6 | 14.3 |
| 45-49 | 8.5 | 8.0 | 12.2 | 11.6 | 11.7 | 14.6 | 12.9 | 51.8 |
| 50-54 | 9.9 | 11.4 | 10.5 | 12.6 | 11.5 | 11.6 | 10.2 | 3.0 |
| 55-59 | 13.6 | 12.7 | 10.6 | 10.6 | 15.7 | 11.0 | 13.0 | -4.4 |
| 60-64 | 14.0 | 15.8 | 12.9 | 18.9 | 10.4 | 12.9 | 12.4 | -11.4 |

SOURCE: *Vital statistics of the United States,* Vol. II, mortality Part A (Published Annually), Mortality Statistics Branch, Division of Vital Statistics, National Center for Health Statistics, Department of Health, Education and Welfare.

NOTE: Rates for 1972 are based on a 50-percent sample of death certificates.

all but the oldest age groups can be clearly discerned by referring to Table 11.1, which presents Black male suicide rates at five-year intervals for the thirty-year period 1947-1977. In the 20-24 age group, the rate increased dramatically (195 percent) from 7.3 to 21.5 per 100,000 Black males. In the peak suicide age range of 25-29, the rate increased nearly 250 percent from 8.2 to 28.5 per 100,000 Black males. Equally as dramatic is the 136-percent increase experienced by Black males aged 30-34 (9.5 to 22.5).

The data in Table 11.1 clearly indicate that the suicide rate of young Black males has been rising steadily since the early 1960s. Until then, the rate fluctuated with no clearly discernible pattern. Before the 1960s, the highest Black male suicide rate was recorded among the oldest age groups. Generally, the data in Table 11.1 indicate that in the most recent decade, suicide has become a growing menace to young adult Black males. It is seen as particularly acute because in the Black community there is the general belief that suicide is a female problem.

Table 11.2 presents age-specific suicide rates by sex for Blacks residing in standard metropolitan statistical areas (SMSAs) for the period 1970-1975. An

## TABLE 11.2
### Age-Specific Suicide Rates By Sex
### (per 100,000 metropolitan Black population: 125 SMSAs)

|  | 1975 | 1970 | Percentage Change |
|---|---|---|---|
| Both Sexes | 9.9 | 9.7 | 2.1 |
| All Males | 16.7 | 15.6 | 7.1 |
| 18-24 | 19.8 | 17.6 | 12.5 |
| 25-29 | 27.0 | 23.0 | 17.4 |
| 30-34 | 20.8 | 21.6 | -3.7 |
| 35-39 | 16.0 | 15.4 | 3.9 |
| 40-44 | 12.6 | 11.9 | 5.9 |
| 45-49 | 11.9 | 18.2 | -34.6 |
| 50-54 | 9.3 | 12.9 | -27.9 |
| 55-59 | 8.3 | 10.7 | -22.4 |
| 60-64 | 11.4 | 9.4 | 21.3 |
| 65 + | 8.9 | 8.9 | 0.0 |
| Males under 35 | 22.4 | 19.8 | 13.2 |
| Males over 34 | 12.0 | 12.6 | -4.8 |
| All Females | 4.2 | 5.0 | -16.0 |
| 18-24 | 4.2 | 6.8 | -38.2 |
| 25-29 | 7.2 | 7.4 | -2.7 |
| 30-34 | 4.8 | 7.2 | -33.3 |
| 35-39 | 4.3 | 5.0 | -14.0 |
| 40-44 | 3.5 | 4.8 | -27.1 |
| 45-49 | 2.9 | 4.4 | -34.1 |
| 50-54 | 6.1 | 3.9 | 56.4 |
| 55-59 | 2.8 | 1.3 | 115.4 |
| 60-64 | 3.3 | 2.8 | 17.9 |
| 65 + | 2.9 | 3.2 | -9.4 |
| Females under 35 | 5.1 | 6.8 | -25.0 |
| Females over 34 | 3.6 | 3.7 | -2.7 |

SOURCE: Computations by author from 1970 and 1975 Mortality Tapes, 1970 County Group Public Use Sample, and 1976 Survey of Income and Education.

SMSA consists of a county or group of counties having a city or twin cities with a combined population of 50,000 or more. These in conjunction with adjacent counties which are metropolitan in character and economically and socially integrated with the central city constitute the boundaries of an SMSA as defined by census data. Although the trends discerned in Table 11.2 are not necessarily durable and permanent, they indicate that the Black suicide rate increased slightly (2 percent) over the six-year period. Among Black males, the suicide rate *increased* by 7 percent, whereas Black females experienced a 16-percent *decrease* in their rate. Indeed, significant declines occurred among metropolitan Black females at all but the oldest age levels. Consistent with our earlier finding, significant increases occurred among young Black males in their twenties. In the 18-24 age group, the suicide rate increased 13 percent (from 18 to 20 per 100,000) and it increased 17 percent (from 23 to 27 per 100,000) in the peak age range of 25-29. Young Black males experienced a 13-percent increase in their rate while the older Black male rate declined by 5 percent.

## METROPOLITAN TRENDS

Metropolitan areas have always been regarded as locales where suicide in general and Black suicides in particular are most frequent. Indeed, Black male suicide rates that are consistently higher than those for Black females in some of the nation's largest and most populated metropolitan centers are commonplace in the suicide literature. In Table 11.3, attention is focused upon approximately fifty of the largest metropolitan centers, primarily those with a Black population of 100,000 or more. Analysis of these data reveals that among Black males, SMSAs accounting for the highest suicide rates at the beginning of the decade—Pittsburgh (41.3) and Columbus (31.5)—were not leading centers of Black male suicides by the middle of the decade. Indeed, significant decreases in both metropolitan areas' male rates (73 percent and 29 percent) were recorded. By 1975, Cincinnati, Nashville, and Buffalo, with rates of 38, 37, and 32, respectively, per 100,000 adult Black males emerged as forerunners. In Cincinnati, suicide increased by more than 150 percent, while Buffalo recorded the most dramatic increase, 376 percent. Nashville's Black male suicide rate increased by a modest 50 percent over the period.

The lowest Black male rates occurred in the same SMSAs recording the lowest total rates, as expected. In 1970 suicide rates of approximately 4.4 per 100,000 characterized Black males in Shreveport, Norfolk, and Charleston. Mobile, the SMSA with the lowest total rate, had an overall male rate of 3.7 per 100,000. By the mid 1970s, Augusta (2 per 100,000) joined Mobile (4.4 per 100,000) in recording the lowest rates. The Augusta SMSA experienced a 60 percent decrease in its Black male suicide rate between 1970 and 1975, propelling the metropolis from its relatively low 1970 male rate of 5 per 100,000 to the status of the SMSA with the lowest Black male rate by 1975.

*(text continued on p. 187)*

## TABLE 11.3

### Trends in Suicide Among Blacks in Metropolitan Areas[a] Rates per 100,000 Black Population[b] by Sex, 1970 and 1975, and Change for SMSAs by Region

| Rank 1970 | Rank 1975 | SMSA | 1970 Both Sexes | Males | Females | Ratio | 1975 Both Sexes | Males | Females | Ratio | Change Both Sexes | Males | Females |
|---|---|---|---|---|---|---|---|---|---|---|---|---|---|
| | | *SOUTH* | 8.7 | 14.2 | 4.3 | 3.3 | 8.9 | 15.0 | 3.8 | 3.9 | 2.3 | 5.6 | -11.6 |
| 15 | 11 | Baltimore, MD | 10.9 | 17.7 | 5.2 | 3.4 | 11.9 | 23.3 | 2.4 | 9.7 | 9.2 | 31.6 | -53.9 |
| 23 | 9 | Washington, DC-MD-VA | 8.0 | 13.8 | 3.0 | 4.6 | 13.2 | 25.3 | 2.8 | 9.0 | 65.0 | 83.3 | - 6.7 |
| 9 | 17 | Richmond, VA | 14.0 | 17.1 | 11.5 | 1.5 | 10.4 | 8.0 | 12.7 | 0.6 | -25.7 | 53.2 | 10.4 |
| 37 | 35 | Norfolk-Portsmouth, VA | *3.1 | *4.3 | *2.0 | 2.2 | 5.3 | 9.4 | *1.6 | 5.9 | 71.0 | 118.6 | -20.0 |
| 27 | 38 | Greensboro-Winston-Salem High Point, NC | 7.0 | 15.8 | 0.0 | 15.8 | 4.6 | *6.6 | *3.2 | 2.1 | -34.3 | -58.2 | 320.0[c] |
| 26 | 37 | *Charlotte, NC | 7.3 | 8.0 | 6.8 | 1.2 | 4.9 | 7.3 | 2.9 | 0.9 | -86.5 | - 8.8 | -57.4 |
| 34 | 18 | *Columbia, SC | 4.1 | 8.3 | 0.0 | 8.3 | 9.5 | 18.3 | 2.8 | 6.5 | 131.7 | 120.5 | 280.0[c] |
| 32 | 41 | *Augusta, GA | 4.8 | 5.0 | 4.6 | 1.1 | 1.2 | 2.0 | 0.5 | 4.0 | -75.0 | -60.0 | -89.1 |
| 23 | 21 | Charlestown, SC | *8.0 | *4.4 | *11.0 | 0.4 | 8.5 | 17.3 | 0.0 | 17.3 | 6.3 | 293.2 | -100.0 |
| 22 | 32 | Jacksonville, FL | 8.6 | *10.1 | *7.5 | 1.3 | 6.2 | 11.1 | *1.5 | 7.4 | -27.9 | 9.9 | -80.0 |
| 19 | 12 | *Fort Lauderdale-Hollywood, FL | *9.8 | *16.0 | *4.6 | 3.5 | 11.6 | 23.9 | 0.0 | 23.9 | 18.4 | 49.4 | -100.0 |
| 17 | 29 | Miami, FL | 10.3 | 14.8 | *6.7 | 2.2 | 6.7 | 9.3 | *4.1 | 2.3 | -35.0 | -37.2 | -38.8 |

## TABLE 11.3

Trends in Suicide Among Blacks in Metropolitan Areas[a] Rates per 100,000
Black Population[b] by Sex, 1970 and 1975, and Change for SMSAs by Region (Continued)

| Rank 1970 | Rank 1975 | SMSA | 1970 Both Sexes | 1970 Males | 1970 Females | 1970 Ratio | 1975 Both Sexes | 1975 Males | 1975 Females | 1975 Ratio | Change Both Sexes | Change Males | Change Females |
|---|---|---|---|---|---|---|---|---|---|---|---|---|---|
| 10 | 8 | Tampa-St. Petersburg, FL | 13.4 | 22.1 | *6.1 | 3.6 | 14.4 | *22.0 | *8.5 | 2.6 | 7.5 | -0.5 | 39.3 |
| 9 | 14 | Atlanta, GA | 14.0 | 24.6 | 5.8 | 4.2 | 10.9 | 15.8 | 6.9 | 2.3 | -22.1 | -35.8 | 19.0 |
| 22 | 15 | Birmingham, AL | 8.6 | 12.8 | *5.5 | 2.3 | 10.8 | 21.5 | *2.7 | 8.0 | 25.6 | 68.0 | -50.9 |
| 25 | 28 | Memphis, TN-AR | 7.6 | 11.8 | *4.5 | 2.0 | 6.9 | 12.3 | 2.0 | 6.2 | -9.2 | 4.2 | 0.0 |
| 11 | 2 | Nashville-Davison, TN | 13.2 | 25.0 | *3.1 | 8.1 | 21.9 | 37.4 | *10.2 | 3.7 | 65.9 | 49.6 | 229.0 |
| 6 | 6 | Louisville, KY-IN | 15.5 | 32.2 | *3.0 | 10.7 | 14.8 | 19.6 | *10.8 | 1.8 | -4.5 | -39.1 | 260.0 |
| 26 | 30 | Dallas, TX | 7.3 | 9.6 | *5.3 | 1.8 | 6.5 | 12.5 | *1.0 | 12.5 | -11.0 | 3.0 | -81.0 |
| 20 | 26 | *Ft. Worth, TX | 8.9 | 20.0 | 0.0 | 20.0 | 7.4 | 18.2 | 0.0 | 18.2 | -1.7 | -9.0 | 0.0 |
| 35 | 16 | *Shreveport, LA | 3.7 | 4.3 | 3.3 | 1.3 | 10.7 | *11.8 | *9.5 | 1.2 | 189.0 | 174.0 | 188.0 |
| 30 | 34 | *Jackson, MS | 6.1 | 8.8 | 3.8 | 2.3 | 5.6 | 7.7 | 3.9 | 2.0 | -8.2 | -12.5 | 2.6 |
| 36 | 40 | *Mobile, AL | 3.6 | 3.7 | 3.6 | 1.0 | 2.7 | 4.4 | 1.2 | 3.7 | -25.0 | 18.9 | -66.7 |
| 7 | 36 | Baton Rouge, LA | 14.7 | 28.2 | *3.8 | 7.4 | *5.2 | *10.1 | 0.0 | 10.1 | -64.6 | -64.2 | -100.0 |
| 24 | 13 | New Orleans, LA | 7.8 | 16.7 | *1.0 | 16.7 | 11.5 | 21.5 | *3.0 | 7.2 | 47.0 | 29.0 | 200.0 |
| 28 | 22 | Houston, TX | 6.8 | 10.8 | *3.4 | 3.2 | 8.2 | 13.4 | 3.7 | 3.6 | 21.0 | 24.1 | 8.8 |

## TABLE 11.3
### Trends in Suicide Among Blacks in Metropolitan Areas,[a] Rates per 100,000 Black Population[b] by Sex, 1970 and 1975, and Change for SMSAs by Region (Continued)

| Rank 1970 | Rank 1975 | SMSA | 1970 Both Sexes | 1970 Males | 1970 Females | 1970 Ratio | 1975 Both Sexes | 1975 Males | 1975 Females | 1975 Ratio | Change Both Sexes | Change Males | Change Females |
|---|---|---|---|---|---|---|---|---|---|---|---|---|---|
| | | *NORTH CENTRAL* | 12.1 | 18.5 | 6.4 | 3.0 | 10.1 | 17.4 | 4.5 | 3.9 | -16.5 | -5.9 | -30.0 |
| 13 | 33 | Indianapolis, IN | 11.6 | 17.1 | *7.0 | 2.4 | 5.9 | *10.1 | *2.2 | 4.6 | -49.1 | -40.9 | -68.6 |
| 18 | 1 | Cincinnati, OH | 9.9 | 15.1 | *5.8 | 2.6 | 22.2 | 38.0 | 10.9 | 3.5 | 124.2 | 151.7 | 87.9 |
| 16 | 23 | Dayton, OH | 10.8 | *12.0 | *9.9 | 1.2 | 8.1 | 16.7 | 0.0 | 16.7 | -25.0 | 39.2 | -100.0 |
| 3 | 31 | Columbus, OH | 18.4 | 31.5 | *3.9 | 8.1 | 6.3 | *8.6 | *4.5 | 1.9 | -65.8 | -72.7 | 15.8 |
| 5 | 6 | Cleveland, OH | 16.0 | 25.6 | 8.4 | 3.1 | 14.8 | 24.3 | 6.1 | 4.0 | -7.5 | -5.3 | -27.4 |
| 13 | 3 | Detroit, MI | 11.6 | 18.3 | 5.8 | 3.2 | 16.8 | 29.6 | 7.2 | 4.1 | 44.8 | 61.8 | 24.1 |
| 21 | 21 | Chicago, IL | 8.8 | 15.2 | 3.6 | 4.2 | 8.5 | 15.0 | 3.6 | 4.2 | -3.4 | -1.3 | -14.3 |
| 4 | 27 | Gary, IN | 16.2 | 27.4 | *6.2 | 4.4 | *7.3 | *12.7 | *3.2 | 4.0 | -54.9 | -53.7 | -48.4 |
| 14 | 17 | Milwaukee, WI | 11.1 | *11.6 | *10.6 | 1.1 | 9.6 | 17.1 | *2.6 | 6.6 | -13.5 | -47.4 | -75.5 |
| 12 | 24 | Kansas City, MO-KS | 12.6 | 18.0 | *8.3 | 2.2 | 7.7 | 11.6 | *4.0 | 2.9 | -38.9 | -35.6 | -51.8 |
| 20 | 39 | St. Louis, MO-IL | 6.1 | 12.0 | *1.7 | 7.1 | 4.2 | 7.4 | *1.4 | 5.3 | -31.2 | -38.3 | -17.7 |
| | | *NORTHEAST* | 9.0 | 18.9 | 3.8 | 5.0 | 13.0 | 26.1 | 3.6 | 7.3 | 44.4 | 38.1 | -5.3 |
| 29 | 20 | Boston, MA | 6.3 | *11.7 | *2.2 | 5.3 | 9.0 | 17.4 | 2.3 | 7.6 | 42.9 | 48.7 | 4.6 |
| 33 | 4 | Buffalo, NY | *4.7 | *6.7 | *3.0 | 2.2 | 15.5 | 31.9 | *5.1 | 6.3 | 229.8 | 376.1 | 70.0 |

## TABLE 11.3

Trends in Suicide Among Blacks in Metropolitan Areas,[a] Rates per 100,000 Black Population[b] by Sex, 1970 and 1975, and Change for SMSAs by Region (Continued)

| Rank 1970 | Rank 1975 | SMSA | 1970 Both Sexes | Males | Females | Ratio | 1975 Both Sexes | Males | Females | Ratio | Change Both Sexes | Males | Females |
|---|---|---|---|---|---|---|---|---|---|---|---|---|---|
| 31 | 25 | New York, NY | 5.2 | 9.8 | 1.7 | 5.8 | 7.5 | 13.4 | 3.3 | 4.1 | 44.2 | 36.7 | 94.1 |
| 1 | 10 | Pittsburgh, PA | 21.5 | 41.3 | *5.3 | 7.8 | 12.9 | 29.3 | *1.5 | 19.5 | -40.0 | -29.1 | -71.7 |
| 23 | 19 | Newark, NJ | 8.0 | 11.3 | 5.4 | 2.1 | 9.4 | 17.8 | 3.5 | 5.1 | 17.5 | 57.5 | -35.2 |
| 25 | 20 | *Paterson-Clifton-Passaic, NJ | 7.6 | 17.3 | 0.0 | 17.3 | 9.0 | 20.1 | 0.0 | 20.1 | 18.4 | 16.0 | 0.0 |
| 19 | 7 | Philadelphia, PA | 9.8 | 15.3 | 5.4 | 2.8 | 14.5 | 26.4 | 6.1 | 4.3 | 48.0 | 73.0 | 13.0 |
| | | *WEST* | 17.5 | 23.8 | 12.5 | 1.9 | 15.2 | 20.7 | 9.8 | 2.1 | -13.0 | -13.0 | -22.0 |
| 2 | 4 | Los Angeles-Long Beach, CA | 21.4 | 25.3 | 18.3 | 1.4 | 15.5 | 21.5 | 9.8 | 2.2 | -28.0 | -15.0 | -46.0 |
| 8 | 5 | San Francisco-Oakland, CA | 14.1 | 22.3 | 6.7 | 2.2 | 14.9 | 19.8 | 9.8 | 2.0 | 6.0 | -11.0 | 15.0 |

SOURCE: Computations are by the author from 1970 and 1975 Mortality Tapes, 1970 County Group Public Use Sample, and 1976 Survey of Income and Education.

* Rates are based on less than 5 cases of suicide.

a. Only SMSAs with 40,000 or more adult Black population in 1970 and 1975, and enough cases of suicide to allow the calculation of stable rates.

b. Since suicide is rare under age 18, all Blacks below this age were excluded from the population of each SMSA. The rates then reflect suicide among adult Blacks 18 and above.

c. These increases are statistical artifacts resulting from the fact that no Black female suicides occurred in 1970.

Turning to Black females, we find that the Richmond, Virginia, SMSA emerges as a consistent "high-risk" area for Black females. Rates of 11.5 and 12.7 per 100,000 were recorded between 1970 and 1975, an increase of 10 percent. The Los Angeles-Long Beach urban area distinguished itself by recording the highest Black female rate known to this investigator in 1970, 18.3 per 100,000. By 1975, however, the rate had decreased 46 percent to approximately 10 per 100,000 adult Black females. Charleston, the SMSA with the third highest female rate in 1970 (11 per 100,000), recorded no mortality among Black females by suicide in 1975. Cincinnati, which reported 10.9, Louisville, which reported 10.8, Nashville, which reported 10.2, and Richmond, which reported 11.5 per 100,000 were the SMSAs with the highest Black female rates in 1975. Cincinnati earned the title of the metropolitan area in which Blacks experienced the greatest risk of suicide in 1975. Earlier, attention was directed to the fact that the highest rates for the total female and male population were found in Cincinnati. It is no surprise, then, to find the second highest female rate in Cincinnati in 1975, an increase of 90 percent over the past six years. The Nashville and Louisville SMSAs recorded more dramatic increases in their rates, but the actual number of suicides is relatively small in both cities at the measured intervals.

Looking at SMSAs with the lowest adult Black female rates, we find that no deaths from suicide among Black females occurred in four of the SMSAs in 1970 (Paterson, Columbia, Fort Worth, and Greensboro-Winston-Salem-High Point). Three others, New Orleans (1 per 100,000), New York (1.7 per 100,000), and St. Louis (1.7 per 100,000), had extremely low rates. In 1975, the number of SMSAs with no Black female suicides increased to six with Fort Worth, Texas, and Paterson, New Jersey, continuing to be metropolitan areas in which Black females are relatively immune to mortality due to self-destruction. Charleston, Fort Lauderdale, Baton Rouge, and Dayton are the remaining four SMSAs. Although the Charleston SMSA had the third highest rate for Black females in 1970, the actual numbers involved are relatively small. Similarly, the Fort Lauderdale, Baton Rouge, and Dayton 1970 rates are based on relatively small numbers of Black female suicides. Indeed, the reduction of these rates to zero merely reflects the fact that from 1970 to 1975 the actual incidence of suicide decreased by two or three cases. Hence, Black females in these urban areas represent a traditionally low suicide-prone group.

Additionally, of the 46 SMSAs in the 1975 sample, 13 had female rates of less than 2 per 100,000. In addition to the six mentioned above, Augusta,

Norfolk, Jacksonville, Dallas, Mobile, Pittsburgh, and St. Louis were the most noticeable. In all of these SMSAs, rates were low in 1970.

The difference in relative rates by sex among Blacks in this sample of SMSAs reflects trends indicating that committing suicide is something that males continue to do more often than females. Data in Table 11.3 indicate that the gap between the suicide rates of males and females has been widening among metropolitan Blacks. Since the beginning of the decade, the ratio of male to female suicide increased 18 percent in the South (from 3:1 to 4:1), 30 percent in the North Central region (from 3:1 to 4:1), and 46 percent in the Northeast (from 5:1 to 7:1). In the West, the ratio remained relatively constant at 2:1, reflecting the narrowest margin between the sexes in the country. In 1970, suicides were most demographically distributed between the sexes in Los Angeles, Charleston, Milwaukee, Dayton, Mobile, Shreveport, Jacksonville, Augusta, and Charlotte. Black males exceeded their female counterparts in suicide rates by ratios ranging from 11:1 to 20:1 in Greensboro-Winston-Salem-High Point, Louisville, Fort Worth, New Orleans, and Paterson. By 1975, there were only three SMSAs (Richmond, Charlotte, and Shreveport) in which suicide was demographically distributed. The highest differentials were found in Charleston, Fort Lauderdale, Dallas, Fort Worth, Baton Rouge, Dayton, Pittsburgh, and Paterson. Clearly, a comparison of the SMSAs with the highest differentials over the six years indicates that the ratio is most unequal in Fort Worth, Texas, and Paterson, New Jersey. On the other hand, the gap between the sexes is narrowest in Charlotte, North Carolina, and Shreveport, Louisiana.

## CHANGE BETWEEN 1970 AND 1975

The interesting pattern of trends observed thus far can be further explored by focusing on changes in metropolitan Black suicide during the first half of the 1970s. The last column of Table 11.3 shows changes for each of the 46 SMSAs between 1970 and 1975. In the metropolitan South, overall SMSA rates remained relatively constant. Rates increased slightly among males and declined by 11.6 percent among females. Twenty-one (46 percent) of the metropolitan areas experienced increases in their total rates in comparison to 25 (54 percent) that experienced decreases. The 1970 and 1975 changes were most pronounced in Columbia and Shreveport. The dramatic rises in their rates are of concern, but the actual numbers involved are relatively small. The most significant changes occurred in Washington, D.C., Nashville, and New Orleans, where there have been marked increases in both rates and percentages of suicides over the six-year period. The respective rates of increase are 65, 66, and 47 percent. Using similar logic, the 65-percent decline in the Baton Rouge SMSA is more significant than the noticeable decreases in Charlotte and Augusta.

Among southern Black males residing in metropolitan areas, large increases occurred in Charleston, Shreveport, Columbia and Norfolk. However, increases in Washington, D.C., Birmingham, Nashville, and Fort Lauderdale are of more substantive interest. For example, the suicide rate among adult Black males in Washington, D.C., rose from 14 per 100,000 in 1970 to 25 per 100,000 in 1975, an increase of 83 percent. Birmingham's rate increased by nearly 70 percent and Black males experienced a 50-percent increase in Nashville and Fort Lauderdale.

The suicide rate decreased by slightly more than half in Richmond and Greensboro-Winston-Salem-High Point. Decreases of 60 percent in Augusta and 64 percent in Baton Rouge were the largest observed. In both instances, relatively few cases of suicide were involved, but the decline in Baton Rouge is more meaningful given the size of its rates. Moderate rates of approximately 40 percent occurred in Louisville, Atlanta, and Miami.

Looking at changes among Black females in the metropolitan South, the problem of small numbers is again encountered when attempting to explain dramatic increases. Black females simply *do not* have a high incidence of suicide. The large increases in Greensboro-Winston-Salem-High Point, Columbia, and Fort Worth are statistical artifacts resulting from the fact that *no* female mortality due to suicide occurred among Blacks in these SMSAs in 1970. In four other SMSAs, Nashville, Louisville, Shreveport, and New Orleans, the number of Black female suicides is less than 5 in both time periods. For example, in 1970 there was only 1 recorded suicide among Black females in Nashville and Louisville. By 1975 the number increased to 4 in both SMSAs.

The most noticeable declines occurred in Baton Rouge, Fort Lauderdale, and Charleston. In each instance, the number of Black female suicides decreased from less than 5 to 0, registering decreases of 100 percent. Fairly large declines (50-90 percent) were recorded in Dallas, Mobile, Birmingham, Jacksonville, Augusta, and Charlotte. However, the actual numbers involved are small in both 1970 and 1975. Although the Black female suicide rate decreased by 54 percent in the Washington, D.C., metropolitan area, the actual number of suicides increased slightly (from 7 to 8) between 1970 and 1975. Increases in the Black female population over the six-year period accounted for this anomaly. Finally, during both periods no Black female suicides were recorded in the Fort Worth metropolitan area, distinguishing it as the southern SMSA in which Black females are most immune to self-destruction.

Among Blacks residing in metropolitan areas of the North Central United States, suicide rates declined by 17 percent among the total adult Black population, by 30 percent among Black females, and by 6 percent among Black males. Cincinnati and Detroit were the only SMSAs in which increases occurred for the total adult Black population. These were 124 percent and 45 percent, respectively. The remaining metropolitan areas experienced declines ranging from a low of 3 percent in Chicago to a high of 66 percent in Columbus.

Gary, Indianapolis, and Columbus recorded the greatest declines in their total rates. Suicide rates declined by two-thirds in Columbus (18 to 6 per 100,000), slightly more than half in Gary, Indiana (16 to 7 per 100,000), and by approximately half in Indianapolis (11.6 to 6 per 100,000). A decrease of 40 percent occurred in Kansas City (12.6 to 7.7 per 100,000).

As noted earlier, Cincinnati, Ohio—the top-ranking SMSA in 1975—recorded the most dramatic increase over the six-year period. Among adult Blacks, the suicide rate more than doubled, from 10 per 100,000 in 1970 to 22 per 100,000 in 1975. In Detroit, the rate increased less dramatically, from 11.6 to 16.8 per 100,000. It should be noted that Detroit was also a leading center of metropolitan Black suicide in 1975.

The most dramatic changes among Black males occurred in two of Ohio's largest metropolitan areas. The suicide rate increased 150 percent in Cincinnati (15 to 38 per 100,000) and decreased by three-quarters (31.5 to 8.6 per 100,000) in Columbus. The rate increased 62 percent (18 to 30 per 100,000) in Detroit and declined by approximately 50 percent in Gary (27 to 13 per 100,000). More moderate declines, 36 and 38 percent, occurred in Kansas City (18 to 38 per 100,000) and St. Louis (12 to 7 per 100,000).

Cincinnati and Detroit are clearly the metropolitan areas accounting for most of the increase in suicide among adult Blacks residing in the North Central region of the country. Hence, it is no surprise to find that the Black female rate increased 88 percent in Cincinnati (6 to 11 per 100,000). However, determining the metropolitan areas in which the most significant declines occurred is more problematic. Nine of the SMSAs in 1970 and seven in 1975 had Black female rates that were based on less than five cases of suicide. Moreover, of those nine in 1970, six had noticeable declines in their rates by 1975. Dayton, for example, which had *no* Black female suicides in 1975 and only three cases in 1970, experienced a decrease of 100 percent. In fact, six of the nine SMSAs had declines of 40 percent or more. Clearly, a comparison of the SMSAs with noticeable decreases in their female rates reveals that none of the metropolitan areas experienced significant declines in their rates other than, possibly, Dayton, Ohio.

In the metropolitan Northeast, the pattern of change observed in the adult Black suicide rate is one of an increasing trend, though rates declined slightly among females. The exploration of changes by region indicates that over the six-year span, adult Black males experienced the sharpest rises in their rates in the Northeast. Although the Black female rate declined, the drop is the smallest among all regions. Overall, rates increased nearly 50 percent among adult Blacks (9 to 13 per 100,000) between 1970 and 1975. As would be expected, Black males experienced the greatest increase, 38 percent (19 to 26 per 100,000), with the Black female rate decreasing 5 percent, from 3.8 to 3.5 per 100,000.

The most dramatic increases occurred in the Buffalo SMSA, where the adult Black rate rose from 4.7 to 15.5 per 100,000, an increase of 230 percent. Black males living in this urban area experienced the greatest increase recorded among the 46 SMSAs (376 percent), from 7 per 100,000 in 1970 to 32 per 100,000 in 1975. Black female rates increased less radically (70 percent), from 3 to 5 per 100,000. These rates are based on fewer than five cases at both intervals. Similarly, the dramatic rise in rates among the total population and the male population cannot be cited without reference to the relatively small number of actual cases of suicide occurring in 1970. For example, among adult Blacks, the frequency of suicide rose from 4 in 1970 to 10 in 1975. The increases in the Buffalo SMSA are worthy of attention, but the actual numbers involved do not warrant the amount of public concern implied by the magnitude of the change.

The New York metropolitan area recorded an increase of nearly 100 percent in the rate of Black female suicides. The rate rose from less than 2 per 100,000 in 1970 to 3.3 per 100,000 in 1975. This change represents a marked increase in actual cases of Black female suicide. The only instance of a decline in suicide rates for Blacks living in the metropolitan Northeast occurred in 1975 in Newark, where the female rate declined by 35 percent, and in Pittsburgh, where rates declined by 72 percent. As in Fort Worth, Black females in the Paterson, New Jersey, SMSA are relatively immune to suicide. No suicides occurred among Black females in either 1970 or 1975.

Boston, New York, and Philadelphia experienced moderate increases in both their total female and their total male rates. Philadelphia, the SMSA with the second largest increase in the Northeast, experienced increases of 48 percent (10 to 14.5 per 100,000) and 73 percent (15 to 26 per 100,000), respectively. Adult Blacks living in New York had an increase in their rates of 44 percent (5 to 7.5 per 100,000), with the Black male rate increasing 37 percent (10 to 13 per 100,000). In the Boston SMSA, total rates increased 43 percent (6 to 9 per 100,000), and Black male rates increased 49 percent (12 to 17 per 100,000). Finally, the Black male rate in Newark increased 58 percent, from 11 per 100,000 in 1970 to 18 per 100,000 in 1975.

As in the North Central region, suicide rates in the West declined for each category for which rates are shown. The bulk of the Black population residing in western metropolitan areas lived in either the Los Angeles-Long Beach or the San Francisco-Oakland SMSAs. Although rates decreased in both areas, the declines were generally sharpest among SMSAs located in the North Central United States.

The suicide rate declined 13 percent among all adult Blacks and also among Black males. The total rate decreased from 17.5 to 15 per 100,000, and the Black male rate moved from 24 to 21 per 100,000. The largest drop (22 percent) occurred among Black females. In 1970, their rate per 100,000 was nearly 13, but by 1975, the rate had slipped to 10 per 100,000 adult Black females.

Los Angeles-Long Beach, the western SMSA with the sharpest drop in rates, recorded an overall rate decrease of 28 percent (21.4 to 15.5 per 100,000), whereas the San Francisco-Oakland rate decreased by only 6 percent (14.0 to 15 per 100,000) in the latter. Declines in male rates are fairly similar in both metropolitan areas: 15 percent (25.3 to 21.5 per 100,000) in the former, and 11 percent (22.3 to 20 per 100,000) in the latter. Finally, Black females in the San Francisco-Oakland SMSA experienced a 15 percent (6.7 to 9.8 per 100,000) increase in their suicide rates. Los Angeles-Long Beach, on the other hand, recorded a 46 percent (18.3 to 9.8 per 100,000) decrease in rates of suicide among Black females.

## DISCUSSION AND CONCLUSIONS

The foregoing analysis of the characteristics and trends of metropolitan-area adult Black suicide during the first half of this decade reveals that suicide within the Black community, as among whites, is primarily a male problem. The data indicate that students of suicide, mental health practitioners, and social commentators should direct their energies toward understanding the dynamics of what has become the third leading cause of death among young adult Black males in their twenties. Analysis of death rates from suicide per 100,000 adult Blacks residing in approximately 50 metropolitan areas reveals that (1) the gap between the suicide rates of males and females has been widening in every region of the country except the West, (2) rates declined among metropolitan Black females in each region of the country, and (3) among Black males, rates *declined* in the West and North Central regions and *increased* in the South and Northeast.

In general, male rates are higher than female rates, and the amount of difference varies from one metropolitan area to another. However, the sex ratio remained practically constant in the West, where males and females are equally exposed to factors producing suicide. The highest sex differentials are found in Fort Worth, Texas, and Paterson, New Jersey, where no Black female deaths from suicide occurred. Since the beginning of the decade, the ratio of male to female suicide increased by nearly one-fifth in the South, by almost a third in the North Central region, and by approximately half in the metropolitan Northeast. Indeed, the Black female suicide rate declined in every region of the country between 1970 and 1975. Changes among Black males, however, were not as consistent and displayed a mixture of trends.

The existence of Black male suicide rates that are consistently higher than those for Black females in metropolitan centers such as Greensboro-Winston-Salem-High Point, New Orleans, Louisville, Charleston, Fort Lauderdale, Dallas, Baton Rouge, Dayton, Pittsburgh, Fort Worth, and Paterson suggests that external circumstances are influencing one sex more than the other. Is it possible that Black females have a greater resistance to suicide because of their higher participation rate and involvement in the traditional institutional structures, groups, and relationships within the Black community (e.g., church, PTA, sororities)? This differential involvement may expose Black females to community support systems that provide participation, purpose, and a sense of belonging. They also offer the possibility of cooperative and self-help approaches to stressful situations that might otherwise lead to self-destruction.

Previous research by this investigator suggested a number of reasons for expecting a weakening of social relations to be strongly related to an increase in Black suicide (Davis, 1978a). Attention was focused on the presumed detrimental consequences of becoming isolated (in part or entirely) from social support systems within the Black community, at either the family, group, communal, or institutional level. The results of this study suggest that improved social status (proxy-education) and isolation from protective social networks (proxy-migration) are strongly · related to the increase in suicide among young (20-34) Blacks. Examination of recent research on the labor market position of young Black males and a review of the established literature on the relationship between social mobility and isolation lend further support to this conclusion. Detailed investigation of the National Longitudinal Survey has found that the occupational position of young Black men entering the job market after 1964 is essentially the same as that of young whites with similar premarket background characteristics (Hall & Kasten, 1973). The 1973 Occupational Change in a Generation Survey has shown marked advances in the relative position of Blacks, particularly those aged 25-34, compared to the 1962 survey (Hauser & Featherman, 1975). Several studies oriented toward other labor-market problems have found that the traditionally large negative impact on one's economic status of being Black has become much smaller than in the past (Astin, 1978; Epstein, 1977; Viscusi, 1976; Wilson, 1978). Hence, young, talented, highly educated and skilled Blacks (primarily "prime-aged Black males" 20 to 44) were most likely to experience upward mobility via the social and economic progress of the 1960s and early 1970s. A fact that has probably not escaped the attentive reader is that this prime age range (20-44) corresponds to the age group in which the majority of Black suicides (mostly males) occur (20-34).

There is also an established body of literature contending that social mobility results in isolation, or at least in the disruption of integration of primary and secondary group relations (Blau, 1956; Durkheim, 1951; Janowitz, 1956; Litwak, 1960; Sorokin, 1927). The disruptive tendency of upward mobility for interpersonal relations received considerable attention from Blau (1956: 290):

> The upwardly mobile individual will have to give up old ties to gain status through association with higher-prestige groups and to avoid being identified with his former group. He may, however, find it difficult to establish extensive ties with individuals on the new level due to a reluctance on their part to accept him as an equal.

Hence, the Black community as a caring and protective system is likely to be less available to young, upwardly mobile Black males. When these young Black males, because of racial differences, envy, personal crises, and the like, begin to experience recurrent stressful social situations, they must do so without access to stable, positive social networks within the Black community.

In addition to the young and upwardly mobile, less fortunate Black males who view their peers' success as an indicator of their self-worth (i.e., if they made it, *I* can make it) internalize their failure and frustration and become isolated from their families, communities, and social institutions, thereby increasing the likelihood of self-destruction. Thus, it seems plausible to conclude that Black male suicide is best explained by institutional and sociological variables highlighting the character of institutions, social patterns, and networks that derive from them.

## REFERENCES

Astin, A. *Four critical years.* San Francisco: Josey-Bass, 1978.

Blau, P. Social mobility and interpersonal relations. *American Sociological Review,* 1956, *21,* 13-18.

Davis, R. *Black suicide and the relational system: Theoretical and empirical implications of communal and familial ties* (Discussion Paper 481-78). Madison: University of Wisconsin, Institute for Research on Poverty, 1978 (a).

Davis, R. *Black suicide in the seventies: Current trends and perspectives* (Discussion Paper 483-78). Madison: University of Wisconsin, Institute for Research on Poverty, 1978 (b).

Davis, R. Black suicide in the seventies: Current trends. *Suicide and Life-Threatening Behavior,* 1978, *8*(3) (c).

Durkheim, E. *Suicide.* New York: Free Press, 1951.

Epstein, W. *Schooling and occupational decisions.* (Doctoral dissertation, Harvard University, 1977).

Hall, R., & Kasten, R. The relative occupational success of Blacks and whites. *Brookings Papers on Economic Activity,* 1973, *3,* 781-798.

Hauser, R., & Featherman, D. *Racial inequalities and socioeconomic achievement in the U.S.* (Discussion Paper 275-75). Madison: University of Wisconsin, Institute for Research on Poverty, 1975.

Janowitz, M. Some consequences of social mobility in the United States. *Transactions of the Third World Congress of Sociology,* 1956, *3*(4), 191-201.

Litwak, E. Occupational mobility and extended family cohesion. *American Sociological Review,* 1960, *25,* 9-21.

Sorokin, P. *Social mobility.* New York: Harper & Row, 1927.

Viscusi, W. *Employment hazards: An investigation of market performance.* (Doctoral dissertation, Harvard University, 1976).

Wilson, W. *The declining significance of race.* Chicago: University of Chicago Press, 1978.

# PART IV
# BLACK MEN AND INSTITUTIONS

In this section, the main question asked is, How do Black men relate to major social institutions? In the opening chapter, James M. Patton examines the impact of the public school on the Black male. He asserts that the same values and behaviors that confront Black males in the broader society are perpetuated in the school system, and that they impact negatively on the achievement and self-concept of Black males. Moreover, he identifies several mechanisms such as norm-referenced tests, the lack of male role models/ teachers, and suspensions, which are widely used to relegate Black males to low-status positions in the educational system. In order to improve the educational opportunities for Black males, Patton suggests the development and institution of value premises for the school system that emphasize valuing interpersonal relationships, fostering self and group development, developing a sense of self and collective respect, and recognizing the need for a unitary, holistic development.

In examining the educational experience of Black men in colleges and universities, John E. Fleming states that Black Americans have traditionally understood and stressed the importance of education to their survival, their growth, and their success in various life activities. After tracing the involvement of Black Americans in higher education and the development of affirmative action, the author contends that predominantly white institutions of higher education have not been sincere about their expressed desires of training Black graduate students or recruiting and hiring Black faculty members. Fleming concludes his chapter by saying that effective, vigorously enforced affirmative action programs are needed to ensure that Blacks achieve equal opportunity in academia.

Although Blacks constitute approximately 12 percent of the U.S. population, it is well known that they are disproportionately represented among the nation's state and federal prisons. In reviewing this problem, Roi D. Townsey asserts that, although the incarceration of Black men throughout the United States is extreme, harsh, and brutal, it is not a new or faltering predicament confronting Black males in general and poor Black males in particular. Citing the results of numerous research studies and judicial decisions, the author states that this dilemma is largely attributable to racial discrimination and the lack of the effective assistance of legal counsel, as well as to the absence of standards, rules, or guidelines for making sentencing decisions. As a result, Townsey claims that Black persons convicted of crimes generally receive harsher sentences than do white persons convicted of the same crimes and who have similar criminal histories.

Bogart R. Leashore, in Chapter 15 is concerned with how social welfare agencies and organizations have treated Black men. He maintains that these organizations have traditionally viewed the Black male paternalistically, pathologically, or with disinterest. Due to the negative attitudes of these agencies, Leashore asserts that Black men are more likely to utilize informal resources, such as family and friends, than they are to seek professional or formal social services. Leashore concludes that social service agencies, organizations, and providers must address several important issues in order to have a positive effect on the lives and well-being of Black men. Foremost among these issues are the role racism and the Anglo-European framework play in service delivery, the relative merits of various service approaches for Black men, the participation of Black males as service providers and as clients, and the development of objective measures by which the provision and outcome of services to Black men can be assessed.

James S. Tinney closes this section with an article on the role of religion in the life of Black men. The author identifies and discusses some of the positive benefits Black men have received from the church and some of the possible reasons for the current low participation rate of Black men in the church. Tinney notes that the Black church has provided opportunities for the Black male that have been denied him in the larger society, and has served as a springboard for his entering leadership roles in education, politics, and journalism. In addition, he claims that the church has been instrumental in developing theologians, philosophers, professors, and writers. The author notes that currently a large number of Black men seem indifferent or hostile to the church. Among the possible reasons for this reaction that Tinney identifies are the following: (1) the church's failure to provide a meaningful role for laypersons; (2) its encouragement of psychological passivity among men—its call to nonviolence, pacifism, nonassertiveness, and so forth; and (3) its failure to develop comprehensive ministries to college and university campuses, to jails, and to the armed services.

# 12

## THE BLACK MALE'S STRUGGLE
## FOR AN EDUCATION

James M. Patton

It should be no surprise to most scholars that there is a paucity of conceptual and empirical literature addressing issues important to the proper elementary and secondary education of the Black male in America. When informed attention has been focused on this subject, the resulting commentary usually reveals an educational system that limits the positive growth of a majority of Black males. Moreover, much of the literature designed to explain the "educational lag" of Blacks in general exists within what Williams (1974) refers to as counterfeit paradigms and assumptions that measure the abilities of Black children vis-à-vis norm-referenced tests and curricula based on Anglocentric traits.[1] Deviations from these norms on the part of Blacks have been interpreted as essentially negative or inferior rather than as differences.

The educational system does not exist in a vacuum. It is an integral part of the social, political, and economic fabric of American society. As the primary societal socializing agent, elementary and secondary education have impacted the achievement, self-concept, and selected dispositional aspects of the Black male as part of a racial whole. The feministic, non-Black structure and dominance of public education, particularly the elementary schools, indicates an essentially negative influence. It is this ad hoc sociocultural environment that has led to dangerous mislabeling and negative tracking of many Black males. It is the author's contention that the educational system as we know it in the United States will have to be altered dramatically if it is to contribute to the total development of Black people in general and the Black male in particular.

There are useful and innovative approaches by which to develop a liberating educational system that mirrors and perpetuates the world views, values, and strengths of Black culture. This system is grounded in the context of the Black experience and is based on African-oriented philosophical assumptions. These assumptions constitute a frame of reference that (1) places a premium on harmony among people and their internal and external environments, (2) fosters self and group development through nurturing the feeling mode, and (3) recognizes the need for unitary, holistic development of Black people. If acknowledged and assimilated, these ideas could ensure the positive and determined lifelong development of a majority of Black males.

## CONTEXTUAL SETTING

The effectiveness or ineffectiveness of education for the Black male can be understood only in the context of its interaction with the social, political, and economic order. The discerning observer understands that schools are largely middle-class enclaves, staffed by middle-class teachers, and designed to inculcate middle-class values to a middle-class white America and to middle-class Black emulators (Picott, 1974). Schools are used to screen and control the future life chances of those who attend them. Despite public declarations and representations of democracy, public educational institutions are basically structured to reflect, confirm, and perpetuate the social order that created them. As such, the purposes of elementary and secondary schools in America have been to systematically inculcate attitudes that reflect the dominant social and industrial values (Katz, 1971).

Several devices are widely used to relegate Black males to low-status positions in the educational system. Norm-referenced tests, other assessment devices, and labeling/tracking tactics are easily recognized as means by which to maintain the system in order to perpetuate the status quo and to limit the life progression of Black males. But Blacks, in particular Black males, are a hearty people. In spite of the negative impact of the educational system on the collective Black male,[2] he has survived. Among the more notable examples of survivors have been Frederick Douglass, Martin Luther King, Jr., Richard Wright, and W.E.B. DuBois. The quantity and quality of Black male survival, however, should not be measured by the ability of a few heroic exceptions who excelled under difficult circumstances. The better measure is the ability of the masses of Black males to achieve.

# THE BLACK MALE AND THE
# EDUCATIONAL SYSTEM

Although education as a means by which to obtain equality of opportunity has been the hope of Black Americans, the historical policy toward Blacks in general and Black males in particular has been described by Jones (1979) as one of "compulsory and voluntary ignorance." Until the end of the Civil War, the prevailing educational policy in the South was one of exclusion for Blacks. Most states employed statutory provisions prohibiting individuals from teaching Black people. As a result, Carter G. Woodson (1968) found that by 1860 only 10 percent of all adult Blacks in the South had obtained some basic elements of an education. Despite historical perceptions, the North was not much better, as that area long practiced separate but unequal education as a model for educating Black people (Jones, 1979).

The 1954 Brown v. the Board of Education of Topeka, Kansas decision was to many Blacks a symbol of renewed hope that an equal educational opportunity would become a reality and that subsequent life chances would be enhanced for them. The struggle for a liberating education commenced during these early days, but remains elusive even today. Statistical research supports the conclusion that elementary and secondary education generally have not worked to the advantage of Blacks, and have been even less advantageous for the collective Black male. The cumulative gap between Blacks and whites in educational achievement levels begins with kindergarten and increases through the postsecondary years (Williams, 1974). Selected research conclusions are indicative of the educational system's failure of Black students.

Before venturing into such findings, a caveat concerning their application and usefulness is warranted. Continuous research that has historically shown Black males to lag in academic achievement, development of a positive self-concept, and other key growth areas has the potential of becoming a self-fulfilling prophecy, since the research applies or transfers data collected from an individual or a specific group to the greater body. Yet, such research does little that would lead to changing the educational conditions that account for such patterns.

Generally, data indicate that Blacks perform below the so-called national mean on achievement tests in the social studies, sciences, mathematics, reading, and career and occupational development. Moreover, the negative norm becomes progressively worse in all learning areas except science and career and occupational development.

Additionally, several studies (Hare, 1979) have found that, although Blacks have significantly lower scores in the aforementioned learning areas, the scores of Black males are demonstrably lower than those of Black females. Hare (1979), in his sample of 10- and 11-year-olds, further found that Black females outperformed their counterparts on measures of achievement orientation. His investigations revealed a hierarchical academic performance structure in which whites (males and females) were ranked highest, Black females in the middle, and Black males lowest.

Studies related to Black self-concept appear more equivocal in their findings. Rosenberg and Simmons (1971), Weinberg (1970), and Hirsch and Costello (1970) all point to the negative self-concepts and low aspirations of the Black child. However, Dales and Keller (1972), Jacobs (1974), and Massey (1975) found that the self-concepts of Blacks are equal to or higher than those of whites. Hare (1979) found that Black females showed a trend toward higher school self-esteem than did Black males, and that they had a significantly higher self-concept of ability than did the Black male. He also found that Black males scored higher than did Black females on the nonacademic dimensions of the importance of social abilities and peer self-esteem.

Hare's recent findings raise more questions and promote much speculation but fail to reach potent conclusions. For example, Black female superiority vis-à-vis Black males in achievement, self-concept, and achievement motivation may result from Black parents' consciously or unconsciously encouraging achievement by females. Also, Black males may be allowed to "get away with more" in the home than Black females, although Black males are punished and negatively reinforced for the same assertive behaviors in school. Hare (1979) makes claims of sex-role socialization differences among Blacks that beg further investigation before we assume their validity as a factor in school performance.

Yet, these claims tend to take on a different dimension when applied to the educational system. If schools reflect the values, norms, and attitudes of the larger society, then it is logical to conclude that the abusive treatment of Black males will be an integral part of the approach to the instructional program within the classroom. A study by Rosenberg and Simmons (1971) found that Black males consistently received lower grades than did Black females, and that grades for Blacks were generally lower than were those of their white counterparts. It was found that white teachers engaged in a pattern of expectations and interaction that resulted in Black students being given less attention, ignored more, praised less, and criticized more than whites were. In addition, Blacks labeled as "gifted" were given the least attention, least praise, and most criticism, even when compared to their "nongifted" Black counterparts (Rubovits & Maehr, 1973). It appears that being Black and gifted had more of a harmful effect on teacher expectations and subsequent treatment than did the mere instance of race. It would seem fruitful to determine whether such effects vary by sex within race (Hare, 1979).

Systematic study exploring the impact the female-dominated environment of the public elementary schools has on the education of Blacks in general and Black males in particular is lacking. However, the latest Equal Employment Opportunity Commission (EEOC) data revealed that 83 percent of all elementary school teachers in 1976 were females, while only 10.1 percent of this number were Black females (EEOC, 1976). Black males constituted only 1.2 percent of the total 17 percent of the elementary teachers who were males. Further, 45.7 percent of all full-time secondary school teachers were female, with Black females making up 5.1 percent of this total and Black males accounting for 3.2 percent of the 54.3-percent male participation rate. When teacher aides were considered, the male/female and Black male/Black female imbalances grew even stronger. The EEOC data indicate that 95.5 percent of all teacher aides were females, with 20 percent of this number being Black females. Black males accounted for 1.3 percent of the remaining 4.5 percent male teacher aides. Based on these figures, it could be concluded that a majority of Black males can spend a whole career in the public schools and have very little interaction with a Black male teacher, counselor, or administrator until the secondary school years. Even then, as a result of the paucity of Black males at the secondary level, this interaction is limited.

The historical and present reality of public school "desegregation" efforts further limits the potential for a Black male student to interact positively with a Black role model, particularly a Black male, in the nation's schools. These efforts have generally been deleterious to the progress of both Black students and educators. Recent analysis of the impact of desegregation efforts on the well-being of Black educators reveals a disturbing pattern of dismissal, demotion, and outright systematic violence toward these individuals. A 1970 National Education Association (NEA) study at the secondary level, conducted in 75 school districts in Louisiana and Mississippi, concluded that between 1960 and 1970 a large proportion of Black administrators and teachers were demoted or otherwise displaced from their positions without justification. For the administrators, the strategies usually were to demote Black secondary school principals to elementary or junior high school principalships or to give them the status of assistant principal for discipline or transportation. Decision-making authority in the areas of policy, administration, curriculum, and instruction was shown to be systematically removed from Black principals in at least the two states surveyed (NEA Task Force III, 1970).

Black teachers have been even more vulnerable to victimization due to desegregation efforts. The NEA report indicated that Black teachers were subjected to either outright dismissal or nonrenewal of their employment contracts. Black teachers surveyed were found to have been forced out of their positions by a system that required them to work at grade levels or in organizational structures for which they were ill prepared. Concurrently, their professional status regressed (Arnez, 1978).

The significance of the absence of substantial numbers of Black male and female elementary and secondary school personnel cannot be underestimated. Some recent research (Banks et al., 1978) offers a concept of the manner in which social influence processes might affect the relationship between value-interest orientations of Blacks and their orientations toward academic tasks and achievement. This research uses Festinger's (1954) social comparison model as a frame of reference. This model has been described as a process of interpersonal assessment by which an individual evaluates the appropriateness and desirability of his or her beliefs, opinions, and attitudes through comparisons with other individuals. These other individuals become, in effect, standards of correctness by which values, interest, and behavior may be acquired or measured. The most appropriate sources of social comparison then become similar others who share values, aspirations, characteristics, and experiences (Banks et al., 1978).

Banks et al. (1977) convincingly suggest that for Black individuals the social influence of similar others (Black teachers, counselors, administrators, coaches, and so forth) may serve to convey the appropriate value orientations to achievement tasks. They argue that positive affective expressions from these similar others would likely result in high interest orientations, characterized by strong intrinsic efforts. Consequently, the effect of dissimilar others (white teachers, counselors, administrators, and the like) can be predicted to have an opposite effect on the interest orientations, aspirations, and achievement of Blacks.

The paucity of Black professionals in our schools and the overwhelming presence of white educators have serious long-range negative implications on the life progression of Black people. White teachers, notwithstanding the best of intentions at times, may be ineffective in transmitting and sustaining the intrinsic value orientations to academic achievement that are instilled by Blacks (Banks et al., 1978). To a large extent, this results from the inability of white teachers to serve as effective standards of social comparison (Banks et al., 1978) and their inability to enhance student-teacher empathy through mutual exchange and sensitization (Brown, 1972).

Other indicators of the net negative consequences of collective Black male participation in the nation's elementary and secondary schools lie in the suspension, dropout/pushout rates, and subsequent college attendance rates of Black males. Concomitant with massive desegregation efforts, suspension and expulsion procedures, particularly as they relate to Black students, have been called into question. To illustrate, Cottle (1975) notes that Black children are suspended three times as much as white children are and for longer periods of time. Similarly, the Children's Defense Fund (1975) has concluded that Blacks are three times as likely as whites are to receive suspensions in the elementary grades, and twice as likely to be suspended in the secondary grades. More recent data prepared for the Office for Civil Rights by Killalea & Associates (1980) further support the pattern of differential disciplinary actions toward Black students (see Table 12.1). These data indicate that Blacks are suspended, are expelled, and receive corporal punishment at rates disproportionate to their percentage of the total public school enrollment. Whereas Blacks constituted 16 percent of the total enrollment, national summaries reveal that they were almost twice as likely as whites to be suspended from school (29 percent), to be expelled (27 percent), and to receive corporal punishment (29 percent). Other minority groups received disciplinary actions relative to their percentage of the enrollment in the schools. Whites were found to receive disciplinary actions on the average of 10 percentage points less than what would be expected from their proportion of the population. Although the data did not provide for an analysis of race by sex, one can infer from the total male/female percentages that Black males were even more likely than were Blacks generally to have been disproportionately expelled and suspended, and to have received corporal punishment.

Moreover, as noted by Arnez (1978), the Children's Defense Fund survey found that some "offenses" punishable by suspension were applicable only to Black children. For example, the possession of a metal Afro pick had been considered a weapons offense. The survey also found that low socioeconomic status and female-dominated households were positively correlated with school suspensions, and that these exclusions were more a function of school policies and practices than negative socialization processes or student behavior.

The negative consequence for Black males is further highlighted in dropout and pushout statistics. Data in Table 12.2 indicate that, while Blacks constituted 15 percent of the total public school enrollment in 1975-1976, they were much more likely to drop out than were their white counterparts. Black male students constituted the highest category of dropouts. Two Southern Regional Council (SRC) reports (SRC, 1974; Egleton, 1976) provide evidence indicating that students who leave public schools by choice or by compulsion are disproportionately Black and overwhelmingly males and poor. Further, the 1974 report emphasized that often the most aggressive Black students were the most likely candidates to be induced to leave school (SRC, 1974). Blacks constituted only 12 percent of the public school graduates in the 1975-1976 academic year, thus effectively reducing the pool of potential college-bound students.

## TABLE 12.1
### Disciplinary Actions by Race/Ethnicity and Sex

| | Amer. Indian Number | PCT of TOT | Asian Amer. Number | PCT of TOT | Hispanic Number | PCT of TOT | Black Number | PCT of TOT | White Number | PCT of TOT | Total Number | PCT of TOT | Male Number | PCT of TOT | Female Number | PCT of TOT |
|---|---|---|---|---|---|---|---|---|---|---|---|---|---|---|---|---|
| **The Nation** | | | | | | | | | | | | | | | | |
| Enrollment | 329430 | 1 | 593597 | 1 | 2825229 | 7 | 6578074 | 16 | 31509927 | 75 | 41836257 | 100 | 21445703 | 51 | 20390554 | 49 |
| Suspensions | 10351 | 1 | 9357 | 1 | 106282 | 6 | 528674 | 29 | 1148533 | 64 | 1803197 | 100 | 1232678 | 68 | 570519 | 32 |
| Expulsions | 239 | 1 | 130 | 1 | 1640 | 6 | 6868 | 27 | 16439 | 65 | 25316 | 100 | 19726 | 78 | 5590 | 22 |
| Corporal Punishment | 10502 | 1 | 1991 | 0 | 74170 | 5 | 413127 | 29 | 939887 | 65 | 1439757 | 100 | 1166233 | 81 | 273524 | 19 |

SOURCE: State, Regional, and National Summaries, Conducted by Killalea Associates for the Office for Civil Rights. An analysis of data from the 1978 Civil Rights Survey of Elementary and Secondary Schools, April 1980.

TABLE 12.2
Dropouts and Graduates (School year 1975-1976)

|                                | Whites | Blacks |
|--------------------------------|--------|--------|
| Percentage of total enrollment | 76%    | 15%    |
| Dropouts                       | 70     | 21     |
| Graduates                      | 83     | 12     |

SOURCE: *Fall Elementary and Secondary School Civil Rights Survey.* Conducted by the Office for Civil Rights (Health and Human Services, formerly HEW) for 1970, 1972, 1974, and 1976. Volume I: Users' Guide and National and Regional Summaries, August 1978.

Other consequences of the systematic assault on the Black male child can be further discerned if one examines college attendance rates. A 1977 study that reported on findings from the National Longitudinal Survey of the high school class (Thomas et al., 1977) showed that overall rates of college attendance were 8 percentage points higher for whites than they were for Blacks. Black females had a rate 5.5 percentage points higher than that of Black males. The study further reported that control within family background and socioeconomic status did not alter this pattern. At every level of educational attainment by the father, white males were more likely to go to college than were white females, while Black males were the least likely to attend college. A more recent analysis of Department of Education statistics reveals similar disparities. As shown in Table 12.3, Black males, when compared with both sexes of whites and with Black females, have the lowest postsecondary education attendance status of all four comparison groups.

## DANGERS OF MISLABELING AND
## TRACKING THE BLACK MALE

In recent years, a groundswell of litigation has attacked the criteria used to label and classify Blacks and other minorities for placement in special programs or tracks. There appears to be a national pattern indicating that current assessment systems continue to result in disproportionately large numbers of Blacks, particularly Black males, being placed into classrooms for the emotionally disturbed or mentally handicapped, while a disproportionately small number are assigned to classrooms for the gifted. In the 1970 Spangler v. Board of Education case, the courts in the Southern District of California found that "at every secondary school in the Pasadena school district a higher percentage of Black than white students were in slow classes in every subject

## TABLE 12.3
### Distribution of Racial/Ethnic Groups in Institutions of Higher Education: Fall 1978

*Percentage Distribution*

| Racial/Ethnic Group | Total | Four-Year Institutions | | | | Two-Year Institutions | | | |
|---|---|---|---|---|---|---|---|---|---|
| | | *Full-Time* | | *Part-Time* | | *Full-Time* | | *Part-Time* | |
| | | *Male* | *Female* | *Male* | *Female* | *Male* | *Female* | *Male* | *Female* |
| White | 100.0 | 24.9 | 21.3 | 9.3 | 10.1 | 6.5 | 6.3 | 9.6 | 12.2 |
| Black | 100.0 | 18.2 | 23.7 | 6.6 | 9.7 | 8.9 | 11.3 | 9.4 | 12.3 |

*Dichotomous Distribution*

| | Total | Four-Year Institutions | Two-Year Institutions | Full-Time | Full-Time | Total | Male | Female |
|---|---|---|---|---|---|---|---|---|
| White | 100.0 | 65.6 | 34.4 | 58.9 | 41.1 | 100.0 | 50.2 | 49.8 |
| Black | 100.0 | 58.0 | 52.0 | 62.0 | 38.0 | 100.0 | 43.0 | 57.0 |

SOURCE: U.S. Department of Health and Human Services (formerly Department of Health, Education and Welfare), National Center for Education Statistics, Fall Enrollment in Higher Education 1978, 1979, and Unpublished Tabulations.

NOTE: Details may not add to totals because of rounding.

matter, and a higher percentage of white than Black students were in fast classes." The courts indicated that one of the principal causes for this situation was the practice of grouping students based on their scores on achievement and "intelligence" tests, which contained Anglocentric norms.

Arnez (1978) reports that in 505 school districts in Alabama, Georgia, South Carolina, Mississippi, and Arkansas, which had classes for those labeled as "educable mentally retarded," over 80 percent of the students so labeled were Black, although less than 40 percent of the total school district enrollment was Black. Similarly, Mercer's (1971) classic study found that, as a result of culturally biased assessment instruments, there were four times more Mexican Americans eligible for special education placement and two times more Blacks eligible for such placement than would be expected from their relative distributions in the school populations. She further found that, although the biased I.Q. test was a major factor producing racial disproportions, the differential vulnerability of Black children to the labeling process persisted into subsequent classification stages. The study indicated that disproportionately more of the "eligible" (based on I.Q. test results) Black children were actually recommended for placement into special classrooms, while disproportionately fewer eligible white children were recommended for such placement. It was also found that the racial distribution of children who were actually placed in special classrooms was even more disproportionate than that for the children found eligible for placement. Of those actually placed in special education classrooms, two and a half times more Black children were placed than would be expected based on their proportion in the school district population. A large percentage of the Black children in this study were found to be Black males.

This research cogently points out that Blacks, particularly Black males, are differentially vulnerable to the total labeling process, which includes the use of Anglocentric clinical measures—for example, standard intelligence tests and perspectives employed by decision makers. Recent research findings by Pickholtz (1977) tend to corroborate Mercer's conclusions. Pickholtz found that a child's racial label, that is, being Black, significantly affected the degrees to which school psychologists believed that a child should be classified as educable mentally retarded. Collectively, these results point to the conclusion that Black students, particularly Black males, are more likely to be labeled, recommended for placement, and actually placed in lower-track programs or special classroom situations than any other race/sex group. Labeling and tracking Black males into programs not consistent with their concrete situations and potentials cannot and should not be justified.

# TOWARD THE DEVELOPMENT OF A
# LIBERATING EDUCATION

The halting contribution of U.S. education to equality and to the complete human development of Black males appears intimately related to the assumptions, philosophies, and ideas of our educational system. It is apparent that to effect any systematic, long-lasting change in the education of Blacks, the very purposes and foundations of the educational system will have to be altered dramatically.

The basic elements of an educational system with the necessary liberating qualities consist of (1) valuing interpersonal relationships; (2) fostering self and group development through nurturing the affective; (3) developing a sense of self and collective respect; and (4) recognizing the need for unitary, holistic development. It must be emphasized that changes that enhance the development of Black males also are applicable to improving the collective lot of Black people.

An education with liberating qualities for Blacks has as a guiding principle the development of positive relationships among people and the reinforcement of the basic interconnection between the individual and the group. In this system, human needs are taught to be preeminent to material needs. The ability to relate to other human beings and assist in their growth is highly rewarded. This perspective reflects what Nobles (1976) has described as a value for collective responsibility, cooperative action, and interdependent existence. This axiological orientation of education relates to being in harmony with other human beings as well as with the total phenomenal world, rather than exercising mastery over others. In essence, a more collective spirit permeates the value system of this type of education.

The acceptance of the value of the affect (feeling) as a knowledge base constitutes a liberating quality of an educational system consistent with the world view of Black people. A guiding tenet of this liberating education is the enhancement of the power of feeling as a means of achieving, knowing, and understanding. The positive rhythmic qualities of Black people are reinforced and built upon in this system rather than denied or denigrated. Certainly, the value of knowing through counting, measuring, and reasoning is allowed and nurtured, but the absolute legitimacy of, and necessity for, the affective to help guide the cognitive is honored.

The development of Black self-respect and respect toward others is an important element of an educational system with liberating qualities. Life progression for Blacks is enhanced through the development of a people who historically respect their existence and those of the masses of Blacks. In this model, the individualistic mindset gives ground to the corporate perspective. An understanding is reached that views the self as an interdependent entity shared by the total group (Nobles, 1974). Developing self-respect then becomes the same as developing respect for the extended self, the collective Black. The development of group respect leads to the enhancement of harmony among Black people and their external environment. The harmony of people and their world is a valued perspective of Black people. The aim of Blacks has historically been to maintain a balance or harmony between human beings and their environment (Dixon, 1976). Harmony with nature, as opposed to mastery over it, is the touchstone of this perspective. Everything in this sense is interdependent (Erny, 1973).

Consistent with this harmonious world view is the recognition in this liberating system of the holistic or unitary development of people and the "wholeness" of relationships among people and their world. Williams and El-Khawas (1978) call this approach a unitary conceptual one. According to these authors, this approach concerns itself with the harmonious relationship among things, concepts, ideas, and human beings and how these elements form a "whole" way of viewing and acting toward life. This liberating education views life progression from a holistic rather than a separate or fragmented perspective. The total mental, physical, spiritual, and emotional growth of Black people is inextricably interwoven in this system and must be approached in a holistic manner.


# CONCLUSIONS


The struggle for a liberating elementary and secondary school education has resulted in an uneven growth on the part of Black males. Many individual Black males have, notwithstanding the present public education system, negotiated the public elementary and secondary school system with success and furthered their lifelong development. Many will continue to do so. Unfortunately, the balance of the struggle is weighted heavily against the life progression of the collective Black male. The relative inability of the public elementary and secondary educational system to positively impact on the lot of Black males has resulted to a large extent from its massive disconnection with the world view of Black people. For Black males to progress and to develop an expectation of progression, it becomes imperative that elementary and secondary education develop qualities and characteristics that are liberating to the collective Black welfare.

Although the historic presence of the Black male in this nation's elementary and secondary educational system has created some positive impact on these institutions, the system in the main has limited the total development of Black people and, hence, the Black male. Empirical and statistical evidence overwhelmingly supports the conclusion that the educational system has been mentally, emotionally, and physically as well as spiritually brutal and oppressive toward the collective Black male. The recurring pattern of achievement indicators, their inherent biases notwithstanding, point to the Black male as the most oppressed group affected by the educational system. Unfortunately, the futile attempts to correct these conditions have generally been piecemeal and replete with solutions that are regressive with respect to the positive development of the Black male.

The effects of a liberating education will be hampered severely without the acceptance and application of aspects of the Black experience and traditional culture to the American system of education. A system that is liberating to the Black male must be built on a world view consistent with, and supportive of, a Black frame of reference. The essential point is that American education must define Black strengths and weaknesses and respond to these realities in ways consistent with the nation's collective essence. To do this would be to make a reality of the promise, pronouncements, and dream of the American system of education. That, indeed, would be revolutionary.

## NOTES

1. Anglocentric traits refer to the tendency of researchers and others to perceive and gauge the existential condition of non-Anglos (Blacks in this case) through assumptions, norms, value systems, paradigms, and frames of reference that usually claim the preeminence of a white middle-class perspective.

2. The term "collective Black male" is used to indicate the majority of Black men who have not escaped the debilitating effects of sociopolitical and economic limitations.

## REFERENCES

Arnez, N. Implementation of desegregation as a discriminatory process. *Journal of Negro Education,* 1978, *47,* 28-45.

Banks, C., McQuarter, G., & Hubbard, J. Talk-liking and intrinsic-extrinsic achievement orientation in Black adolescents. *Journal of Black Psychology,* 1970, *3*(2), 61-71.

Banks, C., McQuarter, G., & Hubbard, J. Toward a reconceptualization of the social-cognitive bases of achievement orientations in Blacks. *Review of Educational Research,* 1978, *48,* 381-397.

*Brown* v. *Board of Education of Topeka, Kansas,* 347 U.S. 483 (1954).

Brown, S. *Emphathic process as a dimension of African reality.* Unpublished doctoral dissertation, Stanford University, 1972.

Children's Defense Fund. *School suspensions: Are they helping children?* Washington, DC: Washington Research Project(s), Inc., 1975.

Cottle, T. A case of suspension. *National Elementary Principal,* 1975, *5,* 69-74.

Dales, R., & Keller, J. Self-concept scores among Black and white culturally deprived adolescent males. *Journal of Negro Education,* 1972, *41,* 31-34.

Department of Health, Education and Welfare. *Trends in Black segregation, 1970-74.* Washington, DC: National Institute of Education, 1977.

Dixon, V. World views and research methodology. In L. King et al., *African philosophy: assumptions and paradigms for research on Black persons.* Los Angeles: Fanon Center, 1976.

Egleton, J. *School desegregation: A report card from the south.* Atlanta, GA: Southern Regional Council, 1976.

Erny, P. *Childhood and cosmos: The social psychology of the Black African child,* New York: New Perspectives, 1973.

Festinger, C. A theory of social comparison processes. *Human Relations,* 1954, *7,* 117-140.

Hare, B. *Black girls: A comparative analysis of self-perception and achievement by race, sex and socio-economic background.* Baltimore: Center for Social Organization of Schools, Johns Hopkins University, 1979.

Hirsh, J., & Costello, J. School achievers and underachievers in an urban ghetto. *Elementary School Journal,* 1970, *39,* 78-85.

*Hobson v. Hansen,* 269 F. Supp. 401 (1967).

Jacobs, P. *Persistence factors in the academic success of low socio-economic status Black community college students.* Doctoral dissertation, University of California, Berkeley, 1974.

Jones, F. *Historic roles of public education.* Washington, DC: Howard University, 1979 (ERIC Document Reproduction Service No. Ed 169 151).

Katz, M. *Class, bureaucracy, and schools.* New York: Praeger, 1971.

Killalea & Associates, Inc. *State, regional and national summaries.* Washington, DC: Office for Civil Rights, Department of Health and Human Services (formerly HEW), 1980.

Massey, G. *Self-concept, personal control, and social context among students in inner city high schools.* Doctoral dissertation, Stanford University, 1975.

Mercer, J. Sociocultural factors in labeling mental retardates. *Peabody Journal of Education,* 1971, *48,* 188-203.

National Education Association Task Force III. *School desegregation: Louisiana and Mississippi.* Washington, DC: Author, 1970.

Nobles, W. Africanity and Black families. *The Black Scholar,* 1974, *5,* 10-17.

Nobles, W. African science: The consciousness of self. In L. King et al., *African philosophy: Assumptions and paradigms for research on Black persons.* Los Angeles: Fanon Center, 1976.

Pickholtz, H. *The effects of a child's racial-ethnic label and achievement differences on school psychologists' decisions.* Unpublished doctoral dissertation, The Pennsylvania State University, 1977.

Picott, R. A quarter century of the Black experience in elementary and secondary education. *Negro History Bulletin* 1974, *37,* 297.

Rosenberg, M., & Simmons, R. *Black and white self-esteem: The urban school child.* In M. Arnold & C. Rose Monograph Series. Washington, DC: American Sociological Association, 1971.

Rubovits, P., & Maehr, M. Pygmalion Black and white. *Journal of Personality and Social Psychology,* 1973, *25,* 210-218.

Southern Regional Council and Robert F. Kennedy Memorial. *The student push-out victims of continued resistance to desegregation.* Atlanta, GA: Southern Regional Council, 1974.

*Spangler v. Board of Education,* 311 F. Supp. 501 (1970).

Thomas, G., et al. *Access to higher education: How important are race, sex, social class and academic credentials for college access?* Baltimore: Johns Hopkins University, 1977. (ERIC Document Reproduction Service No. ED 142 616).

U.S. Equal Employment Opportunity Commission. *Employment opportunity in the schools: Job patterns of minorities and women in public elementary and secondary schools, 1976.* Washington, DC: Author, 1978.

Weinberg, M. Desegregation research: An appraisal. *Phi Delta Kappa*, 1970, *51*, 49-56.

Williams, L., & El-Khawas, M. A philosophy of Black education. *Journal of Negro Education*, 1978, *7*, 177-1991.

Williams, R. Cognitive and survival learning of the Black child. *The survival of Black children and youth.* Washington, DC: Nuclassics and Science Publishing, 1974.

Woodson, C. G. *The education of the Negro prior to 1861.* New York: Arno, 1968.

# 13

## BLACK MALES IN HIGHER EDUCATION

John E. Fleming

The impact of affirmative action on Black males in higher education can best be understood when placed in a historical perspective. Since the revolutionary war, Americans have been plagued with the paradox of wanting a society based upon the ideal of equality while not wanting a society of equals. This paradox surfaces in the debate over affirmative action. While the opponents of affirmative action advance the notion of equal opportunity, their very opposition to affirmative action is a major barrier to bringing about equity in the higher education sector.

The primary reason that the debate about affirmative action in higher education became so vociferous is that higher education opens the door to numerous opportunities. Academia plays a central role in American society. Colleges and universities do more than simply provide employment opportunities. They are responsible for educating America's youth—our future. In an ever-shrinking world, education is too important not to reflect the cultural diversity of American society.

Blacks have always understood the pivotal role education plays in their struggle for survival. Prior to the establishment of the American nation, Blacks sought to lift the burden of slavery through learning how to read and write. Yet the institution of slavery served as an effective barrier to Black educational attainment. By the end of the Civil War, only 28 identifiable

Blacks had a college education out of a total Black population of 4½ million (Quarles, 1961).

The education of 4½ million free Blacks was a monumental task in itself. Faced with the hostility of southern whites, it was at best a losing battle. The federal government made some half-hearted attempts to protect the freedmen and their northern allies during Reconstruction, but the effort was short-lived. The one affirmative effort, the establishment of the Freedmen's Bureau, was also too short-lived and inadequately funded to have a major impact on the plight of the freedmen. The Compromise of 1877, for all practical purposes, ended federal involvement in so-called southern affairs. The former slaves were left to fight their own battles against their former masters. Through white violence and intimidation, Blacks gradually lost most of the freedoms guaranteed by the Thirteenth, Fourteenth and Fifteenth Amendments to the Constitution. Consequently, by the turn of the century, Blacks were disenfranchised and relegated to the bottom of a caste society. The national government sanctioned this process through the Plessy v. Ferguson decision of 1896, in which the U.S. Supreme Court gave its blessings to the policy of "separate but equal" (Fleming, 1976). From 1896 to 1954, it became the national policy to provide separate facilities for Blacks and whites. Blacks were always separate but seldom, if ever, accorded equal treatment.

How soon those who now allege reverse discrimination forget the past. Yet this very inequality in providing education for Blacks demands a commitment to affirmative action. When Blacks were provided with any schools, the terms were shorter than those of white schools, the buildings and other facilities were inferior to those of white students, and the teachers were less prepared and were paid lower salaries than their white counterparts. Even with the passage of the second Morrill Act in 1890, the schools established for Blacks were markedly inferior to the schools established for whites. Under these circumstances, one can conclude that the effort to educate Blacks was no less than a modern-day miracle. Well into the twentieth century, Black colleges, both public and private, had to compensate their students for the failure of the South to provide a network of adequate high schools. As early as the 1930s, the National Association for the Advancement of Colored People initiated a well-orchestrated campaign to dismantle the separate-but-equal system. It was not until 1954 that legally sanctioned segregation ended with the Supreme Court's Brown decision (Fleming, 1976).

It was within this climate of legally enforced segregation that Black males sought admission to predominantly white institutions of higher education. While time does not permit a full examination of this struggle, it is worth reviewing the record of the academic community in awarding the doctorate to Blacks, since most four-year institutions now require the doctorate for entry-level faculty positions.

The doctorate is the highest degree awarded in this country. Although the first doctorate degree was awarded in 1866, a Black male did not receive one from an American institution until 1876. Edward Bouchet received his Ph.D. in physics from Yale University. The record of American institutions in awarding the Ph.D. to Blacks is bleak at best. Only 51 degrees were conferred on Blacks from 1876 to 1929, approximately one per year. While there were numerous Blacks capable of pursuing graduate work, discrimination and racial prejudice in large measure prevented most Blacks from acquiring the necessary educational foundation. Those who did gain graduate and professional education found that opportunities for employment were severely limited. It is inexcusable that American institutions did not offer permanent positions on their faculties to qualified Blacks prior to 1954. Outstanding figures, such as W.E.B. DuBois, E. Franklin Frazier, Ernest E. Just, Rayford W. Logan, and Percy L. Julian, are just a few who were eligible. Yet Blacks continued to struggle to gain higher education credentials for employment primarily at Black colleges (Greene, 1946).

There was a dramatic increase in the number of doctorates awarded to Blacks during the Depression and war years; 316 were awarded during the period 1930 to 1943. However, even this number is insignificant when one considers that between 1926 and 1942, a total of 38,765 doctorates were awarded by American universities. Blacks received 335 or substantially less than 1 percent of these. There are little data on Black doctorates between 1944 and 1969, except for the occasional survey by specific fields. In 1969, the Ford Foundation identified a total of 2,280 Blacks with Ph.D.'s. While the number appeared impressive, the percentage remained less than 1 percent of all Americans with earned Ph.D.'s. The Ford Foundation suggested that the number was not likely to increase in the near future because at the close of the 1967-1968 academic year, less than 1 percent of all Ph.D. candidates were Black (Fleming, Gill, & Swinton, 1978; Ford Foundation, 1969).

Although 85.4 percent of Black doctorates were employed at colleges and universities, the vast majority were in predominantly Black institutions. Prior to 1950, at best there was a token scattering of Blacks on faculties of predominantly white institutions. Even after the U.S. Supreme Court declared the separate-but-equal doctrine unconstitutional, in the Brown decision of 1954, there was little or no movement to integrate white college faculties.

While the legal barriers to integration were slowly crumbling, few colleges and universities were willing to end their discriminatory hiring practices. By 1960, there were 5910 Blacks employed in colleges and universities as faculty members, including those employed in predominantly Black colleges. This

represented slightly more than 3 percent of the total number of college and
university teachers. During the academic year 1968-1969, the percentage of
Black faculty members dropped from slightly more than 3 percent to 2.2
percent of faculty members nationwide (Bayer, 1973; Rose, 1966). This is all
the more startling when one realizes that the 1960s witnessed a rapid
acceleration in the growth of higher education as children born during the
1940s reached college age. Although there was some expansion in the recruitment of Black undergraduate students, it was evident that predominantly
white institutions had not recruited Blacks in large numbers for graduate and
professional schools. The response to the pressure of the Civil Rights movement in the 1960s was small and had little impact on institutions' hiring
practices.

By the early 1970s, the percentage of Black faculty members had not
reached the 1960 level of 3 percent. What this suggests is the failure of
colleges to put forth a good-faith effort to train Black graduate students and
recruit and hire Black faculty members during the 1960s when the academic
marketplace rapidly expanded to accommodate increased student enrollment.
Had colleges and universities been sincere, as they professed to have been,
they would have initiated programs to encourage qualified Black students to
enter graduate schools. The increased Black graduate school enrollment thus
would have contained many Blacks who would have been available for faculty
positions in the 1970s.

Before examining the impact of affirmative action on Black males in
higher education, attention should turn to the impact of racism on Black
males in the general labor force by examining intergenerational mobility. In a
forthcoming publication, two Black social scientists, Al Pinkney and Walter
Stafford, have examined Black occupational mobility (Featherman, 1979).
Dividing the labor force into five job categories—upper-white-collar, lower-
white-collar, upper-manual, lower-manual, and farm occupations—the authors
found that in 1963, only 10.4 percent of Black males whose fathers were in
upper-white-collar occupations were likely to achieve the same status, while
59.6 percent would assume jobs in the lower-manual occupational categories
(See Table 13.1). The authors found that this was almost a complete reversal
of white occupational patterns during the same period.

While in 1973 the occupational patterns of Blacks had changed, Black
males whose fathers were in upper-white-collar occupational categories still
were not able to match their fathers' occupational status in most cases. Only
33.2 percent were able to achieve a status at or above their fathers' level; 21.8
percent were in lower-white-collar jobs, 10 percent were in upper-manual
jobs, and 34.8 percent were in lower-manual job categories. Upward mobility
in the upper- and lower-manual categories was virtually nonexistent for Black
males. Even after the passage of the 1964 Civil Rights Act and the implemen-

## TABLE 13.1
Mobility From Father's (or other family head's) Occupation
to Current Occupation: Black U.S. Men in the Experienced
Civilian Labor Force Aged 20 to 64 in 1962 and 1973 (in percentages)

| Year & Father's Occupation | Upper-White-Collar | Lower-White-Collar | Upper-Manual | Lower-Manual | Farm | Total | Row Percentage |
|---|---|---|---|---|---|---|---|
| **1962** | | | | | | | |
| Upper-white-collar | 10.4 | 10.3 | 19.7 | 59.6 | 00.0 | 100.0 | 4.5 |
| Lower-white-collar | 14.4 | 13.5 | 00.0 | 72.1 | 00.0 | 100.0 | 1.9 |
| Upper-manual | 8.5 | 9.7 | 10.4 | 67.9 | 3.6 | 100.0 | 9.0 |
| Lower-manual | 7.6 | 8.0 | 10.8 | 71.4 | 2.3 | 100.0 | 37.2 |
| Farm | 3.2 | 3.3 | 7.0 | 66.7 | 19.8 | 100.0 | 47.4 |
| Total | 5.9 | 6.1 | 9.1 | 68.3 | 10.6 | 100.0 | 100.0 |
| **1973** | | | | | | | |
| Upper-white-collar | 33.2 | 21.8 | 10.0 | 34.8 | 00.0 | 100.0 | 5.0 |
| Lower-white collar | 23.8 | 17.2 | 12.3 | 45.8 | 0.9 | 100.0 | 3.5 |
| Upper-manual | 15.2 | 14.7 | 15.0 | 54.9 | 0.2 | 100.0 | 10.2 |
| Lower-manual | 12.4 | 11.2 | 13.9 | 61.4 | 1.1 | 100.0 | 46.1 |
| Farm | 5.6 | 6.2 | 16.8 | 62.9 | 8.5 | 100.0 | 35.1 |
| Total | 11.8 | 10.6 | 14.8 | 59.4 | 3.6 | 100.0 | 100.0 |

SOURCE: Published by permission of Transaction, Inc., from D. Featherman, "Opportunities are expanding," SOCIETY, Vol. 16, No. 3. Copyright © March/April 1979 by Transaction, Inc.

tation of the affirmative action requirement in 1965, racism within the work force continued to exercise a dominant influence on Black male upward mobility. As late as 1973, Black males in the highest occupational categories were unable to pass on their economic status to their male children.

While "reverse discrimination" and "job quotas" became popular code words in the 1970s, the affirmative action thrust actually had little impact on academic employment patterns. In 1971, 57 percent of white males (aged 25-34) who entered the labor force were employed in professional, managerial, and craft occupations. One would naturally anticipate change in this pattern thirteen years after the passage of the 1964 Civil Rights bill and nearly ten years after employers were required to implement affirmative

## TABLE 13.2
### EEO-6 — National Summary, 1975: Total Employment

|            | Total     | Total Male | Black Male | Black Female | Total Black |
|------------|-----------|------------|------------|--------------|-------------|
| Employees  | 1,351,438 | 733,909    | 68,814     | 95,282       | 164,096     |
| Percentage |           | 54.4       | 5.1        | 7.0          | 12.1        |

SOURCE: Equal Employment Opportunity Commission's EEO-6 Survey of Employment at Higher Education Institutions, 1975, taken from unpublished summaries of computer printouts, Washington, D.C.

action procedures. Yet the data indicate that in 1977, 57 percent of white males between the ages of 25 and 34 years old still entered the labor force in the higher-paying occupations.

Finally, Pinkney and Stafford indicate that the mobility of Black males is more dependent on national expansion trends than upon Civil Rights laws. In 1940, merely 2 percent of the Black male population were in professional occupations, and regardless of training, they were primarily teachers and musicians. On the eve of the Civil Rights movement, only three 3 percent of employed Black males were in professional/technical occupations. By 1970, the figure had reached 5 percent—not a very impressive or dramatic change.

There have been few dramatic changes within employment patterns in the higher education community. The affirmative action requirement under Executive Order 11246, as amended, was not extended to institutions of higher education until 1972 (U.S. Department of Health, Education and Welfare, 1972). It was not until 1975 when the Equal Employment Opportunity Commission conducted the first national higher education survey that comprehensive data on employment patterns became available (Equal Employment Opportunity Commission, 1975). The 1975 survey revealed that there were a total of 164,096 Blacks employed in institutions of higher education, or 12.1 percent of the total (see Table 13.2). Blacks in 1975 participated in academia roughly at the same rate as their percentage in the total population. Yet an examination of employment distribution suggests that serious equity problems exist. In 1975, there was a total faculty count of 446,034, but Blacks were only 19,574, or 4.4 percent of faculty representation. While that figure is 1.4 percent higher than in 1960, it also represents Black faculty at the 105 historically Black colleges, the elimination of which would decrease both the number and percentage radically.

While Black males accounted for 5.1 percent of the total college employment population, they held only 2.4 of the faculty positions (see Table 13.3). In the professional categories, Black males were represented at the rate of 4.7 percent of the executive/administrative positions. Looking at all categories,

## TABLE 13.3
## EEO-6—National Summary, 1975

| | Total | *11-12 Month Contract*<br>Total<br>Male | Black<br>Male | Black<br>Female | Total<br>Blacks |
|---|---|---|---|---|---|
| Exec./Admin. | 96,924 | 74,650 | 4,566 | 2,235 | 6,801 |
| Median Salary | $18,525 | $20,392 | $17,525 | $14,107 | |
| Percentage | | 77.0 | 4.7 | 2.3 | 7.0 |
| Faculty | 125,930 | 97,376 | 3,174 | 2,438 | 5,612 |
| Median Salary | $19,155 | $20,300 | $18,391 | $15,560 | |
| Percentage | | 77.3 | 2.5 | 1.9 | 4.4 |
| Prof. Nonfac. | 159,394 | 82,196 | 4,891 | 7,222 | 12,113 |
| Median Salary | $12,791 | $14,414 | $13,024 | $11,898 | |
| Percentage | | 51.6 | 3.1 | 4.5 | 7.6 |
| Sec./Clerical | 296,930 | 22,805 | 3,938 | 31,088 | 35,026 |
| Median Salary | $7,373 | $8,166 | $8,042 | $7,274 | |
| Percentage | | 7.7 | 1.3 | 10.5 | 11.8 |
| Tech. Paraprof. | 110,692 | 50,588 | 5,403 | 12,928 | 18,331 |
| Median Salary | $9,359 | $10,544 | $9,194 | $8,173 | |
| Percentage | | 45.7 | 4.9 | 11.7 | 16.6 |
| Skilled Crafts | 50,607 | 48,404 | 4,115 | 548 | 4,663 |
| Median Salary | $10,654 | $10,783 | $9,343 | $7,624 | |
| Percentage | | 95.7 | 8.1 | 1.1 | 9.2 |
| Service/Maint. | 197,857 | 123,894 | 35,291 | 32,582 | 67,873 |
| Median Salary | $7,399 | $7,927 | $7,114 | $6,670 | |
| Percentage | | 62.6 | 17.8 | 16.5 | 34.3 |
| Total Number<br>11-12 Months | 1,038,329 | 499,913 | 61,378 | 89,041 | 150,419 |
| Percentage | | 48.1 | 5.9 | 8.6 | 14.5 |
| *9-10 Month Contract* | | | | | |
| Faculty | 313,109 | 233,996 | 7,436 | 6,241 | 13,677 |
| Median Salary | $15,669 | $16,475 | $14,860 | $12,966 | |
| Percentage | | 74.7 | 2.4 | 2.0 | 4.4 |

TABLE 13.4
EEO-6—National Summary, 1975: Full-Time Faculty by Rank

|  | Total | Total Male | Black Male | Black Female | Total Blacks |
|---|---|---|---|---|---|
| Professor | 98,028 | 88,656 | 1,637 | 502 | 2,139 |
| Percentage |  | 90.4 | 1.7 | .5 | 2.2 |
| Assoc. Prof. | 99,592 | 82,787 | 1,941 | 999 | 2,940 |
| Percentage |  | 83.1 | 1.9 | 1.0 | 2.9 |
| Assist. Prof. | 121,176 | 86,978 | 3,242 | 2,591 | 5,833 |
| Percentage |  | 71.8 | 2.7 | 2.1 | 4.8 |
| Instructor | 83,192 | 48,946 | 2,652 | 3,382 | 6,034 |
| Percentage |  | 58.8 | 3.2 | 4.1 | 7.3 |
| Lecturer | 9,091 | 5,410 | 405 | 398 | 803 |
| Percentage |  | 59.5 | 4.5 | 4.4 | 8.9 |
| Other Faculty | 34,955 | 23,431 | 915 | 912 | 1,827 |
| Percentage |  | 67.1 | 2.6 | 2.6 | 5.2 |
| Total | 446,034 | 336,216 | 10,791 | 8,783 | 19,574 |
| Percentage |  | 75.4 | 2.4 | 2.0 | 4.4 |

SOURCE: Equal Employment Opportunity Commission's EEO-6 Survey of Employment at Higher
Education Institutions, 1975 taken from unpublished summaries of computer printouts,
Washington, D.C.

Black males were congregated in the lower levels of academic employment
primarily in the service/maintenance occupations, where they constituted
17.8 percent of all workers. Adding Black females, the total percentage of
Blacks in this category rises to 34.3 percent of the total.

In examining Black male faculty by rank, of the 10,791 Black faculty
members, the largest number was at the assistant professor level (see Table
13.4). Black males held only 1.7 percent of the full professorships and 1.9
percent of the positions at the associate level. The largest percentage (3.2)
was at the instructor level. Of the 233,498 tenured positions, there were
4,246 Black males, or 1.8 percent (see Table 13.5). There were 4,124 Black
males in nontenured positions, but who were on the tenure track; 2,424 were

TABLE 13.5
EEO-6—National Summary, 1975: Full-Time Faculty by Tenure

|  | Total | Total Male | Black Male | Black Female | Total Blacks |
|---|---|---|---|---|---|
| Tenured | 233,498 | 191,269 | 4,246 | 2,799 | 7,045 |
| Percentage |  | 81.9 | 1.8 | 1.2 | 3.0 |
| Nontenured on tenured track | 129,603 | 90,038 | 4,124 | 3,574 | 7,698 |
| Percentage |  | 42.4 | 3.2 | 2.8 | 6.0 |
| Other Nontenured | 82,933 | 54,909 | 2,424 | 2,410 | 4,834 |
| Percentage |  | 66.2 | 2.9 | 2.9 | 5.8 |

SOURCE: Equal Employment Opportunity Commission's EEO-6 Survey of Employment at Higher Education Institutions, 1975, taken from unpublished summaries of computer printouts, Washington, D.C.

not on a tenure track. While 52.3 percent of all faculty held tenured slots, of the total Black male faculty, only 39.3 percent were tenured (see Equal Employment Opportunity Commission, 1975). Again, if historically Black colleges were eliminated from the statistics, the Black male faculty percentage at predominantly white institutions would be radically lowered.

The latest EEOC survey data now available are for the 1977 school year (Equal Employment Opportunity Commission, 1977). The two EEOC surveys combined reveal that between 1975 and 1977, the total number of Black faculty increased from 19,574 to 19,915 or by 341 persons. During the same period, the total faculty employment rose by 9,886. While Blacks were 3.5 percent of all new employees, this rate of increase was not nearly high enough to alter their percentage of total faculty composition, which remained at 4.4.

There were 73,609 new employees for all categories of employment in higher education between 1975 and 1977. The total number of Blacks increased by 9,512 to raise the overall Black representation to 12.2 percent of the total. The increase is due largely to increased Black female representation. While the total number of Black males increased, their percentage of total employment decreased from 5.1 to 5.0 percent. In fact, the percentage of Black males in all categories decreased, with the exception of 9-10 month contract faculty, where there was a one-tenth of a percent increase, and in the skilled crafts category where there was a four-tenths of a percent increase (see Table 13.6).

## TABLE 13.6
## EEO-6 — National Summary, 1977

| | | *11-12 Month Contract* | | | |
| | *Total* | *Total Male* | *Black Male* | *Black Female* | *Total Blacks* |
|---|---|---|---|---|---|
| Exec./Admin. | 101,487 | 75,648 | 4,647 | 2,586 | 7,233 |
| Percentage | | 74.5 | 4.5 | 2.5 | 7.0 |
| Faculty | 125,434 | 97,519 | 2,832 | 2,188 | 5,020 |
| Percentage | | 77.7 | 2.2 | 1.7 | 3.9 |
| Professional Nonfaculty | 183,792 | 92,610 | 5,291 | 8,202 | 13,493 |
| Percentage | | 50.0 | 2.8 | 4.4 | 7.2 |
| Sec./Clerical | 314,267 | 23,702 | 4,145 | 35,199 | 39,344 |
| Percentage | | 75.0 | 1.3 | 11.2 | 12.5 |
| Tech. Paraprof. | 116,655 | 53,515 | 5,734 | 13,479 | 19,213 |
| Percentage | | 45.8 | 4.9 | 11.5 | 16.4 |
| Skilled Crafts | 52,716 | 50,330 | 4,482 | 578 | 5,060 |
| Percentage | | 95.0 | 8.5 | 1.1 | 9.6 |
| Service/Maint. | 201,388 | 125,140 | 35,762 | 33,291 | 69,053 |
| Percentage | | 62.0 | 17.7 | 16.5 | 34.2 |
| Total Number | 1,095,739 | 518,464 | 62,893 | 95,523 | 158,416 |
| Percentage | | 47.3 | 5.7 | 8.7 | 14.4 |
| | | *9-10 Month Contract* | | | |
| Faculty | 329,308 | 242,659 | 8,125 | 7,067 | 15,192 |
| Percentage | | 73.6 | 2.5 | 2.1 | 4.6 |

SOURCE: Equal Employment Opportunity Commission's EEO-6 Survey of Employment at Higher Education Institutions, 1977, taken from unpublished summaries of computer printouts, Washington, D.C.

It is obvious from the data presented that there has not been a radical change in the employment patterns in institutions of higher education. Blacks are still largely congregated in service/maintenance areas. There seems little doubt that the Bakke case and decision had a chilling effect on both minority hiring and special minority admissions programs.

For example, take the two prestigious fields of medicine and law. There is one white doctor for every 560 whites in the United States, but only one Black doctor for every 3700 Blacks. The ratio of white lawyers to whites is 1:627, while the ratio of Black lawyers to Blacks is 1:1700. After a decade of steady increase, the number of Black students entering law and medical schools has declined. The reason is attributed to the reluctance of admissions officers to accept students with lower academic skills.

According to the Association of American Medical Colleges, minority students were 6.7 percent of first year medical students in 1979, down from 7.5 percent in 1974. The American Bar Association reported that the percentage of first-year Black law students had declined to 4.3 percent in 1979, down from 4.5 percent in 1976. There seems little doubt that Bakke's challenge to special minority admissions programs created a chilling impact on Blacks seeking admissions and on admissions decisions (American Association of Medical Colleges; American Bar Association; New York Times, 1978, 1979).

The new HEW guidelines for implementing affirmative action plans published in *The Federal Register* (October 10, 1979) may bring some clarity to an otherwise cloudy situation. Colleges and universities were told that they can increase their recruitment efforts, provide special tutorial programs where necessary, and establish numerical goals to increase minority enrollment. Quotas are out where an authoritative body has not found an institution guilty of discrimination. An encouraging HEW suggestion is that institutions can modify admissions criteria to predict more accurately the success chances of minority students.

The future impact of affirmative action on Black employment is not so clear. The employment of Blacks generally and of Black males in particular will be determined by their availability in the academic labor market, the overall demand for faculty, and how vigorously affirmative action procedures are enforced.

The Institute for the Study of Educational Policy at Howard University (ISEP) advocates that the number of Blacks enrolled in graduate and professional programs be substantially increased since Blacks are underrepresented in all fields. Black proportional representation varies widely from 1.1 percent in engineering to 6.7 percent in education.

Currently, demand for faculty is primarily based on student enrollment. Enrollments increased by roughly four million students between 1961 and 1971 and are projected to increase only by another three million in the period between 1971 and 1982. ISEP projects that there will be an actual decline in enrollment from 1982 to 1988. While demand for faculty increased annually by 50,000 during the peak demand period (from 1966 to 1971), demand has already decreased and will nearly vanish from 1982 to 1989. Rates of graduation from graduate programs will not taper off as rapidly, which will result in an excess supply. Without affirmative action goals and strong enforcement of affirmative action procedures, the percentage of Black faculty is unlikely to increase and could very well decline, as it did during the peak demand in the 1960s (Fleming et al., 1978).

If the past record of Black employment in higher education is a key to what will happen in the future, the future does not appear to be bright. With low demand and excess supply, educational institutions will have greater hiring flexibility which, in turn, will make it easier to disguise discriminatory hiring practices. While upgrading qualifications may appear racially neutral, the majority of Black males and females remain in entry-level, nontenured positions. New Ph.D.'s will be forced to compete with older scholars for fewer jobs.

Affirmative action, if properly implemented, can have an impact on Black male employment. The minimal impact of affirmative action suggested in this chapter only underscores the urgency of achieving equal opportunity in academia.

# REFERENCES

American Association of Medical Colleges. Selected minority group enrollment in first-year classes in United States Medical schools for selected years. In *Medical Schools Admissions Requirements.*

American Bar Association. Review of legal education in the United States law schools and bar admissions requirements. In *Selection of legal education and admissions to the Bar.*

Bayer, A. *Teaching faculty in academe, 1972-73.* Washington, DC: American Council on Education, 1973.

Equal Employment Opportunity Commission. *Higher education staff information* (EEO-6). Washington, DC: Author, 1975. (Unpublished National Summary)

Equal Employment Opportunity Commission. *Higher Education Staff Information* (EEO-6). Washington, DC: Author, 1977. (Unpublished National Summary)

Featherman, D. Opportunities are expanding. *Society,* 1979, *16*(3), 7.

Fleming, J. *The lengthening shadow of slavery: A historical justification for affirmative action for Blacks in higher education.* Washington, DC: Howard University Press, 1976.

Fleming, J., Gill, G., & Swinton, D. *The case for affirmative action for Blacks in higher education.* Washington, DC: Howard University Press, 1978.

Ford Foundation. *A survey of Black American doctorates: A report.* New York: Author, 1969.

Greene, H. *Holders of doctorates among American Negroes.* Boston: Meador, 1946.

New York Times. December 3, 1978, p. 45.

New York Times. February 14, 1979, p. A23.

Quarles, B. *Black abolitionist.* New York: Oxford University Press, 1961.

Rose, H. An appraisal of the Negro education situation in the academic marketplace. *Journal of Negro Education,* 1966, *23,* 20.

U.S. Department of Health, Education and Welfare, Office for Civil Rights. *Higher education guidelines.* Washington, DC: Government Printing Office, 1972.

# 14

## THE INCARCERATION OF
## BLACK MEN

Roi D. Townsey

There is one major comparative source against which criminal justice authorities assess criminality throughout the United States: the *Uniform Crime Reports* (UCR), *Crime in the United States,* provided by the Federal Bureau of Investigation (U.S. Department of Justice). Although highly criticized as less than accurate, the UCR consistently has shown that Blacks account for a significant portion of all arrests. They are particularly involved in violent crimes (murder, forcible rape, robbery, and aggravated assault) and property crimes (burglary, larceny-theft, and motor vehicle theft). For example, the 1978 UCR indicated that Blacks made up 51 percent of the total arrests for murder in 1977. It also reported that of the persons arrested for forcible rape in 1977, 47 percent were Black. According to the same source, Blacks similarly constituted 57 percent of those arrested for robbery. Overall, the 1978 UCR shows that 2,308,429 Blacks were arrested throughout the United States in 1977, thus accounting for 25.7 percent of the total arrest population (U.S. Department of Justice, 1978b). Similarly, information about the sex and race of those persons adjudicated and formally labeled "criminal offenders" clearly shows that Black men, in particular, are disproportionately represented.

Accessible prisoner data show that there are 306,602 persons incarcerated in our nation's state and federal prisons (U.S. Bureau of the Census, 1979).

Of this strikingly high total, which is an increase of 3 percent above the 1977 year-end prisoner count, 46.8 percent (143,376) are Black. Attention to prisoner gender shows that 95.9 percent (293,882) of those persons held in state and federal prisons are men. As shown in Table 14.1, 46.6 percent (136,893) of these male prisoners are Black. Less than 10 percent (27,975) of all U.S. male prisoners are held under federal authority. Among these federal prisoners, approximately 37 percent (10,424) are Black. Altogether, state prisons incarcerate 265,907 men. Of this number, 47.6 percent (126,469) are Black (see Table 14.1).

Regionally, the largest number of prisoners (130,738 or 42.6 percent) are incarcerated in the South. Of these, 70,842 or 54.2 percent are Black, and 67,801 or 51.9 percent are Black men (see Table 14.2). Capital punishment data show that throughout the nation's 34 jurisdictions condoning the death penalty, 443 persons are being held under the sentence of death (U.S. Department of Justice, 1978a). A little less than 45 percent of these death row prisoners are Black (197), and all are being held under state authority. Only 3, or 1.5 percent, of these Black death row prisoners are women. Black women constitute 37.5 percent of the female death row population. Of the 194 men sentenced to death, 52.2 percent (107) are in southern prisons; 28.3 percent (55) are in north central prisons; 15.4 percent (30) are in western prisons; and 1.0 percent (2) are in northeastern prisons (see Table 14.2. All but 2 of the 194 Black men on death row have been convicted of murder. It is noteworthy that the 130,730 southern prisoners (including the 67,694 Black men sentenced to one year or more and the 106 Black men sentenced to death) constitute a proportion that significantly exceeds the South's 33.3 percent of the nation's population.

During 1977, ten states experienced decreases in their prison populations. The most notable decline (775), a 4 percent decrease, occurred in California. Nonetheless, there are 6,743 (33.4 percent) Black men imprisoned in California. Of these, 21 have been sentenced to death. These 21 Black men constitute nearly 40 percent (38.9) of California's death row population. At year end 1977, Texas ranked first among the top ten states with the most sentenced prisoners. Although this state now has 470 fewer prisoners than New York, there are still 10,015 (42.5 percent of the total) Black men incarcerated in Texas. Of these, 22 are under the sentence of death. As in California, Black men in Texas are disproportionately represented on death row, accounting for 33.8 percent. Also, at year end 1977, South Carolina ranked first among the top ten states with the highest incarceration rate per capita. The latest prisoner count shows that South Carolina still holds this rank, with 4,028 (56.8 percent) Black male prisoners. Two are under the sentence of death, and they represent 50 percent of the total death row population in South Carolina (see Table 14.2).

## TABLE 14.1
### State and Federal Male Prisoners By Race and Region, December 31, 1978

| Jurisdiction | White | Black | American Indian/ Alaskan Native | Asian/Or Pacific Islander | Ethnicity Unknown | Total |
|---|---|---|---|---|---|---|
| U.S. | 151,534 | 136,893 (46.6%) | 2,423 | 667 | 2,365 | 293,882 |
| Federal institutions | 16,111 | 10,424 (37.3%) | 433 | 54 | 953 | 27,975 |
| State institutions | 135,423 | 126,469 (47.6%) | 1,990 | 613 | 1,412 | 265,907 |
| Northeast | 20,318 | 20,707 (50.3%) | 17 | 6 | 136 | 41,184 |
| North Central | 29,932 | 28,140 (47.4%) | 609 | 53 | 594 | 59,328 |
| South | 57,018 | 67,801 (54.0%) | 539 | 9 | 158 | 125,525 |
| West | 28,155 | 9,821 (25.0%) | 825 | 545 | 524 | 39,870 |

SOURCE: Unpublished data, provided by the U.S. Bureau of Census, Washington, D.C., October 1979.

231

## TABLE 14.2
### State and Federal Black Male Prisoners By State and Region
### December 31, 1978*

| Region & State | Total Male Prisoners | Black Male Prisoners Total | Black Male Prisoners Percentage | Total | Death Row** Black Males Total | Death Row** Black Males Percentage |
|---|---|---|---|---|---|---|
| *U.S.* | 293,882 | 136,893 | 46.6 | 443 | 194 | 43.7 |
| *Federal Institutions* | 27,975 | 10,424 | 37.5 | — | — | — |
| *State Institutions* | 265,907 | 126,460 | 47.6 | 443 | 194 | 43.7 |
| *Northeast* | 41,184 | 20,707 | 50.3 | 2 | 2 | 100.0 |
| †Maine | 695 | 8 | 1.2 | — | — | 100.0 |
| †New Hampshire | 277 | 6 | 2.2 | — | — | — |
| †Vermont | 453 | 1 | .22 | — | — | — |
| Massachusetts | 2,738 | 1,008 | 36.8 | — | — | — |
| †Rhode Island | 648 | 152 | 23.5 | 2 | 2 | 100.0 |
| †Connecticut | 3,360 | 1,351 | 40.2 | — | — | — |
| †New York | 19,635 | 10,485 | 54.4 | — | — | — |
| New Jersey | 5,693 | 3,502 | 61.5 | — | — | — |
| Pennsylvania | 7,685 | 4,194 | 55.0 | — | — | — |
| *North Central* | 59,328 | 28,140 | 47.4 | 92 | 55 | 59.8 |
| †Ohio | 12,569 | 6,536 | 52.0 | 87 | 54 | 62.1 |
| †Indiana | 4,754 | 1,376 | 28.9 | — | — | — |
| †Illinois | 10,918 | 6,304 | 57.7 | 1 | 1 | 100.0 |
| Michigan | 14,323 | 8,101 | 56.6 | — | — | — |
| Wisconsin | 3,286 | 1,266 | 38.5 | — | — | — |
| Minnesota | 1,871 | 301 | 16.1 | — | — | — |
| Iowa | 1,985 | 355 | 17.9 | — | — | — |
| †Missouri | 5,455 | 2,728 | 50.0 | — | — | — |
| North Dakota | 196 | 4 | 2.0 | — | — | — |
| South Dakota | 514 | 10 | 1.0 | — | — | — |
| †Nebraska | 1,264 | 422 | 33.4 | 4 | 0 | 0 |
| Kansas | 2,193 | 737 | 33.6 | — | — | — |
| *South* | 125,525 | 67,801 | 54.0 | 255 | 107 | 42.0 |
| †Delaware | 1,261 | 706 | 55.9 | — | — | — |
| Maryland | 7,722 | 5,843 | 75.7 | — | — | — |
| District of Columbia | 2,784 | 2,672 | 95.9 | — | — | — |
| †Virginia | 7,985 | 4,735 | 59.3 | 1 | 1 | 100.0 |
| West Virginia | 1,156 | 180 | 15.6 | — | — | — |
| †North Carolina | 12,718 | 6,856 | 53.9 | 1 | 0 | 0 |
| †South Carolina | 7,086 | 4,028 | 56.8 | 4 | 2 | 50.0 |
| †Georgia | 10,852 | 6,498 | 59.9 | 49 | 25 | 51.0 |
| †Florida | 19,936 | 10,156 | 51.0 | 96 | 40 | 42.0 |
| †Kentucky | 3,279 | 947 | 28.9 | — | — | — |
| †Tennessee | 5,574 | 2,674 | 47.5 | — | — | — |
| †Alabama | 5,213 | 3,116 | 59.8 | 19 | 8 | 42.0 |

TABLE 14.2
State and Federal Black Male Prisoners By State and Region
December 31, 1978* (Continued)

| Region & State | Total Male Prisoners | Black Male Prisoners | | Total | Death Row** Black Males | |
|---|---|---|---|---|---|---|
| | | Total | Percentage | | Total | Percentage |
| †Mississippi | 2,785 | 1,860 | 66.9 | 8 | 6 | 75.0 |
| †Arkansas | 2,511 | 1,304 | 51.9 | 7 | 2 | 28.6 |
| †Louisiana | 7,083 | 5,099 | 71.9 | — | — | — |
| †Oklahoma | 4,010 | 1,139 | 28.4 | 5 | 1 | 20.0 |
| †Texas | 23,570 | 10,015 | 42.5 | 65 | 22 | 33.8 |
| West | 39,870 | 9,821 | 24.6 | 94 | | |
| †Montana | 675 | 10 | 1.5 | 5 | 1 | 20.0 |
| †Idaho | 775 | 17 | 2.2 | 1 | 0 | 0 |
| †Wyoming | 414 | 0 | — | — | — | — |
| †Colorado | 2,419 | 533 | 22.0 | 5 | 2 | 40.0 |
| New Mexico | 1,526 | 172 | 11.3 | — | — | — |
| †Arizona | 3,275 | 641 | 19.6 | 18 | 4 | 22.2 |
| †Utah | 875 | 71 | 8.1 | 6 | 2 | 33.3 |
| †Nevada | 1,274 | 373 | 29.3 | 3 | 0 | 0 |
| †Washington | 4,327 | 843 | 19.5 | 2 | 0 | 0 |
| Oregon | 2,769 | 228 | 8.2 | — | — | — |
| †California | 20,178 | 6,743 | 33.4 | 54 | 21 | 38.9 |
| Alaska | 678 | 176 | 25.9 | — | — | — |
| Hawaii | 688 | 14 | 2.0 | — | — | — |

* Unpublished data provided by the U.S. Bureau of the Census.

** Data are from *Capital Punishment, 1977*. U.S. Department of Justice, November 1978.

† Death penalty authorized as December 31, 1977.

The intention of this chapter is to assert that the incarceration of Black men throughout the United States is *extreme, harsh,* and *brutal.* More important, it is not indicative of a new or faltering predicament.

The predicament of America's 136,893 Black male prisoners is particularly noticeable when attention is focused on the following facts:

(1) Since 1930, 3,861 persons have been executed throughout the United States. Of those executed, 2,051 (53.6 percent) were Black men.

(2) Currently, there are 443 persons under the sentence of death throughout the nation. Of these, 194 (43.8 percent) are Black men.

(3) Black men account for 46.6 percent (136,893) of all male prisoners throughout the United States.

These facts are enlightening, doubtless for more than one reason. Of major note, however, are the glaring disparities between each of the percentages and the nation's Black male population percentage. Comparisons show that although Blacks form approximately 12 percent of America's population, Black men constitute slightly less than 50 percent of all state and federal male prisoners and nearly 45 percent of all persons sentenced to death. Further, the American Black male population percentage has never approximated the percentage (53.6) of Black men executed since 1930. These facts, perhaps better than any others, clearly indicate the incarceration plight of Black men is as bad as previously outlined.

Data show that the current Black male incarceration predicament fits snugly and pathetically within a well-documented history of biased and unduly severe criminal sentencing. Together, the Scottsboro Boys spent more than 100 years in Alabama jails and prisons (Carter, 1969). Marcus Garvey served a five-year sentence for a conviction that usually "produced a sentence that ran from probation to one year in jail" (Vincent, 1972: 203). George Jackson of the Soledad Brothers was sentenced to a term from "one year to life" for stealing $70 from a gas station. He spent eleven years in prison, eight and one-half of them in solitary confinement (Jackson, 1970: Introduction). Malcolm X was sentenced to ten years for burglary, though "the average burglary sentence for a first offender at that time was about two years" (Malcolm X & Haley, 1964: 150). To date, three members of the Republic of New Afrika (RNA) Eleven, having been convicted of waging war against the state of Mississippi, are serving life sentences in the Mississippi State Penitentiary (Hinds, 1978). Together, the initial sentences of the Charlotte Three totaled more than 50 years (Hinds, 1978). Combined, the initial sentences of the Wilmington Ten totaled 282 years. When arbitrarily reduced, they totaled 224 years (Hinds, 1978). Not long ago, Tommie Lee Hines, a Black male, was sentenced to life imprisonment in Georgia. Severely mentally retarded (I.Q. 31), Tommie Lee Hines "cannot tell you what a judge or jury is" (Jones, 1979).

Michael Meltsner (1974) has suggested that it is impossible to separate racism from the death penalty. Atlanta Mayor Maynard Jackson has outlined the severity of the criminal justice system when applied to poor people. A very large number of these are Black (Jackson, 1977). Lennox Hinds (1978) reports in *Illusions of Justice* that in "the history of the United States, no white person has ever been executed for murder, rape, or other capital crimes against a Black person." Hinds notes that the results of a study commissioned by the U.S. Congress indicate that "someone Black and poor tried for stealing a few hundred dollars has a 90 percent likelihood of being convicted of robbery with a sentence averaging between 94 to 138 months. On the other hand, a white business executive who has embezzled hundreds of thousands of dollars has only a 20 percent likelihood of conviction with a sentence averaging about 20 to 48 months" (Hinds, 1978: 44). These assertions are further supported by Dr. George Napper (1977: 14), Atlanta Chief of Police:

> In a case involving the Sherman Anti-trust Act, the executives of seven electrical manufacturing corporations were convicted of a price conspiracy involving over one billion dollars and were sentenced to thirty days in jail each. Meanwhile, seemingly sadistic sentences were meted out to poor people convicted of crimes in the streets. A man in Asbury Park, New Jersey, for instance, was convicted of stealing a $2.98 pair of sunglasses and a dollar box of soap. He was sent to jail for four months. Joseph Sills in Dallas, Texas was sentenced to 1,000 years in prison for stealing $73.10.

Highly publicized events of 1979 show that persons receiving often undue and always excessive criminal sentencing bear the weight of Blackness and/or poverty, whereas those who escape such punishment generally do not. Few did not learn of the 48-year sentence with no possibility of parole imposed upon Robert May (a 14-year-old Black Mississippi youth), found guilty of armed robbery. Further, many are appalled and dismayed at the disparity between the execution of John Spenkelink, a poor drifter, and the manslaughter conviction of Dan White, a former city official of San Francisco. Today, the list of such inequitable sentences is nearly endless, entailing a severe Black male incarceration predicament. More important, there is no indication that the current predicament will soon be corrected, to end a horrible legacy evident in the following incidents.

Since 1930, 455 men have been executed throughout the United States as convicted rapists. Alarmingly, 405 (89 percent) were Black. Records show that 398 (89.8 percent) of the 443 men executed for rape in the South since 1930 were Black. Further, data reveal that for nine of the years between 1930 and 1947, Blacks constituted the entire population of men executed for rape. Also, these data show that for only three of the cited seventeen years does the Black percentage of rape executions fall below 80 percent (Townsey, 1979). William Bowers (1974) has compiled shocking execution data, which include the execution of a Black man for "attempted rape." Black men also constitute 76 percent (23) of those persons executed for armed robbery and 100 percent (11) of those executed for burglary since 1930. Further, when the death penalty was declared unconstitutional in 1972, Blacks accounted for nearly 58 percent of the persons on death row.

Related data show fourteen states to have executed more than 100 persons each. In seven of these states, Black men represented close to or more than 80 percent of those persons executed. In only five of the fourteen states do Black men make up less than 50 percent of those *lawfully* killed. Moreover, in

## TABLE 14.3
### Black Men Executed in Fourteen States
### 1930-1977

| Region & State | Males All Races Number | Black Males Number | Black Males Percentage |
|---|---|---|---|
| *Northeast* | 608 | 175 | 28.7 |
| New York | 329 | 89 | 27.0 |
| Pennsylvania | 152 | 56 | 36.8 |
| *North Central* | 403 | 143 | 33.7 |
| Ohio | 172 | 66 | 38.4 |
| *South* | 2,306 | 1,650 | 71.5 |
| North Carolina | 263 | 197 | 77.7 |
| Georgia | 366 | 297 | 81.1 |
| Florida | 170 | 113 | .6 |
| Kentucky | 103 | 52 | 50.4 |
| Alabama | 135 | 106 | 78.5 |
| Mississippi | 154 | 121 | 78.6 |
| Arkansas | 118 | 90 | 76.3 |
| Louisiana | 133 | 103 | 77.4 |
| Texas | 297 | 182 | 61.3 |
| *West* | 510 | 83 | 16.2 |
| California | 292 | 53 | 18.4 |
| National Execution Totals | 3,827 | 2,051 | 53.6 |

SOURCE: Data are from *Capital Punishment, 1977.* Washington, D.C.: U.S. Department of Justice, November 1978.

only one of the fourteen jurisdictions do Black men constitute less than 25 percent of those executed (see Table 14.3).

Additional and substantive statistics are seemingly in the making, as evidenced by the data in Table 14.2, which show that only one region has a current Black male prisoner population of less than 50 percent of the total. More specifically, and explicative of the point to be made here, throughout 18 states Black men make up over 50 percent and up to 75 percent of the male prisoner populations.

Despite fluctuations within individual state prison populations, Black men constitute the majority of male prisoners held by the two states that have experienced the two extremes. During 1977, in relative terms, Louisiana incurred the largest prisoner population increase (27 percent) and Mississippi experienced the sharpest decrease (18 percent). As might be expected, the latest count shows Black men to form 71.9 percent of Louisiana's male prisoner population. Further, in spite of the state penitentiary's sharp population decrease, Mississippi's proportion of Black male prisoners is 66.9 percent of the incarcerated men.

As in prisons, Black men in city and county jails are represented in gravely disproportionate numbers. *The Preliminary Report on the Census of Jails and The Survey of Jail Inmates for 1978,* provided by the Law Enforcement Assistance Administration (LEAA), U.S. Department of Justice, indicates that the proportion of Blacks in the nation's 3,493 jails far exceeds the general population percentage of Blacks. As of February 1978, there were 158,394 persons held in jails across the country. Blacks constituted 41 percent (65,104) of the inmates. The *LEAA Newsletter* of June/July 1979 reports that nearly 50 percent of the jails holding approximately 43 percent of all jail inmates are in the South. Reportedly, Georgia, Nevada, Alabama, and Louisiana "ranked highest in the ratio of jail inmates to total population." Further, the newsletter reports that California, Texas, New York, and Florida each holds "at least 10,000 persons in jails." It is of note that California, with 26,206 jail inmates, holds more than twice as many as each of the others.

Like prisons, over the last few years, local jails have experienced sizable prisoner increases. The *LEAA Newsletter* for June/July 1979 reported that between 1972 and 1978 the number of persons incarcerated in jails increased by 12 percent. A portion of this increase is attributable to lack of space in overcrowded state prisons. Of the prisoners held at year end 1977 by state authority, 7,048 actually were housed in local jails. Among the ten states housing state prison inmates in jails, only four—Maryland (921), South Carolina (697), Massachusetts (59), and Michigan (58)—counted them as state prisoners. The remaining six—Alabama (2,626), Florida (253), Louisiana (780), Mississippi (575), New Jersey (255), and Virginia (824)—excluded them from their state prisoner count. Hence, the state prisoner totals of these listed states are inaccurate reflections of the number of prisoners actually sentenced to state imprisonment (U.S. Department of Justice, 1979). Nonetheless, data reported in Table 14.2 show that Black men formed over 50 percent and up to 72 percent of the male prisoner populations throughout these six states.

Numerous research efforts concerned with the imposition of the death penalty and other criminal sentencing support the idea that the horror and gravity of the Black male's predicament in being incarcerated is in great part the result of American racism vented through differential sentencing. In noting that "law is the mechanism by which authority implements its intentions," Hinds (1978: iii) described the prosecution of Blacks as an "endless and intricate labyrinth of legal process which hold tantalizing promises of relief but which in practice merely validate the results of proceedings tainted with racism and political expediency." Therefore, it becomes extremely clear why Blacks in gravely disproportionate numbers experience an unfortunate "confrontation with the criminal law and the selective application of its sanctions" (Hinds, 1978: viii). Having acknowledged the impact of discrimination on the imposition of the death penalty, the U.S. Supreme Court in Furman v. Georgia (1978) ruled that the death penalty as then administered was unconstitutional. The court noted that the unbridled discretion allowed to judges and juries in imposing the death penalty buttressed sentencing practices that violated the Eighth and Fourteenth Amendments' prohibitions of cruel and unusual punishment. In great part, majority opinions described the imposition of the death penalty as "random," "wanton," "capricious," and "freakish." Justice Stewart succinctly noted that persons facing execution were "a capriciously selected random handful" (Furman v. Georgia, 1978: 309-310). Indicating that "one searches our chronicles in vain for the execution of any member of the affluent stratum of this society," Justice Douglas made it clear that up to the time of the ruling, "the discretion of judges and juries in imposing the death penalty enabled the penalty to be selectively applied, feeding prejudices against the accused if he is poor and despised and lacking political clout or if he is a member of a suspect or unpopular minority and saving those who by social position may be in a more protected position." Thus, he emphasized that the discretionary death penalty statutes then before the Court were "pregnant with discrimination . . . an ingredient not compatible with the idea of equal protection of the laws that is implicit in the ban on 'cruel and unusual' punishments" (Furman v. Georgia, 1978: 256-257). Justice Stewart also concluded that "the Eighth and Fourteenth Amendments cannot tolerate the infliction of a sentence of death under legal systems that permit this unique penalty to be so wantonly and so freakishly imposed (Furman v. Georgia, 1978: 310). Further, Justice Marshall felt that allowing juries "untrammeled discretion" to impose the death penalty amounted to "an open invitation to discrimination" (Furman v. Georgia, 1978: 365). Juries have seemingly exploited this invitation heartily, as suggested by the following research findings. Combined, Alabama, Arkansas, Florida, Georgia, Louisiana, South Carolina, and Tennessee capital punishment data (Wolfgang & Reidel, 1976) revealed that among 1,265 cases in which the race of the defendant and the sentence were known, nearly seven times as many Blacks were sentenced to death as whites. Among the 823 Blacks convicted of rape, 110, or 13 percent, were sentenced to death. Among the 442 whites convicted of rape, only 9, or 2 percent, were sentenced to death. The statistical probability that such a disproportionate number of Blacks could be sentenced to death by chance alone is less than one in a thousand. Specifically, a statistically significant higher proportion of Black defendants whose victims were white were sentenced to death. From a total of 1,238 convicted rape defendants, 317 were Black defendants with white victims and 921 were all other racial combinations of defendant and victim (including Black-Black, white-white, and white-Black). Of the 137 Black defendants whose victims were white, 113, or approximately 36 percent, were sentenced to death. Of the 921 defendants involved in all other racial combinations of defendant and victim, only 19, or 2 percent, were sentenced to death. In short, Black defendants whose victims were white were sentenced to death approximately 18 times more frequently than defendants in any other racial combination of defendant and victim. Again, the probability of such a distribution or such a relationship between the sentence of death and Black defendants with white victims by chance alone is less than one in a thousand.

Specifics denoting sentencing disparities among Blacks and whites convicted of noncapital crimes sadly mimic the trend outlined above. A study of federal sentences meted out between 1967 and 1970 revealed that Black defendants received harsher sentences than white defendants convicted of the same crimes. For example, the results showed that for postal theft the rate of prison sentencing was below 40 percent for whites and nearly 50 percent for Blacks. Similarly, in interstate theft cases, 48 percent of Black defendants, but only 28 percent of white defendants, received prison terms.

A survey of sentences imposed in South Carolina during 1971 presents particularly varied sentencing patterns. Worth noting are the disparate sentences imposed by one judge in two first-offender marijuana cases. In one case, involving a white youth as the defendant, the judge imposed a sentence of one year's probation and a $400 fine. In the other case, involving a Black defendant, the judge imposed a two-year sentence. The survey also revealed sentencing disparities according to sex and type of crime. A woman who issued a plea of guilty to voluntary manslaughter was sentenced to two years in prison and four years' probation, whereas a male defendant received a sentence of 21 years (both were first offenders). Another defendant pleaded guilty to assault and battery with intent to kill and received a seven-day sentence of imprisonment and five years' probation. Quite differently, a grand-larceny defendant who had stolen two suits was sentenced to seven years' imprisonment. The survey notes in summary that "more of these disparities could be catalogued but that the point is made. There is no policy covering criteria or rationale or objectives for sentencing that are operative among South Carolina's circuit court judges" (*Twentieth Century Fund Task Force on Criminal Sentencing, Fair and Certain Punishment,* 1976: 104). That such sentencing disparities are not indigenous to South Carolina but characteristic of sentencing across the nation leads one to ask how such disparities are able to develop.

It has been noted that "probably the most critical point in the administration of criminal justice" is the imposition of sentence (*Twentieth Century*

*Fund Task Force,* 1976). The sentence, therefore, should reflect the ideal of equity. Sadly, very often it does not. Sentencing throughout the United States is predominantly indeterminate. Indeterminate sentences, which are characterized by a wealth of space between the minimum and maximum penalties authorized by legislatures, include no clearly articulated criteria for determining appropriate sentences. Hence, for the most part, there are no standards, rules, or guidelines for the exercise of sentencing discretion. This being the case, judges are free to manifest their individual notions of what level of sentencing an individual defendant merits. The results are disparate sentences. Certainly, judges rightly entertain a gamut of factors in imposing sentences, and these factors may reasonably account for some sentencing differences. However, if the most determinant factors include social status, sex, or race, the sentencing disparities constitute improper judgments, most of which minority defendants bear in grossly disproportionate numbers.

Without a doubt, every case is different in many significant respects. However, cases involving the same offense, very similar criminal histories, and defendants who differ only by race should result in similar sentences. This is far removed from actuality, as is evidenced by the following. A number of states' armed robbery statutes specify a maximum penalty of twenty years but specify no minimum penalty. It is left to pure speculation if legislators intended probation, one year, five years, or ten years to serve as a minimum. Hence, sentencers lawfully use their discretion to determine the proper sentence for one convicted of armed robbery. Unfortunately, as a result, some first-time offenders receive truly extreme prison terms (such as the 48-year sentence with no possibility of parole), while others with substantial criminal records receive no prison sentence at all (*Twentieth Century Fund Task Force,* 1976). Surely, this level of disparity, resulting from the "capricious and arbitrary nature of criminal sentencing," undermines and weakens the credibility of the entire criminal justice system. Certainly, imposing sentences of life imprisonment upon some first offenders and the one-year probation upon others, when all are convicted of indecent exposure, for example, tremendously discredits the system (*Twentieth Century Fund Task Force,* 1976).

Specifics characterizing the provision of a public defense counsel also undermine the credibility of the system. The American Bar Association (ABA) has reported that nearly half of the 300,000 persons charged yearly with felony offenses cannot afford lawyers. It was ruled years ago in the Scottsboro Boys case, Powell v. Alabama (1932), and reaffirmed in Gideon v. Wainwright (1963), that indigents must be afforded legal counsel for their defense. However, in many jurisdictions counsel is assigned regardless of a defendant's economic status. Although these practices are of great value, they often fall short of what is needed. Louis Knowles and Kenneth Prewitt, authors of *Institutional Racism in America* (1969), reported that most of the

3,100 counties in the United States that provide defense attorneys have only inadequate counsel to offer. Further, those jurisdictions providing defense counsel are often short of the number needed. Because this is the case, most jurisdictions provide counsel only at certain points of the judicial process. This problem is quite widespread. In thirty-two states, courts do not provide counsel at the preliminary hearing. Even more distressing is the fact that in 75 of the 300 counties surveyed by the ABA, there were no definite provisions for counsel at the sentencing stage.

The National Council on Crime and Delinquency (NCCD) gathered data concerning 812 accused criminal offenders represented by public defenders. Nearly 30 percent of the defendants reported that their attorneys spent less than ten minutes with them; 32 percent reported that the public defender spent only ten to twenty-nine minutes with them; and 27 percent stated that the public defender spent one-half hour to three hours discussing their cases with them; only 14 percent reported having conferred with the public defender for more than three hours. Many authorities feel that an adequate defense should include providing the client with a sense of security and the belief that the attorney is doing his or her utmost to protect the defendant. In view of the findings presented by NCCD, there is little wonder that nearly half (49 percent) of all the public defenders' clients "thought that their attorneys were on the side of the state."

Ernest Giles, a 31-year-old Black inmate at the Lorton Reformatory in Washington, D.C., recently spoke in an interview of being "denied adequate legal representation." In a special issue of *Ebony* (1979: 100), entitled "Black on Black Crime," Giles explained:

> I had no money to get a lawyer who would have gathered evidence on my behalf and who could have really gone out and rounded up witnesses to clear me. I met with my lawyer only twice and both times involved only a few minutes. I was brought before Judge Ugast and was convicted in about ten minutes. It was so quick that even the U.S. Marshals in the courtroom did not believe the trial was over. Ten minutes. That was what it took to supposedly hear all the evidence and give me a fair trial, but here I am at Lorton with eight to 24 years hanging over my head.

Few have not acknowledged that sentencing disparities are enormous. Going further, many have also concluded that the enormity of sentencing variations are very often inexplicable and not rationally justifiable. For example, is it a simple matter (if, indeed, it is possible) to explain the findings of the following study or to justify the facts that these findings clearly indicate?

The study, commissioned by the U.S. Court of Appeals for the Second Circuit, entailed supplying fifty federal judges with twenty identical files and requesting that each indicate the specific sentence that he would impose in each case. What have been termed "shocking" disparities developed. In a case concerning the possession of and intent to distribute barbiturates, one judge indicated a five-year sentence while another judge indicated a sentence of probation. In a case involving a union official convicted on several counts of extortionate credit transactions, one judge indicated a sentence of 20 years' imprisonment plus a $65,000 fine. In contrast, another judge indicated a three-year sentence with no fine (*Twentieth Century Fund Task Force*, 1976). Additional research efforts show equally disparate actual sentencing. A study of sentences meted out in Montgomery County, Ohio, revealed that some judges imprisoned defendants twice as often as other judges for the same offense. Further, in very similar robbery cases, one judge imprisoned 17 percent of the defendants while another judge imprisoned 77 percent.

More important, sentencing laws making such disparities possible do not differ in quality or consequence from several states' death penalty statutes. This is made evident by the following.

In Georgia, the death penalty may be imposed for the crime of murder if the jury determines that the offense was "outrageously or wantonly vile, horrible or inhuman in that it involved torture or depravity of mind . . ." (Black, 1974). The foregoing serves as a sentencing *standard* that supposedly guides and confines the exercise of jury discretion. However, as Professor Charles Black (1974) of Yale Law School wrote, "What Georgia has done is to lay down a smoke screen of plenteous words which on hasty reading mask the fact that exactly the same old unbridled jury discretion is there" (Black, 1974). What murder cannot be described as *outrageously* or *wantonly vile* or *horrible* or *inhuman?* Further, what murder cannot be said to have involved *torture* or *depravity of mind* of some kind? Such a statute allows juries a wealth of unbridled and thus dangerous discretion. Consequently, bias is able to run rampant and Georgia juries *lawfully* find Black men to have committed *outrageous and wantonly vile murders* in a proportion which exceeds the proportion of white men convicted in this fashion. (Currently, Black men constitute 59.9 percent of the men under the sentence of death in the state of Georgia.)

The post-Furman Texas death penalty statute allows imposition of the death penalty upon one convicted of a capital crime if the jury concludes "beyond a reasonable doubt . . . that there is a probability that the defendant would commit criminal acts of violence that would constitute a continuing threat to society" (Black, 1974). The vagueness of this language allows the inference that, in Texas, the probability of a convicted capital offender's execution rests significantly upon a jury's *guess* as to his or her future conduct. A number of its aspects debase the Texas death penalty statute. Certainly, it is proper to ask, What does "a probability" mean? Does it mean "a great likelihood" or "a good chance" or "just short of certainty?" Each by definition is correct. Beyond this, offenses that are "criminal act(s) of violence that would constitute . . . continuing threat(s) to society" are very nebulously defined, so nebulously that hitting someone with one's fist may qualify as such an act of violence. Hence, according to Black (1974), it is not unimaginable that a jury in Texas may lawfully decide to "electrocute persons shown to be given to fisticuffs." Apparently, juries *guess beyond a reasonable doubt* that a greater proportion of Black as opposed to white capital offenders would *probably* "commit acts of violence that would constitute a continuing threat to society." This is true insofar as Black men account for 42.5 percent of the men sentenced to death in Texas.

Judges and juries are presumed to assess guilt similarly in noncapital cases, i.e., by concluding *beyond a reasonable doubt.* However, no statutes of any kind define what a consensus or judgment *beyond a reasonable doubt* is, in actuality, or how we are to know this level of certainty has been assuredly reached. It is of note that many believe judges and juries do not approximate meeting but generally do, in fact, meet this challenge (Townsey, 1979). However, even the most ardent supporters of the criminal justice system acknowledge that, on occasion, sentencers may only profess to reach such a judgment or consensus, responding to personal or political biases rather than the facts at hand. Because this happens, however *infrequently,* and because Black men clearly bear the adverse weight of this *infrequency,* it is far from shallow to note in a strict fashion the role of such unbridled discretion in sentencing. It is of note that having focused upon the presence of dangerous amounts of unbridled discretion and the influence of race upon sentencing, criminological research affirms that "criminal courts are arbitrary and discriminatory" in sentencing. Thus, statistics and case dispositions such as those previously discussed develop.

Perhaps the most extreme sentencing disparity is that between sentences imposed upon citizens responsible for the deaths of police officers and sentences imposed for the reverse. Generally, the killing of a citizen by a police officer does not receive nearly as much judicial or state attention as is given to the killing of an officer by a citizen. The *Uniform Crime Reports,* for example, present extensive data concerning the number of killings of police officers by citizens, but do not report killings of citizens by police. However, there are statistics indicating that nonwhite males make up a significant proportion of civilians killed by police officers. As outlined in Table 14.4, minority males constituted up to 43 percent of male police shooting victims for each year of the 1952-1969 period. In fact, minority males made up 50 percent and more of the male shooting victims of police for nine of the eighteen years shown in Table 14.4. Further, statistics for more recent years show disproportionate yearly percentages of victims of police shootings are

### TABLE 14.4
### Male Civilians Killed By Police 1952-1969

| Year | Total Males Killed | White Male Victims | | Nonwhite Male Victims | |
|------|------|------|------|------|------|
| | | Number | Percentage | Number | Percentage |
| 1952 | 252 | 128 | 50.6 | 125 | 49.4 |
| 1953 | 254 | 124 | 48.8 | 130 | 51.2 |
| 1954 | 242 | 130 | 53.7 | 112 | 46.3 |
| 1955 | 225 | 111 | 49.3 | 114 | 50.7 |
| 1956 | 226 | 123 | 54.4 | 103 | 45.6 |
| 1957 | 228 | 119 | 52.2 | 109 | 47.8 |
| 1958 | 228 | 111 | 48.7 | 117 | 51.3 |
| 1959 | 226 | 109 | 48.2 | 117 | 51.8 |
| 1960 | 242 | 124 | 51.2 | 118 | 48.8 |
| 1961 | 235 | 132 | 56.2 | 103 | 43.8 |
| 1962 | 182 | 88 | 48.4 | 94 | 51.6 |
| 1963 | 240 | 111 | 46.3 | 129 | 53.7 |
| 1964 | 274 | 131 | 47.8 | 143 | 52.2 |
| 1965 | 271 | 154 | 56.8 | 117 | 43.2 |
| 1966 | 294 | 150 | 51.0 | 144 | 49.0 |
| 1967 | 382 | 200 | 52.3 | 182 | 47.6 |
| 1968 | 344 | 163 | 47.3 | 181 | 52.6 |
| 1969 | 350 | 160 | 45.7 | 190 | 54.3 |

SOURCE: Arthur L. Kobler, "Police Homicide in a Democracy." *Journal of Social Issues,* 1975, *31*(1): Table 1. Reprinted by permission.

nonwhite civilians. Table 14.5 shows that between 1968 and 1976, the yearly percentages of nonwhite civilians killed by police officers consistently approach or surpass 50 percent. There are also recent research findings showing that Black men, in particular, are the victims of police killings at a very disproportionate rate.

Professor Paul Takagi (1979) of the University of California noted that between 1960 and 1968, 1,188 Black men and 1,253 white men were killed by police officers in an area with a 10-percent Black population. Professor Takagi (1979: 33) also indicated that during the 1956-1974 period, the rates of police shooting deaths "remained consistently at least nine times higher for Blacks" than for whites. Concomitantly, numerous other research findings also show Black men to form a disproportionate number of police shooting victims. For example, Gerald Robin (1963) conducted multiple analyses and

TABLE 14.5
Civilians Killed By Police, 1968-1976

| Year | Civilian Deaths | White Civilian Victims | | Nonwhite Civilian Victims | |
|------|------|------|------|------|------|
| | | Number | Percentage | Number | Percentage |
| 1968 | 343 | 159 | 46.4 | 184 | 53.6 |
| 1969 | 347 | 158 | 45.5 | 189 | 54.5 |
| 1970 | 330 | 154 | 46.7 | 176 | 53.3 |
| 1971 | 409 | 214 | 52.3 | 198 | 48.4 |
| 1972 | 296 | 132 | 44.6 | 164 | 55.4 |
| 1973 | 372 | 185 | 49.7 | 187 | 50.3 |
| 1974 | 370 | 183 | 49.5 | 187 | 50.5 |
| 1975 | 330 | 177 | 53.6 | 153 | 46.4 |
| 1976 | 286 | 146 | 51.0 | 140 | 49.0 |

SOURCE: Unpublished data provided by the National Center for Health Statistics, U.S. Department of Health, Education and Welfare.

concluded that throughout ten cities, Blacks (the vast majority of whom were men) were killed at a rate six to twenty times greater than the rate for whites. In an explanation of these high proportions, police officials have indicated that because Blacks commit a higher percentage of major crimes that often result in citizen killings, they logically constitute a higher percentage of deaths associated with the commission of major crimes. Dr. James J. Fyfe (1978: 144) of the American University, author of *Shots Fired: An Examination of New York City Police Firearms' Discharges*, explains that "Blacks are the mode among New York City police's shooting opponents because they are also the mode among the lower socioeconomic groups which most frequently precipitate extreme police-citizen violence." However, the implication of these and similar substantive explanations is not absolute. In view of data such as those noted by Takagi (1979), Blacks constitute 51 percent of those killed by police officers in 1964 and 1968, while they accounted for only 30 to 36 percent of all arrests in 1964 and 1968 for major crimes. In sum, Takagi (1979: 33) indicated that "no matter how we view crime statistics on Blacks with police killing of Black civilians, the death rate of Blacks is far out of proportion to the situations that might justify it."

Rarely is an officer prosecuted for the death of a civilian, regardless of the victim's race or sex. The vast majority of such deaths are designated as justifiable homicides and the remainder labeled negligent homicides carrying misdemeanor penalties. Information released by the U.S. Department of

Justice shows that throughout every region of the country, indictments have been brought against police officers who, "acting under the color of law, unlawfully shot the victim, taking away his constitutional right not to be deprived of liberty without due process of law." However, 180 (78.9 percent) of the 228 indictments brought against police officers between 1971 and 1975 resulted in acquittals (Takagi, 1979).

A police officer's grant of power to use deadly force (e.g., shooting a fleeing felon during the commission of a felony thought to endanger the life of the police officer or others) excuses the officer from legal liability in the death of a civilian in certain situations. However, there is evidence that strongly suggests many officers exploit this authority by killing minority civilians in practically any situation. Recognizing this, recent court rulings have sought to restrain the authority of officers to use deadly force in certain situations. Takagi (1979) reports that in a recent federal case, Mattis v. Schnarr (1976), a Court of Appeals ruled a Missouri statute concerning the killing of fleeing felons unconstitutional. The case concerned the death of a burglary suspect who was killed by a police officer as he ran from a bare golf course early one morning. The court ruled that the state cannot kill a person committing a nonviolent felony unless, as stipulated, there is strong reason to believe the suspect endangers the life of the police officer or others. In spite of the potential of this ruling, the U.S. Supreme Court vacated it on procedural grounds. However, in a similar case, the Court of Appeals in St. Louis ruled unlawful the use of deadly force against a felony suspect who is not violent. Unfortunately, the impact of Mattis v. Schnarr and similar rulings has been very limited. Hence, civilians, most notably Black men, are often erroneously and viciously killed by police officers who are generally only subjected to written reprimands. Most illustrative of the point to be made here is the 1978 prosecution of three police officers in Texas. In that year, three Houston police officers found to be responsible for the deliberately vicious death of a local Mexican American youth (Joe Torres) were sentenced to probation. In November 1979, in response to great minority protest, they were sentenced to imprisonment for one year and one day. In contrast, in 1979, a 16-year-old Black youth in Prince George's County, Maryland, was sentenced to 25 years' imprisonment when convicted of manslaughter in the death of a local police officer who, as evidence presented in court showed, had physically abused the youth without provocation.

Feodor Dostoevski, the Russian writer, wrote in 1862 that "the degree of civilization in a society can be judged by entering its prisons" (Gibbs, 1979: 44). The state of American civilization, if Dostoevski is correct, is certainly crude. If we are to achieve humanistic rehabilitation, we must at least provide those incarcerated with "adequate food and clothing, reasonably comfortable surroundings, work and recreational opportunities [and] some contact with friends and relatives" (Hartzen, 1974: 134). However, humanitarianism does not, even in fairly general terms, characterize prison conditions. This is true for a significantly large number of the nation's 867 state prisons and 3,493 jails. Thus, to indicate that scores of prisons maintain deplorable conditions only hints at the reality of incarceration. Since the 1960s, however, a number of court orders concerning the quality of incarceration have come into being. Initially, federal court orders directed, albeit in very vague terms, that states devise strategies to upgrade objectionable prison conditions. However, later court orders have specifically outlined minimally acceptable incarceration standards. For example, in 1976 the U.S. District Court for Alabama issued what has become a significant decision concerning incarceration standards. Judge Frank M. Johnson, Jr., ruled that prisoners then incarcerated in Alabama were subjected to cruel and inhuman punishment prohibited by the Eighth Amendment. It may be surprising to some to learn that the Johnson Decision mandated a number of provisions that, although quite basic, were absent previously. In part, this ruling called for the assignment of a meaningful job to each inmate, the improvement of medical services, and three "nutritious" meals daily. It also indicated that each person be provided with "at least 60 square feet of cell floorspace" (U.S. Department of Justice, 1979: 3). Most of the requirements were upheld by the Fifth Circuit Court of Appeals. However, the requirement for 60 square feet of cell floorspace was rejected.

Litigation concerning cruel and inhuman incarceration has been particularly widespread throughout the South. Gates v. Collier (1975, 1977), Newman v. Alabama (1976, 1977), Williams v. Edwards (1977), and Holt v. Sarver (1969, 1970) charged the states of Mississippi, Alabama, Louisiana, and Arkansas with inadequate sanitation and security, racial discrimination in work assignments and religious freedom, improper medical care, lack of recreation, guard brutality, and promotion of inmate violence. They were also cited for numerous other human rights violations. In Gates v. Collier (1975, 1977), Judge William Keady ruled that the housing units at the Mississippi State Penitentiary at Parchman were "unfit for human habitation under any modern conception of decency." The ruling indicated that inmates were subjected to extreme physical abuse when placed in the maximum security unit (MSU). It is reported that in MSU, inmates were "administered milk of magnesia as a form of punishment." Other extremes included "stripping inmates of their clothes, turning the fan on inmates while naked and wet, depriving inmates of mattresses, hygenic materials, and adequate food, handcuffing inmates to the fence and to cells for long periods of time, shooting at and around inmates to keep them standing or lying in the yard at MSU, and using a cattle prod to keep inmates standing or moving while at MSU." The ruling also noted that the incarceration periods of Blacks in particular were significantly harsher. According to Judge Keady, Black inmates received "disparate and unequal treatment." Further, "approximately twice the number of Blacks [were] required to live in the same amount of dormitory space as that accorded to white inmates." It would not be true to indicate that such litigation is confined to the South, for it surfaces in the North, East, and West as well (American Civil Liberties Union Foundation, 1979). In the case of Pugh and James v. Britton (1976), the entire prison system of the state of Alabama was declared unconstitutional. (Black men constitute 60 percent of the men imprisoned throughout Alabama.) Duran v. Apodaca (n.d.) challenges all conditions at the New Mexico State Prison. A major aspect of this lawsuit addresses the operation of the prison food service, which is described as below minimum standards. (Black men form over 11 percent of those men incarcerated in the New Mexico State Prison.) In the case of Ramos v. Lamm (n.d.), the entire spectrum of conditions at the Colorado State Penitentiary is challenged as "inadequate." In view of "a massive amount of discovery," "a serious settlement" is expected. (Black men constitute 22 percent of the men incarcerated in Colorado state institutions.) Stewart v. Rhodes (1979) charges that the conditions, in total, at the Ohio State Prison in Columbus are beneath minimum standards. Thus far, the District Court has ruled on two issues, declaring unconstitutional the practice of segregating prisoners by race and the practice of placing prisoners held in isolation in restraint. It is hoped that this case will be as successful as Palmigiano v. Garrahy (1977) and Trigg v. Blanton (1978), in which the entire Rhode Island and Tennessee prison systems were declared unconstitutional. (Black men account for 52.0 percent, 23.5 percent, and 47.5 percent, respectively, of the state male prisoner populations in Ohio, Rhode Island, and Tennessee.)

Attorney Steven Winter (1979) of the NAACP Legal Defense Fund reported that the Georgia State Prison is a strong example of how horrid the conditions in many state prisons are. According to Winter, even as he spoke conditions at the Georgia State Prison were breeding interracial inmate violence. In 1976, interracial violence at this particular prison was a near-daily occurrence and was cited as primarily due to prison overcrowding. At that time and up to February 1979, the Georgia State Prison, which is equipped to house no more than 2,000 inmates, held more than 3,000 white and Black prisoners in small and inadequate barracks rather than in single cells. These conditions, coupled with guards who purposely aggravated the animosity between Black and white inmates, led to constant outbreaks of prisoner violence. One such outbreak, in 1976, resulted in the deaths of 3 Black inmates and the serious wounding of 23 others. These inmates were ambushed by 100 white inmates as they walked from one section of the prison to another for work. According to Winter, evidence showed that prison guards witnessed the ambush and made no efforts to stop the killings. Between March and July 1978, other Georgia State Prison outbreaks of inmate violence resulted in 7 inmate deaths and the severe wounding of more than 25 others. As late as the spring of 1979, there were recurring reports of rapes and stabbings of male inmates by other inmates and guards. Winter also indicated that to date (1979), the Georgia State Prison had access to the services of only four doctors to provide medical services for more than 3,000 inmates. He reported that not one of the four doctors was a fully licensed physician and that one of the four doctors, serving as the chief medical director, was a prison inmate convicted of supplying illegal drugs to female patients in exchange for sexual intercourse. (Black men constitute nearly 60 percent of the men incarcerated in Georgia state institutions.)

The case of Holt v. Sarver (1969, 1970) documents prison violence at its height. The following is an excerpt from a letter concerning prison conditions, written by NAACP Legal Defense Fund attorneys Steven Winter and Elaine Jones to Senator Edward Kennedy, chairman of the Senate Committee on the Judiciary:

> In *Holt v. Sarver* . . . the court described the everyday violence that occurred in the dormitories of the Arkansas State Penitentiary. Inmates known as "creepers" and "crawlers" would often crawl unseen between the cots in the dormitories and stab sleeping inmates. Physically attractive inmates were "frequently . . . raped in the barracks by other inmates." . . . The only measure of protection afforded these young men was assignment to the rows of cots nearest the front bars of the barracks, known as "punk row." These inmates would often come to the front of the barracks and cling to the bars all night out of fear of sexual assault [Winter & Jones, 1979].

(Black men constitute 51.9 percent of those males incarcerated in Arkansas state institutions.)

Sadly, similarly pathetic incarceration conditions are credited as the norm for many jails. In speaking of jails, a Mississippi County attorney states, "The best I have is worse than the worst conditions at the state pen." Further, according to this attorney, "Asking which jails are the worst is like asking, like kids do, whether you would rather die by burning or freezing."

In the case of Maiorca v. Lamb (n.d.), all conditions of confinement in the Clark County (Las Vegas), Nevada, Jail are challenged as "unfit." (Black men constitute 29.3 percent of Nevada state male prisoners and are of similar proportions in Nevada jails.) Arais v. Wainwright (n.d.) charges the Florida state commissioner with failure to establish minimum standards in Florida's jails. The suit outlines failure to initiate standards governing cleanliness, nutrition, medical care, discipline, exercise, visitation, and the operation of facilities in general. (Black men constitute 51.0 percent of the men incarcerated in Florida state institutions and are also overrepresented in Florida's jails.)

In response to the Johnson decision, several states have announced initiation of action to improve prison conditions. Likewise, the Law Enforcement Assistance Administration (LEAA) of the U.S. Justice Department has awarded a grant to the American Medical Association (AMA) to implement a 24-state jail and prison health care program. Reportedly, the AMA aims to provide and upgrade medical, dental, and mental health services offered in prisons. Other signs of improvement efforts are present in individual prisons, such as the Lorton Reformatory of Washington, D.C., which "has hired a dietician for the first time in its 66-year history" (Gibbs, 1979: 19). (Lorton is a five-part, two-thousand-man reformatory that is 99 percent Black.) Also, the Alabama Board of Corrections has obtained funds to start building three new prisons. Louisiana was slated to open three new 500-bed medium security prisons before year end 1979. There are also plans to build a 1,000-bed prison in Louisiana, as officials foresee further population increases. However, in spite of court orders, federal grants, and individual prison efforts, most prisons operate under the burden of overcrowding, filth, consistent violence, improper nutrition, and inadequate medical services. More important, it has been noted that prisons also operate under the guidance of "corrupt or poorly trained administrators [and] callous guards" (Gibbs, 1979: 18). In 1972 guards at the Mississippi State Penitentiary at Parchman were tested; 40 percent were found to be retarded and 71 percent were found to have personality disorders. In explaining why the Georgia Parole Board had reduced the sentences of most inmates by one year, the chairman of the board indicated that the "situation in some prisons and jails has reached the point that simply being assigned to them constitutes punishment beyond that ordered by the court" (*Twentieth Century Task Fund Force*, 1976: 8).

Although fairly well known, it is worth noting that many prisons have been charged with not providing meaningful jobs for all inmates, particularly minority inmates. Inmates of Attica Prison in 1971, like many in prisons today, received from $.20 to $1.00 a day for their labor. Beyond this, in 1971, 76 percent of the Attica inmates working in the metal shop and 80 percent of those working in the grading companies (both very undesirable jobs) were Black and Spanish-speaking. In contrast, white inmates constituted 74 percent of the workers in the powerhouse and 67 percent of the clerks (the most desirable jobs; *Attica*, 1972). Today, similar prisoner employment exists. Gibbs (1979: 19) reported in "The State of the Black Offender" that, according to the Congressional Black Caucus, "segregation within the prison system remains, especially in regard to certain preferred prison assignments and programs."

Not many persons, particularly those abreast of correction issues, are surprised at the physical abuse to which prisoners are subjected during prison riots. Evidence that during the Attica prison riot inmates were "beaten with clubs and gun butts" and forced to allow "cigarettes to burn out upon their naked flesh" was not found extremely alarming. Even that guards attempted "to jam a Phillips head screwdriver up the anus of an inmate" and that they "dumped wounded inmates off stretchers onto the ground" was not considered extreme. That guards "attempted to insert night sticks into the wounds of inmates" and forced prisoners "to run barefoot over broken glass" was news to only a few (Hinds, 1978: 349). Likewise, to read that working inmates of Soledad Prison were paid "two or three cents an hour," that prisoners on Max Row (maximum security) were "cuffed, chained and belted" and their skin searched whenever they left their cells, and that "human waste" was thrown at inmates who were also fed "rotten food" suggests horror, but only those that are truly naive are surprised (Davis, 1971: 27-43).

Also, that prisoners are abused without the provocation of rioting registers, sadly, as quite *normal*. The Reverend Ben Chavis of the Wilmington Ten reported that while in prison, he witnessed extreme physical brutality:

> I have seen prisoners who were forced to submit to electrical-shock treatment on their brains. I have seen prisoners "watered down" in their cells with a two hundred pound pressure water hose by prison officers. I have seen elderly prisoners made to slave in plantation fields until their limbs give out (often resulting in amputation of their legs) [Hinds, 1978: 183-184].

Incidents just as tragic as those outlined by the Reverend Chavis are reported to occur in a host of prisons and jails throughout the nation. For example, Attorney Elaine Jones of the NAACP, counsel of record in the Tommie L. Hines case mentioned earlier, reported at the Criminal Justice Braintrust meeting of the 1979 Congressional Black Caucus that the mentally retarded youth "had been brutalized and raped" since being imprisoned in Georgia. Equally as tragic is the reported treatment of persons held in the Allegheny County Jail in Pittsburgh, Pennsylvania, evidenced in the case of Owens-El v. Robinson (1978). In the previously cited letter to Senator Kennedy, attorneys Winter and Jones stated:

> In the Allegheny County Jail in Pittsburgh, inmates were held in inadequately heated cells without hot water and lighted only by a 25 or 40 watt bulb. The cots upon which inmates slept were "discolored by blood, vomit, feces, and urine." The jail hospital contained a "restraint

room," which the court found was "being used excessively, inappropriately and as punishment. . . ."

In this bleak room inmates are placed in a hospital gown or naked on a canvas cot with a hole cut in the middle. Their body wastes drop through a hole into the tub on the floor underneath the cot. The tub is emptied twice a day. The inmates are shackled by leather restraints to the canvas cots. . . . The medical logs . . . revealed that inmates have been held in such restraints for as long as 29 days.

(Black men constitute 55 percent of those men incarcerated in Pennsylvania state prisons. They are overrepresented in jails throughout the state as well.)

The horror of incarceration is evidenced only in part by the foregoing reports. More of greater intensity surfaces when attention is focused on incarceration of those persons awaiting death. Death row was originally designed to hold prisoners sentenced to death for only a brief period of time. However, a large number of inmates have spent more than ten years awaiting execution. Inmates are very much aware of the fact that execution is imminent. Not only are they able to watch others on their way to be killed, but many units are arranged in such a way that the death chamber is in full view of the inmates at all times. In a number of prisons there are two corridors on death row (one at each end of the unit) that connect with the death chamber. There is usually little or no ventilation. Hence, the smell and sound of an execution permeate death row for months—some say years.

Death row has been described as "a grisly laboratory, the ultimate in experimental stress in which the condemned prisoner's personality is incredibly brutalized" (Sarat & Vidmar, 1976: 211). Jacobs v. Britton (n.d.) is a recent case that challenged the conditions of confinement on death row in Alabama and evidenced the brutality to which inmates awaiting death are subjected. Meltsner (1974) has cited the case of James Thacker, a Black Georgian. On March 26, 1969, Thacker received a stay of execution from the U.S. Supreme Court. However, officials at the Reidsville Prison facility waited until only hours before the scheduled execution on April 2, 1969, "to tell the trembling man." Still, the brutality of incarceration on death row nowhere approaches the horror of actual execution. Regardless of the method, this is the ultimate terror. The technology used for execution today has been labeled as far below the nation's technological capability. Not one of the four lawful modes of execution, excluding a yet unused drug now being legalized in a few states, is instantaneous, and they all mutilate the body.

Some states employ the classic form of execution—hanging. Testifying before the U.S. Senate in 1968, Warden Clinton Duffy of San Quentin Prison explained that he had witnessed numerous hangings and presented the following account:

> The day before an execution the prisoner is weighed [and] measured for length of drop to assure the breaking of the neck. . . . When the trap door springs, he dangles at the end of rope. There are times when the neck has not been broken and the prisoner strangles to death. His eyes pop almost out of his head, his tongue swells and protrudes from his mouth, his neck may be broken and the rope many times takes large portions of skin and flesh from the side of the face. . . . He urinates and defecates and droppings fall on the floor . . . and at almost all executions, one or more witnesses faint and have to be taken from the witness room. The prisoner remains dangling from the end of the rope for 8 to 14 minutes before the doctor . . . pronounces him dead. A prison guard stands at the feet of the hanged person and holds the body steady, because during the first few minutes there is usually considerable struggling in an effort to breathe [Sarat & Vidmar, 1976: 212].

It has been explained that if the drop is too short, the prisoner strangles to death, and if the drop is too long, the prisoner's head is torn off. Clearly, to die by hanging is horrible. (In the United States at least six persons have been *unlawfully* hanged, later found innocent of their alleged crimes.)

Shooting has been promoted as a "humane" method of execution, but death is not always instantaneous and is far from painless. In most deaths by a firing squad, the upper body parts are completely destroyed. With this method being so brutal, Gary Gilmore's last words, "Let's do it," are inconceivable.

Electrocution is a popular alternative to hanging and shooting, and is somehow thought by many to be "more humane." In preparation for electrocution, the prisoner's hair is cropped very short and a pants leg is slit. The prisoner is then led into the death chamber and strapped into the electric chair. At this point, electrodes are fastened to the prisoner's leg and head. "The eyes, which may come out of their sockets," are masked. Warden Lewis Lawes of Sing Sing Prison described an electrocution as follows:

> As the switch is thrown into its socket there is a sputtering drone and the body leaps as if to break the strong leather straps that hold it. Sometimes a thin gray wisp of smoke pushes itself out from under the helmet that holds the head electrode, followed by the odor of burning flesh. The hands turn red, then white, and the cords of the neck stand out. . . . The initial voltage of 2,000 to 2,200 and the amperage of 7 to 12 are lowered and reapplied at various intervals [Sarat & Vidmar, 1976: 212-213].

Exactly how long it takes to die in the electric chair has not been determined. Often several shocks are required over a period of several minutes. Julius Rosenberg, for example, was pronounced dead after two minutes and three shocks. However, Ethel Rosenberg required four minutes and five applications of the current.

When the body is removed from the electric chair, it is frozen in a grotesque position and must be taken to what is known in one prison as the "sandbag room." There, the body is straightened out so that it can be placed in a coffin.

The application of lethal gas is usually the least disfiguring but is very slow and internally torturous. Effectively, it causes death by asphyxiation. Warden Duffy reports that the prisoner is strapped into a chair and the gas chamber is sealed. Then a cyanide pellet is dropped into sulphuric acid, producing cyanide gas. When the gas reaches the prisoner, "there is evidence of pain and strangling. The eyes pop, the prisoner turns purple and drools. It is a horrible sight" (Sarat & Vidmar, 1976: 213). Experts have indicated that cyanide poisoning causes slow and agonizing strangulation. The last person gassed to death in the United States was Luis Monge. The gassing of Monge occurred in Colorado in June 1967 and produced this eyewitness account:

> He coughed and groaned. . . . The head strained back and then slowly fell down to his chest. . . . The arms, though tightly bound to the chair, strained through the straps and the hands clawed torturously as if he were struggling for air [Sarat & Vidmar, 1976: 213].

Every death row inmate knows that at some point he is to be gassed, hanged, electrocuted, or shot to death. Each also knows of the groaning associated with gassing, the strangulation and mutilation of being hanged, the burning of flesh due to high voltage, and the blasting of being shot. The vast majority (unlike Gary Gilmore and Jesse Bishop) do not welcome the experience of their prescribed methods. Awareness of these facts, along with the general atrocities of prison life, make existence on death row incredibly horrible. (Black men constitute 43.7 percent of those persons awaiting execution throughout the United States.)

The very large and disproportionate number of Black men incarcerated in jails and prisons throughout the United States are clearly faced with constant horror and something inescapably akin to savagery. Those awaiting execution, in particular, are faced with an unimaginably tragic level of existence. Without question, and as projected throughout this document, the incarceration of Black men in the United States is *extreme* and *harsh* and *brutal* and, most appalling, is not indicative of a new or declining predicament.

# CASES

*Arais* v. *Wainwright*, TCA 79-0792 (N.D. Fla.)
*Duran* v. *Apodaca*, C.A. no. 77-721-C (D. N. Mex.)
*Furman* v. *Georgia*, 408 U.S. 238 (1978)
*Gates* v. *Collier*, 390 F. Supp. 482 (N.D. Miss. 1975)
*Gates* v. *Collier*, 548 R.2d 1241 (5th Cir. 1977)
*Gideon* v. *Wainwright*, 372 U.S. 335, 83 S.Ct. 792, 9 L.2d 779 (1963)
*Holt* v. *Sarver*, 300 F. Supp. 825 (E.D. Ark. 1969)
*Holt* v. *Sarver*, (1970) 309 F. Supp. 362 (E.D. Ark. 1970)
*Jacobs* v. *Britton*, C.A. no. 78-70-N (M.D. Ala.)
*Maiorca* v. *Lamb*, C.A. LV-79-30 (HEC D. Nev.)
*Mattis* v. *Schnarr*, 547 F.2d 1007 431 U.S. 171, (1976)
*Newman* v. *Alabama*, 406 F. Supp. 318 (N.D. Ala. 1976)
*Newman* v. *Edwards*, 559 F.2d 283 (5th Cir. 1977)
*Owens-El* v. *Robinson*, 442 F. Supp. 1368 (W.D. Pa. 1978)
*Palmigiano* v. *Garrahy*, 443 F. Supp. 956 (D. RI 1977)
*Powell* v. *Alabama*, 287 U.S. 45 (1932)
*Pugh and James* v. *Britton*, 406 F. Supp. 318 (M.D. Ala. 1976)
*Ramos* v. *Lamm*, C.A. no. 77-K-1093 (D. Col.)
*Stewart* v. *Rhodes*, 473 F. Supp. 1185 (S.D. Ohio 1979)
*Trigg* v. *Blanton*, C.A. no. A-6047 (Fulton County Chancery Court, Tenn., December 20, 1978)
*Williams* v. *Edwards*, 547 F.2d 1206 (5th Cir. 1977)

# REFERENCES

American Civil Liberties Union (ACLU) Foundation, National Prison Project. *A report of activities for the quarter ending September 30, 1979.* Author, 1979.

*Attica, the official report of the New York State special commission on Attica.* New York: Bantam Books, 1972.

Black, C. *Capital punishment: The inevitability of caprice and mistake.* New York: Norton, 1974.

Bowers, W. *Execution in America.* Lexington, MA: D. C. Heath, 1974.

Carter, D. *Scottsboro, a tragedy of the American south.* New York: Oxford University Press, 1969.

Davis, A. *If they come in the morning.* New York: Signet, 1971.

Ebony (1979) Black on Black crime. August.

Fyfe, J. *Shots fired: An examination of New York City police firearms' discharges.* Unpublished doctoral dissertation, State University of New York, 1978.

Gibbs, C. The state of the Black offender. *Metropolitan Magazine,* October 1979, p. 44.

Hartzen, C. *Crime and criminalization.* New York: Praeger, 1974.

Hinds, L. *Illusions of justice: Human rights violation in the United States.* Ames: University of Iowa, 1978.

Jackson, G. *Soledad brothers: The prison letters of George Jackson.* New York: Bantam, 1970.

Jackson, M. Crime as a concern of city hall. In H. Bryce (Ed.), *Black crime: A police view*. Washington, DC: Joint Center for Political Studies, 1977.

Jones, E. Speech given at the Congressional Black Caucus, Washington, D.C., September 21, 1979.

Kobler, A. Police homicide in a democracy. *Journal of Social Issues*, 1975, *31*(1), 163-184.

Knowles, L., & Prewitt, K. *Institutional racism in America*. Englewood Cliffs, NJ: Prentice-Hall, 1969.

Malcolm X & Haley, A. *The autobiography of Malcolm X*. New York: Grove, 1964, 1965.

Meltsner, M. *Cruel and unusual punishment: The Supreme Court and capital punishment*. New York: Morrow, 1974.

Napper, G. Perception of crime: Problems and implications. In R. Woodson (Ed.), *Black perspective on crime and the criminal justice system*. Boston: G. K. Hall, 1977.

Robin, G. Justifiable homicides by police. *Journal of Criminal Law, Criminology, and Police Science*, 1963, *54*.

Sarat, A., & Vidmar, N. Public opinion, the death penalty and the eighth amendment: Testing the Marshall hypothesis. In H. Bedau & C. Pierce (Eds.), *Capital punishment in the United States*. New York: AMS Press, 1976.

Takagi, P. Death by police intervention. In R. Brenner & H. Kravitz (Eds.), *A community concern: Police use of deadly force*. Washington, DC: National Institute of Law Enforcement and Criminal Justice, 1979.

Townsey, R. *Discretionary justice and the differential imposition of the death penalty*. Unpublished doctoral dissertation, State University of New York, 1979.

*Twentieth Century Fund Task Force on Criminal Sentencing, Fair and Certain Punishment*. New York: McGraw-Hill, 1976.

U.S. Bureau of the Census. Unpublished data, October 1979. Washington, DC: Author.

U.S. Department of Justice. *Capital punishment, 1977*. Washington, DC: Author, 1978. (a)

U.S. Department of Justice. *Crime in the United States–1977*. Washington, DC: Author, 1978. (b)

U.S. Department of Justice, National Prisoners' Statistics. *Prisoners in state and federal institutions on December 31, 1977*. Washington, DC: Author, 1979.

Vincent, T. *Black power and the Garvey movement*. San Francisco: Ramparts, 1972.

Winter, S. Interview, New York City, November 5, 1979.

Winter, S., & Jones, J. Personal communication to Senator Edward Kennedy, October 19, 1979.

Wolfgang, M., & Reidel, M. Rape, racial discrimination and the death penalty. In H. Bedau & C. Pierce (Eds.), *Capital punishment in the United States*. New York: AMS Press, 1976.

# 15

## SOCIAL SERVICES AND BLACK MEN

Bogart R. Leashore

The extent to which public and private social services have been extended to and utilized by Black males is a much neglected area in the literature on American social welfare. With reference to the literature on social services in general and service delivery in particular, Black males have received limited and sparse attention. However, much more can be found regarding Black families, especially those living in poverty (Barrett, 1976; Orcutt, 1977; Minuchin, 1967; Sager, 1968).

The neglect of Black males in the social welfare literature poses a dual paradox. The first suggests that the general well-being of Black families, as well as Black communities, is not related to the social and psychological well-being of Black males. The second suggests that, despite the general ideological aim of helping agencies, organizations, and professionals to provide services regardless of race, class, or sex, Black males are generally excluded or ignored.

This chapter focuses on the provision of social services to Black males, as well as the attitudes and responses of Black males to these services. Factors

AUTHOR'S NOTE: The author gratefully acknowledges the assistance provided by Ms. Cleopatra Howard, Mr. Rudel M. Briscoe, and Ms. Vanessa Williams in the preparation of this chapter.

related to the provision and utilization of services are also examined. Special reference will be made to a study of Black males that included information on their utilization of social service agencies. The chapter concludes with several recommendations which may be used by agencies, organizations, and individuals to provide quality services to Black males.

It should be emphasized that social services are herein used in the broad context of service activities rendered by agencies and organizations which espouse the social and psychological well-being of individuals, groups, and communities. These services include mental health, child welfare, individual and family counseling, psychotherapy, public assistance, legal assistance, housing, job placement, and medical care. Further, although concern is primarily with social services for adult Black males, there are explicit and implicit ramifications for the Black male child or adolescent, as well as for Black females.

## HISTORICAL PERSPECTIVE

In addressing the treatment of Black clients by social service providers and social scientists, Jones (1979) states that there has been a tendency to apply an Anglo-European framework that is ethnocentric in character. This framework is assumed to be culturally superior and is therefore used as the definitive model for assessing the attitudes and behavior of Blacks. Reference to low-income Blacks as "culturally deprived," is an example of the use of this framework.

Another position (Miller, 1969: 68) characterizes the general posture assumed by American social welfare agencies and institutions toward Black people in general and Black males in particular as "philanthropic colonialism." This posture summarizes white America's assessment of Blacks as follows:

> The Negro was brought to this country . . . in chains after having been torn from his African culture. He was dispersed . . . exploited in the most barbarous of fashions . . . brutalized, emasculated, looked upon as a nonperson and robbed of his heritage . . . [He] has become more and more marginal to the mainstream of American life.

The assessment concludes that the solution to the marginal status of Blacks is to "uplift" them through social services and institutions. Paternalism and clinicalism have been two means by which "philanthropic colonialism" has been actualized. The former views the Black male and the Black female as children in need of guidance, while the latter views them as psychologically damaged. In both instances, the goal has been to "uplift" them (Miller, 1969).

Both the Anglo-European framework and "philanthropic colonialism" reflect the values and norms of the broader American society. With respect to role expectations as defined by American society, Black males have historically not been accorded status or opportunity equal to that of white males, despite the fact that the same role expectations have been prescribed for both—for example, as economic provider for the family and as authority figure. Social service agencies and organizations reflect the broader society when they view the Black male paternalistically or pathologically, or when they simply ignore his existence. By so doing, these agencies and organizations perpetuate the second-class or inferior status accorded Blacks throughout America's history.

With specific reference to the social work literature, Hopkins (1973: 53) states that there is a consistent theme suggesting that "something is wrong with Black men, either directly or indirectly" since this literature has neglected to mention them. Furthermore, traditional social science research concerning the influence of Black fathers on their children has typically addressed the negative consequences of the fathers' absence (Burton & Whiting, 1961; Hetherington, 1966; Moynihan, 1965; Shinn, 1978; Biller & Meredith, 1974). Researchers and practitioners have ignored the fact that, despite the rise in Black female-headed families, in 1978 approximately half of all Black children 18 years old and under lived with both parents (U.S. Bureau of the Census, 1979). Only in the last few years has there been a recognition by social scientists and practitioners that Black males represent a major resource of the Black community (Tuck, 1971; Chestang, 1970; Hopkins, 1973).

## SERVICE APPROACHES

For the most part, the service approach used with Black males has been the same regardless of his socioeconomic status. The most noticeable variation in approaches may be found when one considers the type of agency or organization providing services. Using the broad dichotomy of public and private agencies, the former are likely to use a coercive approach with Black males, while the latter are likely to ignore him unless compelled to do otherwise.

"Witch-hunts", or intensive field investigations, which were used to determine the existence of welfare fraud in the Aid to Families with Dependent Children (AFDC) program and general assistance cases, represent a classical illustration of the public or coercive approach. In this particular illustration, welfare officials made surprise searches at night to determine if fathers were present, since their absence was a prerequisite for receiving benefits (Bell, 1968). Clearly, practices and policies such as these provide little in the way of service; rather, they force temporary or permanent disruption of families.

Public agencies and organizations that provide services in the areas of child welfare, especially out-of-wedlock pregnancy, have historically used the coercive approach. For the most part, this approach involves efforts to force the male to assume responsibility, especially financial, for his spouse and/or child(ren). For example, the Social Security Act was amended in 1950 to require public assistance agencies to notify law enforcement officials of cases involving parental desertion or abandonment in order for families to receive Aid to Dependent Children (later known as AFDC). A subsequent study in 1955 showed that fathers subjected to court-ordered support payments contributed less frequently than did those who agreed to do so of their own volition (Kaplan, 1960). In recent years, the Child Support Enforcement Program has provided another illustration of the coercive approach (U.S. Department of Health, Education and Welfare, 1976).

While private agencies or organizations are not excluded from the use of the coercive approach, their approach is typically to ignore the Black male. This essentially involves their unwillingness to reach out to Black males; instead, he may be feared, viewed as unimportant, or seen as an intruder. These attitudes have been attributed to several factors: stereotypes of Black males; insecurity rooted in a lack of knowledge about Black males; unwillingness to engage in interpersonal relationships with Black males; and a lack of commitment (Hopkins, 1973).

In those cases in which the Black male cannot be ignored—for example, with regard to fees for service agencies—there may be a disinterest in having him actively participate in the service process. Conscious and unconscious, direct and indirect efforts may be made to minimize or eliminate his participation. For example, appointments, as well as agency hours, may be scheduled for times that may conflict with his working hours; he may be assigned to service providers who are culturally insensitive; or services may be prematurely terminated.

Minimizing the participation of Black males, ignoring them, or using force in the provision of services are negative approaches and do little to promote the well-being of Black males. On the contrary, such approaches fail to give recognition to the humanity of Black males in the holistic sense. Agencies and organizations utilizing these approaches render themselves ineffective with Black males and ultimately communicate to them that contact should be avoided.

# UTILIZATION OF SOCIAL SERVICES

Given the approaches that social service agencies, organizations, and providers have traditionally used with Black males, it is not surprising that research is beginning to document greater utilization of informal, rather than formal, resources by Black males (Pugh & Mudd, 1971; Warren, 1976). Informal resources typically include assistance provided by family and friends, while formal resources refer to services provided by agencies and organizations. It should be noted that the utilization by Blacks of informal resources (Hays & Mindel, 1973; McAdoo, 1977) may be viewed as a continuation of an African value system.

In recent years, there has been an increasing interest in the extent to which Blacks utilize professional or formal social services (Willie et al., 1973; Shapiro, 1975; Cannon & Locke, 1977). Generally, it has been shown that Blacks tend to be overrepresented with respect to utilization of public and often involuntary services, and underrepresented with respect to private and voluntary services. For example, age-adjusted national data for 1975 show that Black males had higher rates of admissions to state and county psychiatric hospitals than did all other groups. Moreover, when compared to all groups, the median age for Black males (30.5 years) was the lowest (Milazzo-Sayre, 1977).

Although additional national data are available regarding the utilization of other types of social welfare institutions and services, they generally involve public institutions and services that are involuntary—for example, the legal system and schools. Information concerning public and private voluntary social services is much less available. To date, research studies and other works in this area have been limited to special target groups within the Black male population or to special areas of concern. For example, Johnson and Staples (1979) studied a group of young, inner-city, minority males, including Blacks, who participated in a service program related to family life education, family planning, and parental concerns. Glasgow (1969) has described an indigenous community organization of Black males who became a positive force for community improvement. Other studies have focused on services directed toward Black males who were fathers (Hopkins, 1973; Tuck, 1971; Leashore, 1979).

Recognizing the need for research on the utilization of public and private voluntary social services by Black males, the Mental Health Research and Development Center at Howard University included this area in its exploratory study of adult Black males. The study was conducted in 1978 and consisted of 142 Black males between the ages of 18 and 65 years who resided in the metropolitan Washington, D.C., area. The respondents were asked whether or not they had sought the services of each of the following types of agencies or organizations over the past year: clinics or hospitals, social security offices, poverty agencies, civil rights organizations, legal services, private social services, welfare offices, unemployment offices, and other social services. Each who had been to any of these agencies or organizations were also asked four questions about the quality of service he had received: (a) Did he trust the staff of the agency/organization? (b) Did the staff seem to know what they were doing? (c) Did the staff show him respect? (d) Were they helpful to him?

Most of the men reported that they had not been to many of the agencies or organizations. Specifically, 54 percent of the sample (77) reported that they had been to a hospital or clinic for treatment, while 26 percent (38) had been to an unemployment office and less than 25 percent had been to the remaining agencies and organizations within the last year. Figure 15.1 presents the frequency distribution of respondents who had utilized each of the agencies or organizations within the previous year. As so few men utilized most of the agencies mentioned, only analyses of those who went to a clinic or hospital will be discussed.

Most (88 percent) of the men who had been to a hospital or clinic reported that they trusted the staff; similarly, most (86 percent) reported that the hospital or clinic staff seemed knowledgeable. Nearly all the men who had been to a clinic or hospital reported that the staff was respectful and helpful (92 percent and 95 percent, respectively). Additional analysis of data for the men who had been to a hospital or clinic showed that those under 35 years of age were more likely than were those 35 years or older not to have been to a hospital or clinic within the last year ($X^2$ = 5.3, df = 1, p < .02). Education, marital status, employment status, and family income were not significant.

The results of the Center's study indicated that, with the exception of health services, few of the men used the services of the various agencies or organizations. However, as it was an exploratory study, combined with the fact that there has been little research in this area, there remains a need for additional research. In the main, social service agencies and organizations should assess the degree to which they promote or fail to promote the well-being of Black males in their service delivery.

## ADVANCING SOCIAL SERVICES FOR BLACK MALES

In order for social services to affect the lives of Black males positively, it is incumbent upon agencies, organizations, and service providers to address

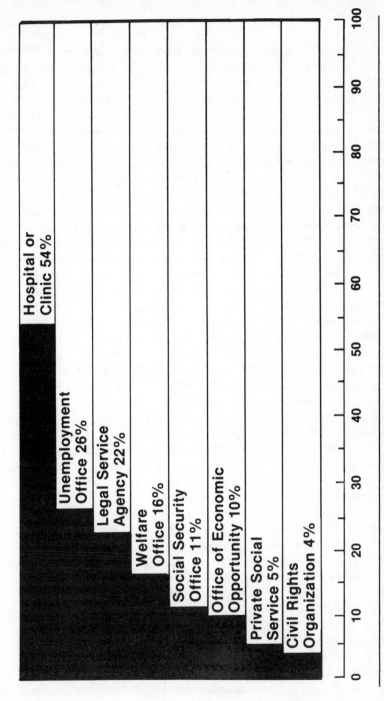

Figure 15.1 Frequency Distribution of Utilization of Social Service Agencies and Organizations in 12 Months During 1977-1978

several important issues. However, they should first make a firm commitment to rid themselves of racism at both the organizational and the personal levels. This involves more than a mere reaffirmation of ideology or professional codes of ethics; it requires a genuine commitment to recognize and appreciate the richness and the value of Black cultural beliefs, norms, and values. Likewise, there must be a recognition that the white American way of life has its merits, but that it is not culturally superior to that of others.

While the conventional route to such a commitment might be learning more about the experiences of the Black male in America, a more direct route should involve full self-examination. This examination should include four basic questions: (1) How has the agency (and the individual within it) maintained racism with respect to Black males in particular and Black people in general? (2) What services does the agency (and the individual) offer Black males? (3) If services are offered to them, in what ways are they offered? (4) What, if any, are the service outcomes for Black males? These questions should be asked and answered by service providers, administrators, and especially policy makers.

In responding to the first question, every possible effort should be made to eliminate elements of racism, including staff who either overtly or covertly practice the same. Efforts should be made to identify and change policies that adversely affect Black males in particular and Black people in general. Line and support staff can assist in this effort by identifying areas of service delivery that negatively impact on the lives of Black men.

If the answer to the second question is that very little in the way of services is offered to the Black male, efforts should be made to develop services from which he can benefit. Direct input from the Black community, especially from Black males, as to particular service needs can be a most effective means for accomplishing this. To ascertain this input, agencies and organizations should go directly to the community—for example, to churches, schools, and Black male organizations. For those agencies that have direct contact with Black women, inquiry can be made of them concerning areas and ways in which services for Black men can be developed. Input can also be obtained by conferring with Black professional organizations, for example, the National Association of Black Social Workers and the Association of Black Psychologists. These efforts should be ongoing.

The third question involves an assessment of how services are offered to Black males. In this regard, it is imperative that agencies, organizations, and providers recognize that the Black male is a person in his own right. This being the case, he should be respected as a person who can decide what is best for him. Thus, the role of the helper is that of facilitator; coercive and punitive approaches in assuming this role should be viewed as unnecessary and inappropriate. Further, approaches that tend to blame the individual for his circumstances should be avoided. Instead, approaches that identify, reinforce, and build individual strengths should be used. Direct efforts should also be made by agencies, organizations, and providers to advocate service to Black males in the broader societal arena.

In providing social services for Black males, agencies and organizations should make special efforts to recruit Black males as service providers. Recruitment efforts should be made directly with Black institutions that train people for social services. Black organizations and media with large Black audiences—for example, Black-owned newspapers and Black-oriented radio stations—may be sources for recruiting Black males, not only as service providers, but also as clients.

Agency hours and the location of services should be adjusted to accommodate Black males as clients, so that services are readily accessible. In addition, efforts should be made to schedule appointments as soon as possible after requested so that long waits are avoided. When agencies cannot locate in close proximity to where Black males live or work, consideration should be given to utilizing facilities within the client's community: churches, schools, community centers, and the like.

Finally, none of the aforementioned suggestions for advancing the quality of services for Black males can be successfully implemented without some mechanism for evaluating them. Since many social agencies have standard procedures for self-evaluation, the provision of services to Black males should be incorporated in the same. As much as possible, objective measures should be made to assess efforts, services, and outcomes as they relate to Black males.

## BROAD SOCIAL WELFARE CHANGES

Although there are many ways existing social service agencies can alter themselves to ensure quality service delivery for Black males, there remains a need for broad changes in the American system of social welfare. Foremost among these changes are an adequate guaranteed income, an adequate program of national health insurance, and full employment. These changes can greatly alter the life circumstances of Black males as well as others. Individuals and organizations should actively lobby for the implementation of these services. Legislation related to each should be comprehensive and available to everyone in need. With specific reference to welfare reform, the National Urban League (1980) has outlined five goals which form a new welfare system:

(1) The system should be adequate, equitable, and universal.
(2) It should be federally administered and funded.
(3) The benefits should not be work-conditioned.

(4) They should be cash rather than in-kind.

(5) The goal of the new program should be income maintenance.

Other areas in which there is a need for broad changes which directly affect Black males include (1) deinstitutionalization, (2) social security reform, (3) the portrayal of Black males in the media, and (4) the establishment of Black-controlled social service agencies and organizations.

The deinstitutionalization of Black males in the criminal justice system and psychiatric care facilities can be actualized by eliminating social and economic circumstances that lead to institutionalization. Measures should be taken by the social security system to afford Black males benefits at an earlier age in view of the fact that they die at an earlier age than those of other groups. Stereotyped and distorted portraits of Black males in the mass media need to be eliminated, and the diversity found among them should be illuminated.

Finally and most important, Black Americans should continuously endeavor to create and maintain Black-owned institutions that can effectively render social services to Black males. In order to accomplish this, coalitions of Blacks that are committed to the survival of Blacks in America should be formed. This commitment should include time, knowledge and skills, and money. Existing Black institutions and organizations can contribute by developing and investing their resources toward the goal of assuring the quality of life for Black Americans is enhanced and sustained.

# REFERENCES

Barrett, B. Enterprising principles in counseling the low-income Black family. *Journal of Non-White Concerns in Personnel and Guidance.* 1976, *5*(1), 14-22.

Bell, W. The rights of the poor: Welfare witch-hunts in the District of Columbia. *Social Work,* 1968, *13,* 60-67.

Biller, H., & Meredith, D. *Father power.* New York: Daniel McKay, 1974.

Burton, R., & Whiting, J. The absent and cross sex identity. *Merrill-Palmer Quarterly,* 1961, *7,* 85-95.

Cannon, M., & Locke, B. Being Black is detrimental to one's mental health: Myth or reality? *Phylon,* 1977, *33,* 408-428.

Chestang, L. The issue of race in casework practice. In *Social Work Practice.* New York: Columbia University Press, 1970.

Glasgow, D. The emerging Black community: A challenge to social work. In W. Richan (Ed.), *Human services and social work responsibility.* Washington, DC: National Association of Social Workers, 1969.

Hays, W., & Mindel, C. Extended kinship relations in Black and white families. *Journal of Marriage and the Family,* 1973, *35,* 51-57.

Hetherington, E. Effects of paternal absence on sex-typed behaviors in Negro and white males. *Journal of Personality and Social Psychology,* 1966, *4,* 87-91.

Hopkins, T. The role of the agency in supporting Black manhood. *Social Work,* 1973, *18,* 53-58.

Johnson, L., & Staples, R. Family planning and the young minority male: A pilot project. *The Family Coordinator,* 1979, *28,* 535-543.

Jones, D. African-American clients: Clinical practice issues. *Social Work,* 1979, *24,* 112-118.

Kaplan, S. *Support from absent fathers of children receiving ADC, 1955.* Washington, DC: Government Printing Office, 1960.

Leashore, B. Human services and the unmarried father: The forgotten half. *The Family Coordinator,* 1979, *28,* 529-534.

McAdoo, H. *The impact of extended family variables upon the upward mobility of Black families: Final Report.* Columbia, MD: Columbia Research Systems, Inc., 1977.

Milazzo-Syre, L. Admission rates to state and county psychiatric hospitals by age, sex and race. In *Mental Health Statistical Reports, Note 140,* Washington, DC: U.S. Department of Health, Education and Welfare, 1977.

Miller, H. Social work in the Black ghetto: The new colonialism. *Social Work,* 1969, *14,* 65-76.

Minuchin, S., et al. *Families of the slums: An exploration of their structure and treatment.* New York: Basic Books, 1967.

Moynihan, D. *The Negro family: The call for national action.* Washington, DC: U.S. Department of Labor, 1965.

National Urban League. *The state of Black America, 1980* (J. D. Williams, Ed.), New York: Author, 1980.

Orcutt, B. Family treatment of poverty level families. *Social Casework,* 1977, *58,* 92-100.

Pugh, T., & Mudd, E. Attitudes of Black women and men toward using community services. *Journal of Religion and Health,* 1971, *10*(3), 256-277.

Sager, E., et al. Selection of engagement of patients in family therapy. *American Journal of Orthopsychiatry,* 1968, *38,* 715-723.

Shapiro, R. Discrimination and community mental health. *Civil Rights Digest,* 1975, *7,* 19-23.

Shinn, M. Father absence and children's cognitive development. *Psychological Bulletin,* 1978, *85,* 295-324.

Tuck, S. A model for working with Black fathers. *American Journal of Orthopsychiatry,* 1971, *41,* 465-472.

U.S. Bureau of the Census. *The social and economic status of the Black population in the U.S.: An historical view, 1790-1978* (Series P-23, No. 80, 1978). Washington, DC: Government Printing Office, 1979.

U.S. Department of Health, Education and Welfare. *First annual report to congress on the child support enforcement program.* Washington, DC: Government Printing Office, 1976.

Warren, D. *Neighborhood and community contexts in help-seeking, problem coping, and mental health: Data analysis monograph.* Ann Arbor: Program in Community Effectiveness, University of Michigan, 1976.

Willie, C., et al. (Eds.). *Racism and mental health.* Pittsburgh: University of Pittsburgh Press, 1973.

# 16

## THE RELIGIOUS EXPERIENCE
## OF BLACK MEN

James S. Tinney

One might argue that the Black church is a women's institution. Uncontrovertably, women make up the largest proportion of its membership and an even larger proportion of its active participants (Brown & Walters, 1979). However, since the church is an association whose conditions of membership and ministry are determined by men, and since its internal relationships are ordered by men and structured with men as its chief powerholders, the church is, in the final analysis, a male institution (Moberg, 1962).

This discrepancy between numerical representation and power lies at the heart of any discussion of the Black church and the Black male. It provides a basis for examining both the strengths and weaknesses, the successes and sins, of the church's outreach to persons of both genders. Most specifically, it suggests three hypotheses for present discussion: (1) Black men have benefited positively from the Black church; (2) at the same time, and especially more recently, many Black males seem uninterested in, or hostile to, the Black church; and (3) part of the explanation for the apparent paradox between hypotheses 1 and 2 may be found in an examination of the intertwining of racism and sexism in American society. A closer look at each of these ideas will better illustrate the subject under consideration.

First, let it be said unequivocally that Black men owe a great deal to the Black church for promoting male welfare. Not only has this social institution been the mainstay of Black communities in the past, and not only has it contributed immensely to the social and political advancement of the race, but it has also specifically benefited its lay*men* in numerous ways (Tinney, 1979). Such spheres as psychological liberation, leadership development, intellectuality, the family, economics, and social networking, all reflect the church's contribution.

In terms of psychological liberation, the Black church has done more than can be imagined. Whether as a result of inculcating middle-class values (Johnson, 1961), or as a consequence of "conversion," it has delivered thousands of men from the debilitating use of drugs, excessive reliance on alcohol, and similarly negative lifestyles seemingly endemic to social conditions of hopelessness and oppression. Untold numbers of young men, whose lives seemed marked by despair and self-destructive anger, have been emotionally healed and had their energies redirected into positive channels of purposeful protest and creative activity by the church's ministry (Nelsen & Nelsen, 1975; Wilmore, 1973). Many other men have come off the "Tally's Corners" so plenteous in every inner city, and changed from street life to productive living because of the influence of some storefront sanctuary or urban cathedral (Liebow, 1967). That the Black church has not been totally successful in this realm simply indicates the limitations of personalized change in structurally induced deprivations; that the churches have been as successful as they have, in the midst of such odds, is itself ample proof of their merits.

In terms of leadership development, the Black church has been the most important single positive force. It has provided opportunities for men to assume leadership roles denied them in the larger society. It was the "main area of social life in which Negroes could aspire to become the leaders of men . . . in which the struggle for power and the thirst for power could be satisfied. This was especially important for Negro men who had never been able to assert themselves and assume the dominant male role . . . as defined by American culture" (Frazier, 1964). In addition, the Black church not only propelled men into larger arenas of leadership in education, politics, and journalism; it also provided the constituency necessary for the success of male political and social leaders outside the church. Thus, the following gained by nonelectoral, political movement leaders, such as Marcus Garvey, was drawn from the churches and supported by Black clergy (Burnett, 1978).

Intellectually—a quality denied Black men by American society as a whole—was another area fostered by the Black church. At a time when whites refused to recognize the intellectual capabilities and contributions of Black males, the church fostered male genius. Evidence of this abounds in the records of white sociologists and historians who have described the Black church as chiefly a means of sublimating or deflecting social frustration into emotionalism. (No less a scholar than Gunnar Mydral proclaimed this distorted appraisal.) Yet the Black church, even with its emotional aspects, was developing theologians, philosophers, professors, college and seminary presidents, and writers with "a unique and distinct conceptualization" relating "Black religion to the political, social, educational, economic, and cultural structures of society" (Young, 1979: 15). More recently, the church has witnessed the arrival of a full-blown, distinctly Black theology, which "not only tends to be about Blacks, but also tends to be only about Black males" (Russell, 1978: 256).

Another way the church benefited Black males was its encouragement of male authority in the home. If slavery disrupted the Black nuclear family as a unit (a fact Blassingame, 1972, feels has been overstated), and if many Black families tended to be organized as functional matriarchies (a proposition that was the subject of debate among Black academicians), the church was the primary factor in reversing these trends, lending its approval to male-headed families. On the positive side, this occurred as the church fostered "a sense of common unity that transcends individual and family disorganization" (Washington, 1967: p. 225). On the negative side, this occurred as the church fostered male authoritarianism. It gave not only "moral support for a patriarchal family to be found in the Bible," but also "holy sanction to the new authority of the Negro man in the home" (Frazier, 1964: 33, 43).

Neither should the economic role of the Black church in providing actual jobs for men be overlooked. To a large extent, this situation was encouraged by the family role assigned to men, as mentioned previously. "The new economic position of the man was consolidated by the moral support of the Negro church" (Frazier, 1964: 43). Perhaps not all congregations were large enough to be able to hire twenty-four persons full-time, as did the Olivet Baptist Church in Chicago in 1920; but in their own way, thousands of smaller churches and even storefronts were providing financial remuneration for the thousands of men who also served in them as pastors. Furthermore, the organizational and business skills learned through participating in local church affairs provided many more men with skills transferable to the secular world of work. By raising $50,000 in one year to buy a college that the state of Ohio could not raise enough funds to continue, the African Methodists were providing not only an educational future for youth, but also employment for scores of men ranging from maintenance workers to instructors. The same may be said for all church projects: establishing other schools, welfare agencies, insurance societies, and printing plants.

Finally, the Black church, through these efforts and others, was instrumental in social networking—creating all types of attendant opportunities and social institutions and services with men at the helm or as chief beneficiaries. Male fraternal orders were among these. The clergy organized the Knights of

Liberty as early as 1824, and the Grand United Order of True Reformers in 1876. Other more enduring lodges, including the Prince Hall Masons, the Odd Fellows, and the Knights of Pythias, were begun and/or joined largely by men from the churches (Frazier, 1964). Prince Hall, responsible for originating the Masonic Order among Afro-Americans, was himself a Methodist minister.

Since the Black church has been a positive benefactor to Black men, if not a male-dominated institution, it is worth considering why it has failed to enlist a larger number of men as active members. The fact is that large numbers of men seem indifferent to the church, and many are openly hostile to it.

While some surveys in the Washington, D.C., area have revealed that less than one-third of church members were men (Brown & Walters, 1979), other observers project an even lower representation of males. "In the Black church, the female population far exceeds that of the male. In some churches, the ratio is as high as eight [women] to one [man] and in smaller churches this ratio is much worse" (Bland, 1977: 12). What is more, this problem may worsen if present youth participation is an indicator of future male participation. Teenage males are "practically absent or highly diminished" in both church attendance and membership, another study states (Bowden, 1980). Among all ages, Black men who describe themselves as "religious nonaffiliates" outnumber Black women nonaffiliates four to one (Welch, 1978).

There are some who suggest that these low rates of male affiliation and participation are no cause for alarm, since men of all races exhibit lower percentages of church attachment than do women. There are important cultural differences, however, that negate such an argument. For one thing, African Americans share a religious tradition dating back to Africa itself—a large heritage that finds life steeped in religious meaning in a holistic manner. Such a tradition contrasts sharply with the Euro-American one, where the sacred and secular are separated and where the culturally male virtue of rationality is opposed to religious feeling. For another thing, the percentage of Black women involved in religious structures exceeds that of white women, which makes the low Black male involvement even more striking.

It would probably not be helpful to consider all the complaints that have been lodged from time to time against the Black church. The church is, after all, an evolving institution; and some of the most pertinent criticisms made about it in the past have since become obsolete or at least tempered. Other complaints (such as those registered by Franklin Frazier and Joseph R. Washington, Jr.) are based on ideas of assimilationism now largely rejected by most Black Americans (Frazier, 1964). This is not to suggest that there are no legitimate grievances about today's Black church. But this chapter, as a matter of relevance and practical brevity, will concern itself only with those grievances relating to gender—those that affect Black males by design or deficit.

One of the most common accusations against the church concerns its failure to provide a meaningful role for lay*men*. Black denominations as a whole have no internal mechanism for empowering the nonministerial members and giving them a voice in the church equal to the voice of the clergy. (Not a single Black denomination, for instance, has a "house of the laity," as does the Episcopal Church, for example.) Even at the local level, male members are severely restricted in their power. Many congregations are "ruled" (for all practical purposes) by the pastor; even where boards of trustees or deacons exist, the number of members so designated to serve on these boards is limited. But what about the man who is not a preacher or deacon or teacher? What significant part does he play in the average Black church? Usually not a major one. Only in the smaller Black churches, where every male member may be "called to preach" or exhort or testify, does the lay*man* have a prominent role in worship; and even there, a trend exists for those "called" to simply sit en masse on the platform, inactively sharing the space surrounding the pulpit.

Another complaint is that the Black church encourages psychological passivity among men, contrary to the cultural norms of American males as a whole. The call to nonviolence, pacifism, nonassertiveness, and adoration of a "meek and mild" Christ runs counter to the real-life situations one faces in both the ghetto and the larger, competitive, capitalistic order. Sometimes this personal passivity is logically extended to political interaction—although this is not generally true of the Black church (Staples, 1973). Nevertheless, the emphasis on personal attributes characteristic of a contemplative, rather than a socially active, life becomes a negative factor for many Black men, lessening the relevance of the church for them.

Similarly, many Black men feel that the legalistic pietism proclaimed in many pulpits somehow strikes at their masculinity. The gospel, if one were to believe some preachers, is an endless list of prohibited behaviors: don't smoke, don't drink, don't curse, don't dance, don't engage in sex other than in the married state, ad infinitum (Yates, 1971: 45-46). Obviously, these prohibitions (whether defensible or not) strike at activities characteristically associated with cultural norms of being "macho" or masculine. (The intention here is not to judge the "rightness" or "wrongness" of such activities, nor to judge these as appropriate or inappropriate concerns of a church, but only to point out that ethical rigor centering on cultural symbols of masculinity alienates some men from the Black church.)

Also, the Black church as a whole has failed to develop comprehensive ministries to college and university campuses, to jails and prisons, and to the armed services—places where hundreds of thousands of young Black males spend significant portions of their lives (Saucer, 1977). This neglect not only deprives the church of a resource pool of talent, but also gives Black men a feeling that the church is unconcerned about them. When they return to their communities from these institutions, they understandably return the "favor" of unconcern to the Black church.

Finally, one must consider that the male-centered myths, rituals, and polity of the Black church, while benefiting the male leadership of the church (primarily pastors and bishops), may in fact have been a major "turn-off" for Black males at the lay level, particularly those not actively participating in churches. In a word, sexism has been the church's undoing as far as Black men (not in the churches) are concerned, even as it may likely prove to be a hinderance to ministry among women in the future (Cone, 1979).

Such sexism is implicit in nearly every criticism of the Black church mentioned under the second proposition already discussed. The implication is that, consciously or unconsciously, pastors and evangelists have not attempted to fashion a ministry to unaffiliated males in the community. Some suggest that pastors enjoy their personal "kingdoms" and do not want too many males around them who might compete for the attention of the female membership or for a share in authority (Hoover, 1979). Unfortunately, many women churchgoers have not consciously considered the negative effects of such male-centered (that is, pastor-centered) religion on themselves either.

The sexist nature of the Black church was, of course, learned and borrowed from the model of the white church. White "missionaries" had a vested interest in ensuring that a small, elitist class of Black male ministers would reserve power for themselves. This prevented the rise of a mass movement of resistance to racial oppression by placing many Black men outside the influence of the religious leadership. It also effectively encouraged divisions between Black men and Black women by neutralizing Black women's potentially shared authority and fostering resentment between men outside the church and women inside the church. "Unfortunately, neither the Black man nor the Black woman understood the true nature of the forces working upon them." (Beale, 1979: 368-371).

Even Black women theologians seem not to have considered the effects sexist religion has had on furthering the alienation of Black men (as well as women) from the Black church. Staples (1973: 171-172), while not considering this as sexism, admits that the "image of the Black minister is sexual . . . and many women find sexual appeal in his prestigious status, command of oratory, wealth, and flamboyance." This tends to be so, even if the minister does not carry through his sexual image in "illicit" relations.

Women subconsciously "find themselves accepting the pastor as being much more than just a pastor," particularly those who may be divorced, separated, or otherwise unhappily married. "These women often seek a strong male figure [such as the] pastor because it appears that pastors are usually happily married and thus, become the immediate targets of admiration" (Bland, 1977: 12).

The Black husband (or male friend) obviously resents the fact that women appear to love Jesus (or the church) more than they love their husbands; that women sometimes prefer to spend more time at church than they do at home; that women "serve" the preacher more readily than they serve others; and that they often give inordinate amounts of money to the church and pastor.

If the husband is not a church member, then "he would like to know exactly what is going on. He is actually being driven farther and farther away from the church" by such sexist devotion. "The Black man who is not . . . in the church is made to feel like a 'nobody' regardless of his position (or job) outside the church. Even if the husband is in the church, he will begin to feel inferior because he realizes that he is constantly being compared to the pastor, who in the eyes of his wife can never say or do anything wrong" (Bland, 1977: 13-14).

The solution is not to exchange authoritarianism in the church for authoritarianism in the home. Sexism is wrong wherever it occurs; but perhaps nowhere is the link between sexism and racism more clear than in the relations between Black men and women in the church (Murry, 1979). Whites did an effective job of foisting a "spiritualized" version of theology on the Black church. Thankfully, the 1960s ushered in a period when the Black church recaptured its roots, or as C. Eric Lincoln (1974) suggested, the Negro church became the Black church. In addition, whites effectively stratified women and men within the church order in ways which, in the final analysis, ended up alienating lay*men*; themselves from the sacred institution. Only as male clergy relinquish their sexist roles and content themselves with spiritual and political leadership will men now outside the church be persuaded to join the Black church, and only then will the Black church be able to minister effectively to men.

# REFERENCES

Beale, F. Double jeopardy: To be Black and female. In J. Cone & G. Wilmore (Eds.), *Black theology: A documentary history, 1966-1979.* Maryknoll: Orlus, 1979.

Bland, E. *The Black church in conflict.* New York: Bland, 1977.

Blassingame, J. *The slave community: Plantation life in the Antebellum South.* New York: Oxford University Press, 1972.

Bowden, L. First phase of the Black church study completed (press release of PCPC church study), 1980.

Brown, D., & Walters, R. *Exploring the role of the Black church in the community.* Washington, DC: Institute for Urban Affairs and Research, Howard University, 1979.

Burnett, R. *Black redemption: Churchmen speak for the Garvey movement.* Philadelphia: Temple University Press, 1978.

Cone, J. New roles in the ministry. In J. Cone & G. Wilmore (Eds.), *Black theology: A documentary history, 1966-1979.* Maryknoll: Orlus, 1979.

Frazier, E. The Negro church in America. New York: Schoken, 1964.

Hoover, T. Black women and the churches: Triple jeapardy. In J. Cone & G. Wilmore (Eds.), *Black theology: A documentary history, 1966-1979.* Maryknoll: Orlus, 1979.

Johnson, B. So holiness sects socialize in dominant values? *Social Forces* (May), 1961, 306-316.

Liebow, E. *Tally's corner.* Boston: Little, Brown, 1967.

Lincoln, C. E. *The Black church since Frazier.* New York: Shocken, 1974.

Moberg, D. *The church as a social institution.* Englewood Cliffs, NJ: Prentice-Hall, 1962.

Murray, P. Black theology and feminist theology: A comparitive view. In J. Cone & G. Wilmore (Eds.), *Black theology: A documentary history, 1966-1979.* Maryknoll: Orlus, 1979.

Nelsen, H., & Nelsen, A. *Black churches in the sixties.* Lexington: University Press of Kentucky, 1975.

Russell, L. A feminist looks at Black theology. In C. Bruce & W. Jones (Eds.), *Black theology II: Essays on the formation and outreach of contemporary Black theology.* Lewisburg, PA: Bucknell University Press, 1978.

Saucer, B. Crises and challenges of institutional ministry. In D. Jones & W. Matthews (Eds.), *The Black church: A community resource.* DC: Institute for Urban Affairs and Research, Howard University, 1977.

Staples, R. *Introduction to Black sociology.* New York: McGraw-Hill, 1973.

Tinney, G. The Black church and mental health. *Urban Research Review,* 1979, *5*,(1), 1-4.

Washington, J. *The politics of God: The future of Black churches.* Boston: Beacon Press, 1967.

Welch, M. The untouched: Black religious non-affiliates. *Journal for Scientific Study of Religion,* 1978, *15*(3), 291.

Wilmore, G. *Black religion and positive radicalism.* New York: Anchor, 1973.

Yates, L. The God-consciousness of the Black church in historical perspective. In J. Gardner & J. Roberts (Eds.), *Questions for a Black theology.* Philadelphia: Pilgrim, 1971.

Young, J. *Major Black religious leaders: Since 1940.* Nashville, Abington, 1979.

# CONCLUSION

Lawrence E. Gary

In the previous chapters, we have examined the current status of Black men in a number of areas, such as education, economics, family relationships, religion, the military, the penal system, social services, and physical and mental health. In this concluding section, we plan to identify strategies and solutions for reducing the high social, health, and economic risk status of Black men in our society. Basic to developing any strategies to improve the quality of life for Black men is the need for more research. Given the paucity of reliable information or data on Black people, particularly Black men, it is crucial for social scientists and practitioners to begin to do serious research on the conditions and behaviors of Black men within the context of their families and their communities. Moreover, the Black community must develop strategies for strengthening the role and position of Black men in their respective communities and families and in the broader society. These strategies should involve family members, friends, voluntary associations and clubs, churches, and fraternal groups. These social units must give appropriate consideration to teaching functional values and the importance of group identity to this important sector of our society. In addition, external strategies directed at changing some of the policies and programs of the major social institutions, such as education, politics, health, social welfare, and the penal system, are necessary in order to reduce their negative impacts on Black men.

277

# INSTITUTIONAL OPPRESSION

In recent months there has been an increase in the number of violent incidents directed at Black males in cities such as Youngstown, Buffalo, Cincinnati, Detroit, Indianapolis, Salt Lake City, Atlanta, and Portland (Sheppard, 1980). Of particular concern are the murders of Black children in Atlanta. As of February 1981, eighteen Black children had been found dead (two were missing) over a nineteen-month period ("Atlanta Skeleton Identity Learned," 1981). These children were between the ages of 7 and 15 years old and all but two of them were males. Moreover, there has been a resurgence of the Ku Klux Klan in recent months, and many of their activities are directed against Black men. Some Black leaders believe there is a conspiracy against Black people and have requested that the federal law enforcement agencies play a role in helping to stop these violent acts against Black people. To a large extent, there are historical precedents for these attacks on Black people. According to Rowan (1979: A9),

> no one ought to be surprised by these Klan depredations; they are merely history repeating itself. And in a cruelly ironic way, they are a barometer of Black progress or attesting [to] the progress that some whites perceive Blacks to be making. The clear history of American race relations is that whenever Blacks appear to be making substantial political and economic gains—however trifling these gains may seem to Blacks—someone riles up the most violently ignorant elements of white America and the Klan rides again.

These attacks on Black males as the economy retrenches point to the tenuous status they hold in the American society. Several chapters in this volume document the systematic process by which Black males are removed temporarily or permanently from their families and communities through the operations of the major social institutions of our society. As pointed out by several authors, these institutions use a variety of techniques designed to make Black males dysfunctional in regard to their role performance. Due to racial oppression, many Black families have experienced considerable difficulties in preparing their male offspring for meaningful roles in this society. Figure C.1 depicts the process by which Black men express negative reinforcement from the major institutions. When the Black male leaves his family for an education, he is confronted with a system that is unsympathetic to his needs and concerns. In this volume both Patton and Gary have discussed how the public school system operates to retard the intellectual and psychosocial growth of young Black males. In too many cases, these young men are given negative labels, which often lead them via the health system to social welfare institutions. Data clearly show that Black males, including children and

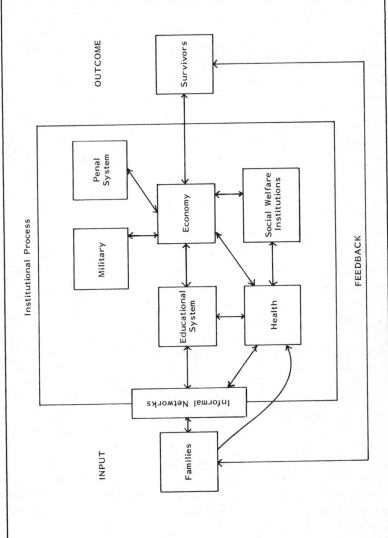

**Figure C.1  A Model of Institutional Oppression of Black Males**

279

youth, are overrepresented in all types of institutions, such as detention homes, training schools for juvenile delinquents, homes for dependent and neglected children, and homes for the mentally handicapped (U. S. Bureau of the Census, 1979).

Many Black males, as discussed by several authors, drop out of school and seek employment. Due to their limited skills, racism, and other factors, these persons experience considerable frustration trying to find jobs. For those who find jobs, the pay is often inadequate for them to support themselves or their families. Therefore, many Black men are forced to earn a livelihood through the irregular economy by gambling, stealing, robbing, and selling stolen goods and drugs, to name a few activities. Often, these activities create unanticipated problems—homicide, suicide, substance abuse, and arrest records that often lead to the penal system. Negative impacts of the economy on many Black males include a decline in their health, and often the health system transfers them to social institutions—mental hospitals, community mental health clinics, or regular hospitals and clinics—or they become burdens to their families.

While it is true that the majority of Black men are able to survive the frustrations of dealing with the economy, a large percentage of them, in comparison to white men, do not. As pointed out earlier, many Black men engage in the irregular economy and often end up in the penal system. The data show the negative consequences of the penal system. In general, this system does not provide adequate training or skills for the inmates. Consequently, once they are released they are still unable to find appropriate jobs, and many again seek personal income through the operations of the irregular economy. Thus, they eventually return to the penal institutions or become burdens to their families. In some cases, these men are routed to other social institutions, including mental health agencies. Data were presented which suggest that many Black men who have difficulty dealing with the economy often join the armed forces. For the most part, these men have positive experiences in the military, but in comparison to white men too many are expelled or incarcerated. Once these persons return to civilian life, they continue to experience economic frustrations, as shown in the unemployment rates for veterans. What this means is that Black families are forced to protect these individuals or they engage in the irregular economy, which often leads them to the penal system.

This institutional process of systematically increasing the social and psychological risks of Black men has a tremendous impact on the stability of Black families. The inability of a large number of Black men to survive the institutional assault on their being creates many problems for them in their relationships with wives, children, parents, lovers, and friends. These social frustrations, rooted in the racist structures of our institutions, are primarily responsible for much of the violence and unrest in many Black communities. Many social agencies are reluctant to intervene in this institutional process, for such action will threaten their own survival. As a result of the lack of institutional support, many Black men have tried to use informal networks as a means of buffering the negative effects of these institutions (Anderson, 1976; Gary, 1980; Keil, 1966; Liebow, 1967). Unfortunately, we do not know very much about the linkages between informal networks and the development of survival skills on the part of Black men. We do know that many Black men are able to deal very effectively with the social, political, and economic institutions and have been able to protect and develop their families. Again, we lack information on the coping strategies of successful Black men.

## THE NEED FOR RESEARCH

Throughout this volume, authors have called for more research on the status and behavior of Black men in the United States. Many Black scholars and practitioners are beginning to realize that research plays an important role in developing programs and policies in our society. In fact, science is considered to be a major value in this society, as reflected in the amount of funds allocated for research. For example, in 1979 it was estimated that $51 billion were spent for research and development (National Center for Education Statistics, 1979). Of this amount, the federal government allocated $25.7 billion for these activities. With such a large financial outlay for research, it should come as no surprise that politics play an important role in research development and utilization (Gary, 1978; Horowitz, 1975; Weiss, 1972; Wilcox, 1970; Yette, 1971). An important question is, Who gets these research funds? Colleges and universities get a large share of the funds for research. Unfortunately, Black colleges and universities do not get their fair share of research funds from the federal government (Gary, 1975; Gary & Howard, 1979). Hollis (1980) estimated that Black colleges receive less than 1 percent of all research funds granted to colleges and universities, although they constituted more than 3 percent of all institutions of higher education in fiscal year 1979.

While there are factors that mitigate against the involvement of Black colleges and universities, based on their competencies they should be more involved in research activities than they have been (Gary, 1976; Royster et al., 1972). When one looks at the National Institute of Mental Health (NIMH), one can observe that minority principal investigators—regardless of whether they are located at Black colleges or predominantly white schools—have only a limited involvement in research (see Table C.1). It is interesting to

## TABLE C.1
### Known Minority Principal Investigators on
### NIMH Research Grants Active as of July 28, 1977

| | Total PIs | Known Minority PIs | |
|---|---|---|---|
| | | n | % |
| *Division of Biometry and Epidemiology* | | | |
| Center for Epidemiologic Studies | 30 | 3 | 10 |
| *Division of Extramural Research Programs* | | | |
| Applied Research Branch | 75 | 6 | 8 |
| Behavioral Science Research Branch | 345 | 7 | 2 |
| Clinical Research Branch | 163 | 4 | 2 |
| Psychopharmocology Research Branch | 177 | 13 | 8 |
| Small Grants Section | 125 | 4 | 4 |
| *Division of Mental Health Service Programs* | | | |
| Mental Health Services Development Branch | 80 | 8 | 10 |
| *Division of Special Mental Health Programs* | | | |
| Center for Studies of Crime and Deliquency | 38 | 0 | 0 |
| Center for Studies of Metropolitan Problems | 48 | 2 | 4 |
| Center for Minority Group Mental Health Programs (CMGMHP) | 38 | 36 | 95 |
| National Center for the Prevention and Control of Rape | 29 | 0 | 0 |
| Total NIMH | 1148 | 83 | 7 |
| NIMH excluding CMGMHP | 1110 | 47 | 4 |

SOURCE: Unpublished data, National Institute of Mental Health, 1977.

note that in 1977 the Center for the Studies of Crime and Delinquency and the National Center for the Prevention and Control of Rape did not have one known minority principal investigator. This is most unfortunate, given the overrepresentation of Black people, especially Black males, in these two areas of deviance. In fact, the Minority Center of the National Institute of Mental

Health was responsible for 43 percent of all the known minority principal investigators who received grants from NIMH in 1977. In an analysis of the review process at NIMH, Gary and Howard (1979: 22-73) concluded that the process is controlled by white male scientists from the leading private and public colleges and universities. They state:

> Black scholars have not received their fair share of funds . . . . There is a need to develop policy alternatives which would make the pathway to funding more accessible to Black scholars. . . . It will be necessary to foster policies which would change or significantly modify the structure of the research funding process. . . . We need an affirmative action plan at NIMH for increasing the number of top Black research administrators and of Black scholars on review committees.

## A RESEARCH AGENDA

It is assumed that if funds were made available to Black scholars, they would conduct research dealing with many of the issues and problems confronting Black men. In developing a research agenda for the survival of Black men, it is important for us to understand that the Black male population is diversified; that is, there are different cultural, political and class subgroups. Moreover, researchers dealing with the Black male condition must understand any serious research cannot be conducted in isolation from Black women and children. It is important for researchers who are seeking to develop more reliable knowledge on the behavior of Black people to give appropriate attention to both sampling and nonsampling errors; at the same time, they should appreciate the need to develop alternative theoretical paradigms.

Although we have emphasized the need for research, one has to be cognizant of the fact that many Black people, including Black men, have suffered psychological and social damage as a result of research projects. The infamous Tuskegee syphilis study ("Compensation Deadline Drawing Near for 23 Duped in Syphilis Study," 1978) is a case in point. This study began in 1932 and ended in 1972 due to public outcry after the disclosure of the project. The researchers involved 600 poor, uneducated Black men in an experiment in which 400 participants with syphilis were not treated in order to study the effects of the untreated disease on the human body. The other 200 men, who were used as a control group, did not have syphilis. These men were not told the purpose of the study, and from all indications the participants were duped. It has been estimated that about 100 of them died as a result of the experiment. A lawsuit was initiated and the U. S. government agreed to pay

$9 million to the known surviving participants and relatives of those who died. Of course, the government can never adequately compensate these victims of human experimentation. Even though the government has developed more refined procedures for safeguarding the rights of human subjects, experimentation on human beings, especially on veterans, prisoners, drug addicts, and mental patients, continues in our society (Bronstein, 1976; Cottle, 1975; Lawthers, 1979; London, 1979; Porter, 1978). Given that Black men are overrepresented in prisons, mental institutions, and the armed forces, and are more likely to be drug addicts than are white men, it is necessary for the Black community and others closely to monitor research projects involving human beings.

In earlier chapters, authors identified specific areas where more research is needed in order to gain a better understanding of the problems and issues confronting Black men and to provide a framework for developing strategies for problem resolution. With respect to health, more research is needed in the area of cancer. As pointed out earlier, there has been a sudden rise of cancer in Black men, especially cancer of the lungs, stomach, esophagus, larynx, prostate, tongue, liver, penis, and pancreas. We should study why there is a disparity between whites and Blacks in regard to cancer survival rates. What factors account for the fact that Black men are less likely to get the current cancer treatment and follow-up care? Since Black male workers are more likely than are whites to be assigned to the most toxic exposures and hazardous conditions in the work place, greater emphasis needs to be placed on occupational health research. We suspect that the work place might be responsible for the high incidence of cancer, respiratory illness, heart disease, hypertension, and stroke among Black men. In regard to occupational health, research is needed to answer the following questions: What conditions cause special job hazard problems for Black workers? Are Black people aware of the connection between work place hazards and their health status? What is the interrelationship of job-related illnesses and death rates among Black workers? What role do discriminatory employment practices play in the job placement of Black male workers? How adequate are state and federal laws for protecting the health of workers? What types of approaches or strategies can be developed to address these problems?

Other areas where more research funds should be allocated include hypertension, infant mortality, veneral disease, diabetes, liver disease, nutrition, and tuberculosis. In regard to hypertension, it is important for us to study the relative effectiveness of various treatment techniques for this condition and its relationship to stress, especially in young Black men. As has been discussed by several authors in this volume, Black men are experiencing considerable stress in our society. Living conditions for many Black men, especially those in the urban centers of this country, make them particularly susceptible to the impact of stress-producing factors. The prevalence of overt and covert discrimination by whites makes many Black men consistently open to assaults on their tranquility as well as on their material status. In simple terms, we need to conduct research that speaks specifically to the needs and concerns of the Black man, the different environments in which he works, and the responses he makes to the multitude of stress-producing factors he encounters in his daily life. Follow-up research questions should be asked: What are the common stressors found in the environment of Black men? What are their frequencies of incidence? What responses to these stressors are included in the repertoires of Black men? What are their frequencies of use? What are the rules and conditions governing the choice of particular responses to various stressors? Given situational constraints, how "adequate" are the typical responses made to stressors? In instances in which the responses are inadequate, what are the origins of the inadequacies? Finally, can measures be taken to increase the use of adequate stressor responses by Black men in a given environment? We need to know the precise effect of stress and frustration on the behavioral responses of Black men so that we can teach them appropriate skills for coping with institutional oppression.

With the rise of suicide among young Black men, we need more reliable information on this problem. As we develop a psychosocial profile of suicide victims, it is important for us to examine this problem from a political as well as from an economic perspective. Given the high level of unemployment in the Black community, we need research that identifies the relationship between the economy and suicide and other adaptive strategies of Black men. It is believed that there is a close relationship between homicide and suicide. With respect to the economy, we need more in-depth and longitudinal studies that examine the relationship between the rate of unemployment and the incidence of illness and criminal behavior in the Black male community. What are the social and economic costs of unemployment for Black communities in terms of suicide, homicide, incarceration, admissions to mental institutions, and so forth? It has been suggested that recession or unemployment literally kills thousands of Black people and makes others seriously ill. As a consequence, many Black people end up in mental hosptials or clinics. Therefore, more research is needed that examines racial differences among persons utilizing psychiatric facilities, racial differences in the diagnoses of mental disorders, effective treatment modalities used with Black patients, and the distribution and utilization of Black mental health manpower. Of course, our suggested health research agenda is incomplete. For example, we need more research into the area of the impact of lifestyles on health-related behavior and on how to develop effective health maintenance programs in Black communities.

Several authors in this volume have discussed the importance of gaining a better understanding of interpersonal dynamics within Black communities. Of all the institutions in the Black community, the family has received the most attention with respect to research and targets of intervention. As noted by several authors, most studies of Black family life have used a pathological frame of reference; that is, there is a tendency to focus on weaknesses rather than on strengths and to focus on mothers and their children. Future family research in the Black community should give greater priority to the role of the Black man in his family. Other research questions include: What impact do poverty and racism have on all aspects of family life in the Black community? What accounts for the significant rise in the number of unmarried male persons in the Black community? How do Black fathers relate to their children? What are the necessary conditions for improving the interpersonal relationships between Black men and women? What has been the effect of interracial dating on Black male and female relationships? Are there alternative marital arrangements for the Black community? What is the role of the boyfriend in selected family settings? How are authority decisions and tasks distributed among men, women, and children in Black families? Finally, what strategies can be developed for strengthening the kinship bond within the Black community?

Earlier in this volume, we mentioned that voluntary associations and clubs, fraternal groups, and churches have played important functions in helping Black men to cope with institutional oppression. Further research is needed in these areas so that appropriate strategies can be developed for promoting the growth and development of these social units within Black communities. An important aspect of the life of Black men is their informal networks—friends, fictive kin, fellow workers, peer groups, and associates in bars and barbershops. These networks, as suggested by several authors in this volume, have assisted many Black men in developing the necessary skills for functioning in a hostile racist environment. Yet, little research has been conducted to determine the significance of social networks in Black communities. The following questions should be considered for research in this area: What are the significant qualities that Black men look for in friends? How are friends integrated with the family life of Black men? What have been the positive mental health aspects of social network systems in the Black community? What is the relationship between values established in peer groups and those established in the family? Is the rise in drug usage in the Black community directly related to the decline of peer groups and gangs? Is there a relationship between the rise in crime and violence among the 18-25-year-old Black male group and the declining influence of the social network apparatus? Finally, has the tolerance level of stress and ambiguity been directly affected by the dispersion of gang and peer groups and the declining influence of the church among Black males?

In conclusion, we have not identified all the areas in need of research so that appropriate strategies can be developed to reduce the high social, health, and economic risk status of Black males in our society. Policy research can play an important role in this regard. More consideration should be given to studying the impact of federal and state policies on all aspects of the Black community. Special attention needs to be given to documenting the extent to which governmental policies and programs promote and support the values and cultural imperatives of the Black community.

## A RESEARCH FRAMEWORK

Given our interest in the role of research in helping to define the parameters for the development of programs to strengthen the social, economic, and political position of Black men, it is important to suggest a framework for integrating these research concerns. A conceptual model is crucial for guiding a research and development effort that focuses specifically on understanding problems in Black communities. Social and behavioral scientists have used a variety of models, theories, and constructs to study behaviors in Black and other communities. According to some scholars and practitioners (Billingsley, 1968; Boykin, Franklin, & Yates, 1979; Gary, 1978; Hill, 1980; Solomon, 1976), only a few of these conceptual schemes have been useful in producing meaningful research on problems and issues confronting Black communities. A major criticism of research on Black people concerns the theoretical assumptions which guide such activities.

To a large extent, this research framework is designed to clarify the relationship among social forces and conditions, sociocultural processes and behaviors, and social outcomes, and is based on the ideas of a number of scholars and researchers (Billingsley, 1968; Blackwell, 1975; Dye, 1972; Eaton, 1965; Parsons, 1964; and others). This model draws on several theories of behavior, such as role theory, labeling theory, societal reaction theory, and systems theory (Anderson & Carter, 1974; Becker, 1963; Lemert, 1967; Morton, 1957; Perruci & Wallace, 1975; Scheff, 1966; Siegler & Osmond, 1976; Szaz, 1961; Whittaker, 1974). Since many of the research questions discussed can be classified as related to mental health, we shall treat this model as a scheme for studying the mental health of Black people.

As depicted in Figure C.2, the model portrays mental health (illness) as an output (or outcome) of sociocultural processes and social forces and conditions of our society. This implies an identifiable set of behaviors and activities

### Figure C.2
### A Conceptual Framework for Studying
### the Mental Health of Black People.

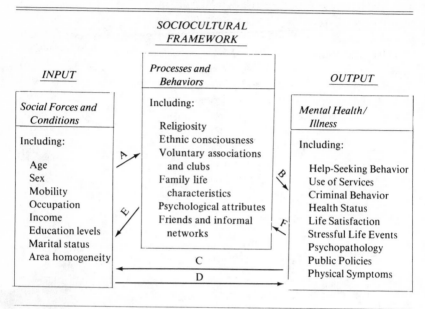

Linkage A: The effect of forces and conditions on sociocultural processes and behaviors in the Black community.

Linkage B: The effect of sociocultural processes on mental health and illness.

Linkage C: The effect of environmental forces and conditions on mental health/illness.

Linkage D: The effect (feedback) of mental health/illness on social forces and conditions.

Linkage E: The effect (feedback) of sociocultural processes and behaviors on social forces and conditions.

Linkage F: The effect (feedback) of mental health/illness on sociocultural processes and behaviors.

in Black communities that function to transform demands (pressure points) from social conditions into mental health outcomes, whether they are positive or negative. The model also implies that the input and output elements are interrelated and that the system can respond to forces in its environment and that it will do so in order to preserve itself.

The social forces and conditions are identified as input variables and manifest their presence in the form of demands. In conducting research studies, these variables should be treated as control factors. At the analysis stage, these factors may be treated as dependent or independent variables. Controlling for variables such as age, sex, income, marital status, and so forth allows for definitive generalizations about the selected study group. In studying the behavioral processes of Black people, one must acknowledge culturally specific modes and patterns of negotiating life circumstances. These modes of coping are different from those of the dominant culture and embrace constructs of (a) religiosity, (b) informal networks, (c) social participation, and (d) ethnic consciousness, to name a few.

The mental health/illness dimension of this model depicts the outcomes of the interactions evidenced by pressures from social forces and conditions as well as the operative behavioral processes. The model assumes that sociocultural processes can mediate the impact of social conditions on the mental health of people. Through the feedback mechanisms, the model further assumes that social conditions can mediate the effect of sociocultural processes and behaviors on the mental health of people. Realizing that there is no general agreement on ways to measure mental health or illness, it is important to use a multidimensional approach for assessing mental health status. Hence, the output measures of mental health include help-seeking behavior, use of mental health services, psychopathology, attitudes toward mental health, physical symptoms, and so forth. The value of using this conceptual approach to studying the mental health of Black communities lies in the questions it poses, namely: (a) What are the significant dimensions of the environment that generate demands upon (and supports of) the sociocultural system in Black communities? (b) What are the significant characteristics of the sociocultural system that enable it to translate/transform demands into mental health outcomes (positive and negative) and to preserve itself over time? (c) How does environmental input (demand and support) affect the character and nature of mental health outcomes? (d) How does environmental input affect mental health output? (e) How does mental health outcome affect, through feedback, the character of the sociocultural process?

Research into these areas is supported by the following: (a) Black people live in an environment significantly different from that of other racial/ethnic groups in the United States. These environments are particularly stressful and the opportunity structure restricts the psychological well-being of Black people, (b) Norms for the study of human behavior, particularly the interpretation of specific types of behavior designated as functional or dysfunctional, require knowledge of the social and cultural traits of the target population under study. Norms of the general population, particularly the middle-class, are typically not applicable to Black subpopulations, (c) Strategies for intervention and treatment should be based on research that amplifies positive patterns prevalent in the lifestyle of Black clientele.

In conclusion, it should be noted that all problems cannot be solved by means of a research approach, for social problem resolutions are fundamentally related to politics. Therefore, in order to improve the quality of life for Black men, Black people and others must become more involved in the political process. Policies and programs are developed as a result of political pressures in this society. In this regard, Black people must make community, state, and federal officials aware of their unique health and social problems by testifying at hearings, writing position papers, appealing to the mass media, writing letters to the editors of newspapers and magazines, and participating in demonstrations and marches. Moreover, Black people must support, through financial donations, public-interest organizations that institute legal suits and force public agencies to be more responsive to the concerns and needs of Black people. Although the conditions facing Black men are difficult, based on past experiences, Black men will survive and continue to make significant contributions to all aspects of American civilization.

# REFERENCES

Atlanta skeleton identity learned. *The Washington Post*, February 16, 1981, p. 1.

Anderson, E. *A place on the corner*. Chicago: University of Chicago Press, 1976.

Anderson, R., & Carter, I. *Human behavior in the social environment: A social systems approach*. Chicago: Aldine, 1974.

Becker, H. *Outsider: Studies in the sociology of deviance*. New York: Free Press, 1963.

Billingsley, A. *Black families in white America*. Englewood Cliffs, NJ: Prentice-Hall, 1968.

Blackwell, J. *The Black community: Diversity and unity*. New York: Dodd, Mead, 1975.

Boykins, A., Franklin, A., & Yates, J. (Eds.). *Research directions of Black psychologists*. New York: Russell Sage, 1979.

Bronstein, A. Rights of prisoners versus the state. *Current History*, 1976, *80*, 40-45.

Compensation deadline drawing near for 23 duped in syphilis study. *The Washington Post*, March 11, 1978, p. D2.

Cottle, T. Science atrocities. *New Republic*, 1975, *173*, 5-6.

Dye, T. *Understanding public policy*. Englewood Cliffs, NJ: Prentice-Hall, 1972.

Eaton, D. *A framework for political analysis*. Englewood Cliffs, NJ: Prentice-Hall, 1965.

Gary, L. The significance of research for the survival of Black colleges. *Journal of Black Studies*, 1975, *6*, 35-53.

Gary, L. A mental health research agenda for the Black community. *Journal of Afro-American Issues,* 1976, *4,* 50-60.

Gary, L. (Ed.). *Mental health: A challenge to the Black community.* Philadelphia: Dorrance, 1978.

Gary, L. *Suicide and support systems in Black communities: Implications for mental health practice.* Paper presented at the Symposium on Black Suicide, Chicago, Illinois, April 22-23, 1980.

Gary, L., & Howard, C. Policy implications of mental health research for Black Americans. *Urban League Review,* 1979, *4*(1), 16-24.

Hill, R. Social work research on minorities: Impediments and opportunities. In D. Fanshel (Ed.), *Future of social work research.* Washington, DC: NASW, 1980.

Hollis, M. *Report on the President's Black college initiatives for fiscal year 1979.* Unpublished report of the U.S. Department of Health, Education and Welfare, Washington, D.C., 1980.

Horowitz, I. (Ed.). *The uses and abuses of the social science* (2nd ed.). New Brunswick, NJ: Transaction, 1975.

Keil, C. *Urban blues.* Chicago: University of Chicago Press, 1966.

*Known minority principal investigators on NIMH Research Grants as of 7/28/77.* Washington, DC: National Institute of Mental Health, 1977. (Unpublished data)

Lawthers, W. Uncle Sam wants you stoned: Army's use of soldiers to test drug BZ in 1965. *Macleans,* 1979, *92,* 29-30.

Lemert, E. *Human deviance: Social problems and control.* Englewood Cliffs, NJ: Prentice-Hall, 1967.

Liebow, E. *Tally's corner.* Boston: Little, Brown, 1967.

London, P. Experiments on humans: Where to draw the line. *Psychology Today,* 1979, *11,* 20.

Morton, R. *Social theory and social structure.* New York: Free Press, 1957.

National Center for Education Statistics. *Digest of education statistics: 1979.* Washington, DC: Government Printing Office, 1979.

Parsons, T. *The social system.* New York: Free Press, 1964.

Perruci, R., & Wallace, S. Models of mental illness and duration of hospitalization. *Community Mental Health Journal,* 1975, *11,* 271-279.

Porter, M. Veterans as guinea pigs. *New Times,* 1978, *11,* 13-14.

Rowan, C. The Klan and Black progress. *The Washington Post,* November 12, 1979, p. A-9.

Royster, E., et al. *Research and learning centers among Black colleges in the human services: A feasibility study.* Washington, DC: Department of Health, Education and Welfare, 1972 (Grant No. 10-P-5606/3-01)

Scheff, T. A sociological theory of mental disorders. In J. D. Page (Ed.), *Approaches to psychopathology.* Wolfe City: Texas University Press, 1966.

Sheppard, N. Perception growing among Blacks that violent incidents are linked. *New York Times,* November 30, 1980, pp. 1, 64.

Siegler, M., & Osmond, H. *Models of madness, models of medicine.* New York: Harper & Row, 1976.

Solomon, B. *Black empowerment: Social work in oppressed communities.* New York: Columbia University Press, 1976.

Szaz, T. *The myth of mental illness: Foundation of a theory of personal conduct.* New York: Hoeber-Harper, 1961.

U.S. Bureau of the Census. *Statistical abstract of the United States: 1979* (100th ed.). Washington, DC: Government Printing Office, 1979.

Weiss, C. (Ed.). *Evaluating action programs.* Boston: Allyn & Bacon, 1972.

Whittaker, J. *Social treatment: An approach to interpersonal helping.* Chicago: Aldine, 1974.

Wilcox, P. Social policy and racism. *Social Policy,* 1970, 41-46.

Yette, S. *The choice: The issue of Black survival in America.* New York: Putnam, 1971.

# ABOUT THE CONTRIBUTORS

WALTER R. ALLEN earned his Ph.D. in sociology from the University of Chicago, received postdoctoral training in public health and social epidemiology from the University of North Carolina, and has been the recipient of several research grants. Presently, he is an assistant professor in the Department of Sociology and Center for Afro American and African Studies at the University of Michigan. His research interests and publication activities focus on the Black family and socialization outcomes. Some of the journals in which his publications have appeared include the *Journal of Negro Education,* the *Journal of Marriage and the Family,* the *Journal of Comparative Family Studies,* and the *Sociological Quarterly.*

MOLEFI K. ASANTE, who received his Ph.D. from the University of California, is a professor in the Department of Communication at the State University of New York, Buffalo. His research interests focus on interpersonal communications and development of an Afrocentric consciousness in human relationships. He has published numerous articles, which have appeared in the *Western Journal of Black Studies,* the *Journal of Black Studies,* the *Journal of Communication, Encore: The Journal of NADSA,* and the *Journal of Black Psychology,* and has also published numerous books. Two of his most recent books are entitled *Contemporary Black Thought: Alternative Analysis in Social and Behavioral Sciences* (coeditor with A. S. Vandi) and *Afrocentricity: The Theory of Social Change.*

RONALD L. BRAITHWAITE is the Associate Director of the Institute for Urban Affairs and Research, Howard University. He earned his Ph.D. in counseling and educational psychology from Michigan State University and his M.S. in rehabilitation counseling from Southern Illinois University. Among his major research interests are studies on achievement, educational attainment, human development, and diversity.

ROBERT DAVIS received his Ph.D. in sociology from Washington State University. He is an associate professor of sociology at North Carolina A&T State University, and is affiliated with the Institute for Research on Poverty and the Center for Demography and Ecology, both at the University of Wisconsin, Madison. Mortality and Black suicide are among his major research interests. Black suicide is also the focus of his publication activities.

JOHN E. FLEMING holds the position of project administrator at the National Afro-American Museum and Cultural Center Project, Columbus, Ohio. He earned a Ph.D. from Howard University in U.S. history since 1865. His major research interests include education and Afro-American history. He has published several articles and books, including *The Education of Black Americans: A Profile of North*

*Carolina Central University* and *The Lengthening Shadow of Slavery: Historical Justification for Affirmative Action for Blacks in Higher Education.*

LAWRENCE E. GARY is the director of the Institute for Uuban Affairs and Research and the Mental Health Research and Development Center at Howard University. He received his Ph.D. in political science from the University of Michigan. His research interests and publications are in the areas of mental health, administration of justice, public policy, and education. He has published numerous articles in journals such as the *Journal of Politics, Social Work,* the *Journal of Black Studies,* the *Urban League Review,* and *Public Health Reports.* He has also written a book entitled *Mental Health: A Challenge to the Black Community* and coauthored with L. P. Brown another book, *Crime and Its Impact on the Black Community.*

LELAND K. HALL is Chief of Health Planning and Development in the Commission of Public Health, Washington, D.C., Department of Human Resources, Mental Health Administration. He received his Ph.D. in psychology, specializing in mental health administration, from Union Graduate School. He has published several papers dealing with the Black community.

FREDERICK D. HARPER holds the position of professor in the School of Education at Howard University. He obtained his Ph.D. in counselor education from Florida State University and his postdoctoral training at HEW's National Institute on Alcohol Abuse and Alcoholism and at George Mason State University of Virginia, in experimental psychology. Some of his major research interests include guidance and counseling, Black students—particularly at predominantly white universities—and alcoholism. He has published a number of articles in various journals, such as the *Journal of College Student Personnel,* the *Journal of Black Studies,* the *Journal of Negro Education,* the *Journal of Non-White Concerns in Personnel & Guidance*, and the *Personnel & Guidance Journal.*

LEO E. HENDRICKS holds a Ph.D. in epidemiology from the University of North Carolina at Chapel Hill. Currently, he is a senior research associate in the Mental Health Research and Development Center at the Institute for Urban Affairs and Research, Howard University, and an assistant professor in the Urban Studies Program at the Institute. His research interests and publications are in the areas of family and health, teenaged fathers, and mental health. His articles have appeared in *Social Work,* the *American Journal of Public Health,* and *Adolescence.*

BOGART R. LEASHORE is a research associate in the Mental Health Research and Development Center of the Institute for Urban Affairs and Research at Howard University, and an assistant professor in the Urban Studies Program at the Institute. He received his Ph.D. in social work and sociology from the University of Michigan. He has published in *The Family Coordinator,* and his research interests include Black men and the Black family.

JOHN L. McADOO is an associate professor in the School of Social Work and Community Planning at the University of Maryland. He obtained his Ph.D. in educational psychology with an emphasis on mental retardation from the University of Michigan, his postdoctoral training in mental health epidemiology at Johns Hopkins University, and his training in evaluating school effectiveness at Harvard

University. He has published several articles and has authored, with other writers, a monograph entitled *An Evaluation of the Effect of Decentralization on the Delivery of Income Maintenance and Social Services.* Most of his research is in the area of the Black family, aging, research and evaluation, social services, and Black preschool children.

JAMES M. PATTON holds an Ed.D. in education from Indiana University and obtained his postdoctoral training in improving teaching through the use of various forms of instructional media from an Eli-Lilly Postdoctoral Grant at Hampton Institute. He currently chairs the Department of Special Education and Rehabilitation Services at Virginia State University. His major research focuses on education and teaching. He is the author of several publications and has obtained several grants.

RONALD L. TAYLOR, who received his Ph.D. from Boston University, is an associate professor in the Department of Sociology at the University of Connecticut. He has published several articles and two books, *The Black Male in America: Perspectives on his Status in Contemporary Society* and *The Black Worker in Post-Industrial Society.* His articles have appeared in various journals, including the *American Journal of Orthopsychiatry, Issues in Adolescent Psychology,* the *Journal of Black Studies,* the *Social Science Quarterly,* and the *American Journal of Sociology.* The focus of his research is on the Black male, psychosocial development, and Black youth.

JAMES S. TINNEY completed his Ph.D. in political science at Howard University. He is not only a political scientist but also an educator, an editor-publisher, a leading Black Pentecostal historian and lay theologian, and an assistant professor in journalism at Howard University. He has coauthored several books, written chapters in books, and is currently preparing two book manuscripts. Among his coauthored books are *In the Tradition of William J. Seymour, A Selected Bibliography of Afro-American Religious Organizations, Schools and Periodicals,* and *Issues and Trends in Afro-American Journalism.* He has also published more than 1,000 articles in journals, magazines, and newspapers, including *Black Scholar,* the *Journal of the Interdenominational Theological Center,* and *Spirit: Journal of Issues Incident to Black Pentecostalism.*

ROI D. TOWNSEY is a program research associate at the Police Foundation in Washington, D.C. She earned her Ph.D. in sociology from the State University of New York at Stony Brook. Her research interests are in the sociology of law and criminal justice.